CAMBRIDGE STUDIES IN AMERICAN LITERATURE
AND CULTURE

# T. S. Eliot: The Modernist in History

# CAMBRIDGE STUDIES IN AMERICAN LITERATURE AND CULTURE

*Selected books in the series*
Charles Altieri, *Painterly Abstraction in Modernist American Poetry: The Contemporaneity of Modernism*
Douglas Anderson, *A House Undivided: Domesticity and Community in American Literature*
Sacvan Bercovitch and Myra Jehlen (eds.), *Ideology and Classic American Literature**
Michael Davidson, *The San Francisco Renaissance: Poetics and Community at Mid-Century*
George Dekker, *The American Historical Romance**
Stephen Fredman, *Poets' Prose: The Crisis in American Verse, 2nd Edition*
Susan Friedman, *Penelope's Web: Gender, Modernity, H.D.'s Fiction*
Albert Gelpi (ed.), *Wallace Stevens: The Poetics of Modernism**
Richard Godden, *Fictions of Capital: Essays on the American Novel from James to Mailer*
Russell Goodman, *American Philosophy and the Romantic Tradition*
Richard Gray, *Writing the South: Ideas of an American Region**
Ezra Greenspan, *Walt Whitman and the American Reader*
Alfred Habegger, *Henry James and the "Woman Business"*
David Halliburton, *The Color of the Sky: A Study of Stephen Crane*
Susan K. Harris, *19th-Century American Women's Novels: Interpretive Strategies*
Robert Lawson-Peebles, *Landscape and Written Expression in Revolutionary America: The World Turned Upside Down*
Robert S. Levine, *Conspiracy and Romance: Studies in Brockden Brown, Cooper, Hawthorne, and Melville*
John Limon, *The Place of Fiction in the Time of Science: A Disciplinary History of American Writing*
John McWilliams, *The American Epic: Transformation of a Genre, 1770–1860*
Susan Manning, *The Puritan-Provincial Vision: Scottish and American Literature in the Nineteenth Century*
David Miller, *Dark Eden: The Swamp in Nineteenth-Century American Culture*
Michael Oriard, *Sporting with the Gods: The Rhetoric of Play and Game in American Literature*
Tim Redman, *Ezra Pound and Italian Fascism*
Eric Sigg, *The American T. S. Eliot: A Study of the Early Writings*
Brook Thomas, *Cross Examinations of Law and Literature: Cooper, Hawthorne, Stowe, and Melville**
David Wyatt, *The Fall into Eden: Landscape and Imagination in California**

*Now available in hardcover and paperback

*For a complete list of books in the series, see the pages following the Index.*

# T. S. Eliot:
# The Modernist in
# History

edited by
RONALD BUSH
*California Institute of Technology*

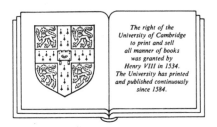

CAMBRIDGE UNIVERSITY PRESS
*Cambridge*
*New York   Port Chester   Melbourne   Sydney*

Published by the Press Syndicate of the University of Cambridge
The Pitt Building, Trumpington Street, Cambridge CB2 1RP
40 West 20th Street, New York, NY 10011, USA
10 Stamford Road, Oakleigh, Melbourne 3166, Australia

First published 1991

Printed in the United States of America

*Library of Congress Cataloging-in-Publication Data*

T.S. Eliot : the modernist in history / edited by Ronald Bush.

p.    cm. – (Cambridge studies in American literature and
culture)

"Shorter versions of these papers were delivered at a conference
at the California Institute of Technology on September 27, 28, and
29, 1988" – Acknowledgments.

Includes index.

ISBN 0-521-39074-5

1. Eliot, T. S. (Thomas Stearns), 1888–1965 – Criticism and
interpretation.   2. Modernism (Literature)   I. Bush, Ronald.
II. Series.

PS3509.L43Z87247     1990

821'.912 – dc20                      90–39425
                                                    CIP

*British Library Cataloguing in Publication Data*

T. S. Eliot : the modernist in history. – (Cambridge studies
in American literature and culture).

1. Poetry in English. Eliot, T. S. (Thomas Stearns), 1888–1965
I. Bush, Ronald
821.912

ISBN 0–521–39074–5 (hardback)

*In Memoriam*
*Raymond J. Bush*

# Contents

# CONTENTS

# *Acknowledgments*

---

Shorter versions of these papers were delivered at a conference at the California Institute of Technology on 27, 28 and 29 September 1988. I wish to thank Caltech and especially David Grether, Chairman of the Division of Humanities and Social Sciences, and Susan Davis, his administrative assistant, for their generous support. I would also like to give special thanks to Betty Hyland, who helped with much of the conference's organization and planning. My one regret about this volume is that one of the finest papers of the conference, "Paralyzed Woman: The Painful Case of Vivienne Haigh Eliot," could not be included. Elliot and Sandra Gilbert, the authors of that paper, made a brilliant case for the importance of Vivienne's voice in Eliot's poetry, and their contribution provoked a great deal of interest.

Thanks are also due to the people who shepherded the essays into print. The enthusiasm of Albert Gelpi, the general editor of this series, meant a great deal. I am also grateful to Andrew Brown, whose shrewd critical eye guided the first stage of publication through a bramble of problems. And I could never have completed the book without the tolerance and encouragement of my wife, Marilyn, and my son, Charles.

# Contributors

RONALD BUSH (California Institute of Technology) is the author of *The Genesis of Ezra Pound's Cantos* and *T. S. Eliot: A Study in Character and Style*.

CAROL CHRIST (University of California, Berkeley) is the author of *The Finer Optic: The Aesthetics of Particularity in Victorian Poetry* and *Victorian and Modern Poetics*.

LYNDALL GORDON (St. Hilda's College, Oxford) is the author of *Eliot's Early Years, Virginia Woolf: A Writer's Life*, and *Eliot's New Life*.

A. WALTON LITZ (Princeton University) is the author of numerous books on modernist literature, including *Eliot in His Time, The Art of James Joyce*, and *Introspective Voyager: The Poetic Achievement of Wallace Stevens*.

JAMES LONGENBACH (University of Rochester) is the author of *Modernist Poetics of History: Pound, Eliot and the Sense of the Past* and *Stone Cottage: Pound, Yeats and Modernism*.

JOHN T. MAYER (Holy Cross College) is author of *T. S. Eliot's Silent Voices*.

MICHAEL NORTH (University of California, Los Angeles) is the author of *The Final Sculpture: Public Monuments and Modern Poets* and *Henry Green and the Writing of His Generation*.

LAWRENCE RAINEY (Yale University) is the author of *Ezra Pound and the Monument of Culture*.

ALAN WILLIAMSON (University of California, Davis) is a poet and the author of *Pity the Monsters: The Political Vision of Robert Lowell* and *Introspection and Contemporary Poetry*.

# Introduction

In a landmark volume of 1965, Richard Ellmann and Charles Feidelson looked back at the heyday of modernism and announced the movement had "already passed into history." Twenty years later that remark is no less true, but its implications have undergone a sea change. Ellmann and Feidelson looked forward to an extended "perspective in time" that would permit them the vantage they needed to see the past "in historical depth." They expected that once we *knew* more, modernist writing would finally be explained by a context of historical facts and literary documents once obscured by literary polemic. And at least in part, they were right; sixty-some years after the publication of *The Waste Land* and *Ulysses*, we do know a great deal more about what they called *The Modern Tradition*. Yet it is also true that in 1990 the productions of modernism look *different* from the way they did in 1965 — and not just because of a deepened perspective. Writing history involves not only facts but narratives, and

1

narratives imply a set of interests that color even the most closely packed set of facts. In the words of the historian Lynn Hunt, history must be understood as "an ongoing tension between stories that have been told and stories that might be told." And our reasons for telling ourselves the story of modernism in the fifties and sixties are not only different from the reasons that obtained in the twenties, they are also different from today's. To appropriate an important but little-known remark of Eliot's from the last essay in this book, history, like literature and all the humanities, "is always turned toward creation; the present only, keeps the past alive." Put another way: the pressure of present values shapes our knowledge of the past.

Which goes some way toward explaining the force behind the post-structuralist reevaluation of modernism, a push that began in the sixties and has gained influence year by year. Under its influence, the critic Richard Poirier, once a powerful proponent of modernist writing, now calls it a "snob's game." And just as striking, in the introduction to a book on modernist impersonality, Maud Ellmann, the daughter of one of the authors of *The Modern Tradition*, opposes the "democratic" readings of Marxist and post-structuralist critics to "Pound and Eliot's authoritarian alternatives." Given these statements and others, nothing could be clearer than that it is impossible in the postmodern 1990s to consider T. S. Eliot our contemporary.

Yet it is by no means evident that the present reassessment of Eliot need necessarily adhere to the contours suggested by the post-structuralists. Ideological competition in the present is no less intense than it ever was, and the post-structuralists, made giddy by their own theory, are sometimes less than assiduous historians. As I argue below, many of their assertions reproduce the simplifications of the politically conservative New Critics, who also blurred over Eliot's contradictions for their own political purposes. The history of modernism the nineties will produce is too important, I believe, for that pattern to be repeated. And so I present the essays in this book with some hope that they might keep a dialogue open. Far from consistent in approach, they have in common a commitment to the discipline of history. Continuing the best efforts of Richard Ellmann's generation, many of them take issue with Eliot's self-presentation and include documents

Eliot chose not to emphasize. Some press the limits of literary and intellectual history and enter areas of cultural practice, stressing the institutions of publishing and the social processes of gender formation. And all reevaluate Eliot with a self-conscious awareness of the pressure of the eighties, whether it concerns the plight current writers (where do we go from here, and which of our several Eliots will help us?) or women readers (what does this self-professed masculinist poetry have to do with us?) or denizens of the hotly contested waters of cultural politics (were modernism's social values consistent and were they inimical to liberal and radical visions of the future?).

Perhaps the easiest way to suggest the way the essays in this book help resituate Eliot is to begin with the essays on Eliot and women. Accused by Leavis and others of being against life, Eliot has lately been portrayed as more specifically misogynist, both in his life and his work. In part this has to do with reading Eliot's attitudes in an age more sensitive to women's concerns than his own and would apply to almost any male writer of his generation. But once one has decided to emphasize the way Eliot suppressed the voice of his first wife, it is relatively easy to connect this chauvinism with modernism's authoritarian poetics and flirtation with fascism. Still, what *were* Eliot's relations with women, and how, precisely, did he represent them? After careful study of a considerable body of unpublished material, Lyndall Gordon argues that, although sometimes unattractive, they were more complicated than either Eliot's proponents or detractors would assume. Moreover, as Carol Christ argues, the issue of voice in *The Waste Land*, at the center of current controversies about whether modernist works tend toward open or patriarchal structures, is not as simple as it looks. Yes, it is gender related, but the implications of gender for Eliot's voices, Christ maintains, are surprisingly unpredictable.

The contradictions that emerge in Eliot's representation of women also can be discovered in the composition of those centerpieces of the modernist project, *The Waste Land* and its related poems. Taking a biographical perspective and making use of manuscript evidence and uncollected prose, James Longenbach demonstrates that Eliot's quatrain poems in *Ara Vos Prec* are as shot through with ambivalence as *The Waste Land* itself. *Tours de force* of formal clarity, these poems have been used to bolster endorsements of Eliot's technical mastery that shade into moral and political arguments. Yet their genesis shows a very different sort of impetus and suggests why they have inspired strong passions in their readers, ranging from collusion to disgust. Similarly John T. Mayer's essay investigates Eliot's attempts in 1910 and 1911 to organize fragments into a long poem and uncovers precisely those tensions recent criticism has discovered in *The Waste Land:* Eliot's poetry notebooks suggest one set of intentions leading toward a prophetic quest poem and the other pulling in the direction of skepticism and despair.

What philosophical tensions existed in Eliot's modernist innovations, however, were soon conditioned and complicated by the process of transmission and reception as his work entered his history and ours. And rarely has this part of the historical process been demonstrated with such particularity as in Lawrence Rainey's essay, "The Price of Modernism: Publishing *The Waste Land.*" Looking at records of *The Dial* magazine transferred in 1988 to the Beinecke Library, Rainey discovers a pattern of expectations in letters between *The Dial*'s owners, Scofield Thayer and J. S. Watson, Jr., that focused the way *The Waste Land* was presented to the American audience. These expectations had everything to do with commercial considerations and help explain why the modernist idiom cornered the market. In Rainey's words, for Eliot, his supporters, and publishers, "the question of publishing [*The Waste Land*] did not necessarily mean an appreciation of its quality or sympathy with its substantive components . . . but an eagerness to position" the poem in the world of financial and ideological power.

The collection concludes with two essays that examine the aesthetic and philosophical contradictions of Eliot's modernism in political terms. Michael North observes the sometimes uncanny similarities between the shifting positions of Eliot and Georg Lukács and suggests that the fault lines of modernism were not very different from those of revolutionary socialism. "Modernist literature," he concludes, was "prevented from solidifying [into its most reactionary premises] precisely because it [could not] solve the political and cultural problems of modernism [i.e., modern life]. That it continues to try keeps it both modern and antimodern at the same time." My own effort examines the politics, literary and otherwise, that conditioned the writing of modernism's history in the thirties and the seventies and suggests what energies these stories left out.

But before this conclusion two essays appear that consider Eliot from a literary point of view and suggest how different Eliot as poet is from the way he first presented himself. Both A. Walton Litz and Alan Williamson address Eliot's mythic allusiveness, and both demonstrate that it serves more subtle purposes than Cleanth Brooks's "rehabilitation of a system of beliefs." Williamson argues that, in *The Waste Land* no less than in *Burnt Norton,* Eliot's transcultural allusions have to do with intrapsychic depth and the processes of psychological growth. And Litz rehearses the steady alteration of Eliot's allusive techniques and suggests that especially at the end of Eliot's career the practice was related to Eliot's personal need to yield himself "to a more pervasive appropriation of other voices, other personalities. . . ."

## PART ONE

# Eliot's Women/ Women's Eliot

# Eliot and Women

## LYNDALL GORDON

T. S. Eliot's first love, Emily Hale, saw him not as a mild English gentleman, old buffer of the clubs, or jolly joker, but as "a man of extremes."[1] This view does fit Eliot's poetry, which jolts us from visionary "hints and guesses,"[2] on the one hand, to horror, despair, and futility, on the other. The women in the poetry and plays emphasize this extreme pattern. Only in his final work, *The Elder Statesman* (1958), does Eliot present a woman who evokes, for the first time, at the very end of his career, ordinary human love. This coincides, of course, with Eliot's own discovery of human love through a happy second marriage to his secretary, Valerie Fletcher, in the last eight years of his life. This was the last of four quite different relationships with women who were all remarkable and who entered his work in different ways.

The first and most long-lasting tie was with a Bostonian called Emily Hale. Eliot declared his love for her before he left for Europe in 1914 but had no impression that his feelings were returned. A year after his impulsive marriage to the English Vivienne Haigh-Wood in June 1915, Eliot came to believe, as he put it in a retrospective paper of the sixties, that he was still "in love with Miss Hale,"[3] a nostalgia that may have been in part a reaction against his "misery" with Vivienne. Curiously, Eliot forecast a separation in "La Figlia che Piange" (1912) as a beautiful, unmessy parting with a girl whose arms are full of flowers. The speaker does muse about how they might have come together but prefers to possess her in memory as the material of art. As such, she reappears, through memory and desire, as a source for the hyacinth girl in *The Waste Land*, who prompts a non-wasteland moment, "looking into the heart of light, the silence."[4]

In 1927, at the time of Eliot's conversion, he and Emily Hale renewed a sustained contact, and almost at once he transformed her in his imagination as a Beatrice figure, an elevating Lady of silences.[5] As such, she was to be vital to the dramas of the poet's new life. Her letters show an unfamiliar Eliot in a long-lasting but ultimately unfulfilled relationship that had to be subordinated to the unhappy fact of his first marriage, his private penitence, and his public mission.

The second woman in Eliot's life was his first wife, Vivienne. His private papers of the sixties tells us that all he had actually wanted of Vivienne was "a flirtation or a mild affair: I was too shy and unpractised to achieve either with anybody." Under Pound's influence, Eliot was persuaded that the marriage would help him burn his boats and commit himself to poetry by staying in England. In fact, the very misery of the marriage brought, as Eliot put it, "the state of mind out of which came *The Waste Land*." Pound wrote next to the neurasthenic drama in the manuscript of Part II: "photography?" The mutual torment of the couple, their irreconcilably different dramas, their powerplay, the impossibility of communication, provide the personal background to the pervasive futility of *The Waste Land*. For Eliot, horror mounted swiftly to a vision of hell: He spoke of "horror of life" as "a mystical experience."[6] For Vivienne, horror came from hidden motives: women rattling carriages behind her in the street might be "dying to propagate their own loathesomeness."[7] Their menace complements Eliot's "red-eyed scavengers . . . creeping / From Kentish Town and Golder's Green".[8]

Vivienne, with her swift hatred and lashing words, reflected in her articulate, blown-up way Eliot's most disturbing private thoughts. He was, Virginia Woolf saw, "thrown like an assegai into the hide of the world."[9] The violence of feeling, controlled by the perfection of his manners, appears in the early poetry as disgust with rotting cities and intellectual pretension, a disgust extended, in Eliot alone, to Jews, sexual license, and woman as "the enemy of the absolute."[10] This fallen world he transmutes into *The Waste Land*'s vision of a disorderly hell, of which Vivienne, with her anarchic abandon, was arch-embodiment. After Eliot left her in 1933, she said that he had made her feel "a sort of super-being."[11] His poetry displays her in powerful, doomed roles, playing – or overplaying – the Duchess of Malfi[12] or Cleopatra[13], a "lady of situations,"[14] wilfully vocal in contrast to his ideal Lady of silences. In 1936, taking up a new career as a student at the Royal College of Music, she exulted in her discovery of a "*huge* voice" as a singer.

A third woman entered Eliot's life at exactly the time that Vivienne was certified and put away for life in a mental home in the summer of 1938. Mary Trevelyan, then aged forty, was less important for Eliot's writing. Where Emily Hale and Vivienne were part of Eliot's private phantasmagoria, Mary Trevelyan played her part in what was essentially a public friendship. She was Eliot's escort for nearly twenty years, until his second marriage in 1957. A brainy woman, with the bracing organizational energy of a Florence Nightingale, she propped the outer structure of Eliot's life, but for him she, too, represented something. He liked introducing her to his sister Marian as "the Vicar's daughter."[15] She was indeed the devout eldest daughter of the Reverend George Philip Trevelyan, who had built various churches of his own High Anglican persuasion. I think that Mary Trevelyan must have represented for Eliot the inherited traditions of the faith to which he had converted in 1927. Without much spiritual imagination, she was an appropriate companion for the regimen that Eliot prescribed for himself in 1941 of "prayer, observance, discipline, thought and action,"[16] and she accompanied him to all services.

Mary Trevelyan has left an unpublished but highly intelligent, humorous, and readable memoir of their friendship that

Boswellizes their conversations in the late forties and early fifties. "The Pope of Russell Square" is the fullest record we shall have of Eliot during his most inscrutable years as a public figure, when his fame, following the Nobel Prize, seemed to preclude close ties. Nursing Eliot was too minor a job for Mary's vigorous talents, and her busy-ness came to be mildly irritating, like the guardianship of the bossy Julia in *The Cocktail Party*. "Oh, it's YOU again, Julia," Eliot greeted her in 1949 in a chemist's in Southampton Row.[17]

Finally, in the mid-fifties, Eliot turned to Valerie Fletcher, who was the source, I think, for the loyal, supportive Monica in the last play, written during their courtship and first year of marriage. She brought relief and some return to simplicity of heart after a long spiritual trial and long-held guilt for "things ill done and done to others' harm."[18] Eliot's last poem was "A Dedication to My Wife," which describes an ideal union of body, mind, and soul.

Of these four women, Emily Hale is both the least-known and most important for the religious search in Eliot's mature work. Almost throughout his career, she alone seems to have been able to generate the all-important "hints and guesses,"[19] the rare, mystical glimpses of something beyond him. And though the bulk of his writing seems to recount horror and trial, it is essential to recognize that it is not routine modernist disillusion and alienation, but that feelings of *"The horror! the horror!"* have their counterpoise in the search for divine love. Why Emily Hale was so important was that for brief but essential moments her memory, transformed as pure light, took a hollow man out of the futile waste of his existence.

In 1923 Eliot ventured to send Emily Hale the first of many gifts.[20] It was a copy of *Ara Vos Prec* (1919), inscribed "For Emily Hale with the author's humble compliments, T. S. Eliot, 5. ix. 23. SIETI RACOMMENDATO / IL MIO TESORO / NELLO QUAL VIVO ANCOR / E NON PIU CHIEGGO / POI SI REVOLSE." This is from Dante's *Inferno*, Canto 15, where Dante tells Brunetto Latini, "[Y]ou taught me how man makes himself immortal," and Latini calls back, from the burning fastness of his hell, of his work *Il Tesoro*. His *Treasure*, in French, is a kind of encyclopedia; his *Little Treasure*, in Italian, tells of an allegorical journey, which may have suggested Dante's poem. After a crisis in his marriage, when

Eliot considered leaving Lloyds Bank without an alternative position, he was calling back to Emily Hale through the tortured voice and gesture of Latini: "[M]ay my 'Treasure' be entrusted to you, my 'Treasure' in which I am still living. And I do not ask more than this. Then he turned around. . . ." Two decades later, Eliot was to return to "Ser Brunetto" in his first draft of the climactic encounter with the ghost of his immortal other self, near the end of the work that he considered his masterpiece, *Four Quartets*.[21]

In 1927, when Emily Hale and Eliot began their sustained correspondence, he sent her his essay on *Shakespeare and the Stoicism of Seneca*. Helen Gardner once remarked to me that it contained a personal message to Emily Hale: "What every poet starts from is his own emotions," which may be "his nostalgia, his bitter regrets for past happiness." These regrets may become for a "brave" poet the basis of an attempt to "fabricate something permanent and holy out of his personal animal feelings – as in the *Vita Nuova*."[22]

Emily Hale had first met Eliot as a family friend through his cousin Eleanor Hinkley, who liked to organize family theatricals. One one occasion, in 1913, Eliot played the hypochondriacal Mr. Woodhouse and Emily Hale the snobbish Mrs. Elton in a scene from *Emma*. Though Emily Hale was keen to go on the stage professionally, her Boston brahmin family would not allow it, and she had to content herself with amateur performances and directing for the rest of her life. She had a natural stage presence and a resonant voice that were to prove effective in commanding comic roles, as shown in one review of her performance as Lady Bracknell while she was teaching drama at Scripps College in California in 1933: "Miss Hale as Lady Bracknell dominated the play with one sweep of her lorgnette. She . . . combined social rapacity with a most imposing glare."[23]

When Emily Hale and Eliot restarted[24] their correspondence at the time of his conversion, his imagination at once conjured up a woman's spiritual presence in "Salutation" (1927), which begins "Lady. . . ." This is where he assigns the role of "Lady of silences." The frail memory of love – "Rose of memory" – supports the end of a tormented life with a promise of renewal. The bare bones of the lost self may yet live through the Lady's watchful fidelity. The poem concludes with a renewal of visionary power as the poet looks to a promised land that is his rightful inheritance. God speaks to him, as to Moses: "This is the land." A poem that begins with a Lady and ends with the voice of God may be the formula for the central imaginative drama of Eliot's mature years. In this, the Lady is to be the initiating influence and prime listener. It is always a woman who is the recipient, or the potential recipient, of poetic confession, which makes women matter to Eliot in rather a different way from their appearance in his first volume, as Laforguian butts of ironic dismissal, or in his second volume, as butts of a sense of sin. Although in early years Eliot does dismiss some women as animals and pity others as victims of male lust, he later calls on the Lady's intelligent receptivity, as eventually the hollow-hearted Elder Statesman will come to depend on the staunch backing with which his daughter, Monica, receives his hesitant confession.

"Salutation," originally written on its own, came to be the second part of the long sequence, *Ash Wednesday*, where a penitent's ordeals culminate in the temptation to erotic love. Looking out on the past, through a window of memory "bellied like the fig's fruit," a man recalls a woman's sweet brown hair but must hold back from its distraction. The music of a flute must play, not to the senses, but to the spirit, while the still "silent" woman bends her head in assent to a higher love. The veiled woman continues to preside, together with the ghosts of New England forebears, until the fountain of the spirit shoots up and the renewing waters flow.

The initial impulse for a long poem, with its protracted and recurring effort of renewal, is an encounter with a nameless, faceless, and silent woman. The impulse recurs in the *Quartets* and goes back to Prufrock's need to confess to a woman – not love, but vision and madness in the manuscript draft, called appropriately "Prufrock Amongst the Women."[25] The confessional content of these encounters with women is a brooding sense of fate: a man whose life marks time for some overwhelming insight. To society women who come and go, this private conviction would seem absurd, and Prufrock finds no woman in the Boston of 1911 in whom he can confide. But between "Prufrock" and "Gerontion," written in 1919, Eliot came to know, trust, and leave Emily Hale.

14

In "Gerontion" a silent listener is there, addressed only as "you," to hear a rapid, low-voiced confession:

I would meet you upon this honestly.
I that was near your heart was removed therefrom. . . .
I have lost my passion. . . .

He has lost the acuteness of his senses and asks pitifully: "How should I use them for your closer contact?" The loss of an un-fulfilled experience is part of a larger drama for this speaker: the loss of a special destiny signified by his youthful premonition of "Christ the tiger." Although the poem is, of course, aesthetically intact, it may have been also some sort of literary letter, in which he allowed himself, under the cover of poetic license, to explore a profounder and more complex understanding of love than he would have permitted himself in a personal form of discourse like the thousand-odd letters that Eliot sent directly to Emily Hale.[26]

Their eventual reunion, when she came to England in 1930, was propelled by a dream that was given the space of long separa-tion to take hold. To dream of meeting an old love after many years was, for the poet, a replay of Dante's meeting with Beatrice on the verge of paradise, as Eliot saw it, the recrudescence of old passion in a new emotion, in a new situation that "comprehends, enlarges, and gives meaning to it." In an essay on Dante (1929) that Eliot owned to be autobiographical[27] he quotes and trans-lates these moving lines: "Olive-crowned over a white veil a lady appeared to me. And my spirit . . . without further knowledge by my eyes, felt, through the hidden power which went out from her, the great strength of the old love." Eliot once discussed with a priest and mentor, W. F. Stead, the way that Dante's love for Beatrice passed over into love of God in the *Vita Nuova.* "I have had that experience," Eliot said eagerly and rather shyly.[28]

While Emily Hale was in England in the summer of 1930, Eliot wrote "Marina" in which a voyager resigns his present stale life for the New World, as he homes in hope, "lips parted," toward a pure woman. The lone voyager, battered, almost broken as he crosses from one life to another, comes at last to a haven of domestic love, but it is not ordinary love, and the woman is not human in the ordinary sense. In this meeting some emotions have been purified away so that others, ordinarily invisible, become apparent. The woman on the New England shore appears as the embodiment of a divine call.

Eliot was refining his idea of love to pose an almost unattainable ideal. This began as early as 1910 with a ruthless rejection of the body's uncleanness. Long before Eliot's conversion, his fierce disgust for the flesh appeared in his unpublished "First Debate Between Body and Soul," in the violence of three martyr poems of 1914–15 ("The Burnt Dancer," "The Love Song of St. Sebastian," and "The Death of Saint Narcissus"), and yet again in *The Waste Land*'s ruthless "Burning burning burning burning" of the polluted flesh. The only way that Eliot could admit a renewed love in 1930 was with reverence and chastity. His idea of love does not fit our usual categories, sexual or romantic. "The love of man and woman," he said in 1929, "is only explained and made reasonable by the higher love or else is simply the coupling of animals."[29] He wished to transform the energy of desire into something absolute and lasting and said that he had to go back to the late Middle Ages for a state of exalted feeling which, he insisted, we no longer experience. Eliot, then, wanted nothing less than perfect love, part of his longing for "the impossible union."[30] This is how he explained it in one of his numerous buried essays: "I mean the turning away of the soul from desire . . . of drugged pleasures, of power, or of *happiness*. I mean 'love', in the sense in which 'love' is the opposite of what we ordinarily mean by 'love' (the desire to possess and to dominate or to be dominated by)."[31]

In the second half of his life, Eliot was more concerned with love than in his early years: love's essence in memory, which prompted the poetry of the new life; divine Love; and much later, marital love. The automatic disgust with almost all women in the early poems came from hardly seeing them: they are slotted into place as inciters or as prey of low desire. Emily Hale was exempt from low desire. Though not ethereal herself and not in the least silent as a teacher of speech and drama, she was a model for silent, ethereal women in Eliot's poetry, la Figlia, the hyacinth girl, the Lady of silences, all of whom elevate the poet's spirit. To consummate such a love would tarnish the dream that made the art or, more accurately, art's climax – moments of light and silence – so Emily Hale was set to play roles of virgin and kinswoman watching faithfully for the battered traveler. This was hard on Emily Hale, for as no real woman fits Eliot's reductive Grishkin image of rank temptress, so no real woman could approximate his dream of purity.

There were two crucial meetings. In the winter of 1932–3 Eliot crossed the continent by train to visit Emily Hale at Scripps College. This meeting is solely of biographical importance for, at this point, Vivienne lost touch with her husband's movements.[32] The other occasion had literary consequences: Emily Hale took a year's leave to be in England in 1934–5, and in September 1934 she and Eliot went together to view the rose-garden of the Gloucestershire country house, Burnt Norton, a visit that, in a sense, set off Eliot's poetry for the next eight years during which he wrote his masterpiece, *Four Quartets*. In the first quartet, *Burnt Norton*, written in 1935, it is a time of autumn heat, both literally – the roses in their second flowering – and as a metaphor for a mature love.

Some momentous experience at Burnt Norton was reshaped into three accounts: the unpublished and fragmentary "Bellegarde" sketch that Eliot sent to his brother in the spring or early summer of 1935,[33] *Burnt Norton* itself, and the rose-garden encounter between Harry and Agatha in *The Family Reunion* (1939). Each account relates a similar experience of love from a different angle. "Bellegarde," written first, is the most physical: a man experiences "leaping pleasures"[34] that release him from a mood of futility, reach a "matchless moment," and then fade all too fast. The opening and conclusion of *Burnt Norton* rework the rudimentary "Bellegarde" material as a deeply emotional encounter with a love from the past. The rapport is so acute that the ghosts of their former selves seem to walk toward a moment that transcends love with a glimpse of eternity, "the still point of the turning world," as they walk the aisle of roses toward a pool filled with light. In 1934 the same woman, now in the flesh, elicited the same visionary moment that is recalled in the hyacinth girl episode of *The Waste Land*. Again, the poet looks into the heart of light. Whatever actually happened at Burnt Norton, the finale to the poem, as well as the finale to *Four Quartets* as a whole, completed in 1942, record a darting, breathless, unforgettable bliss: "Quick now, here, now, always —

Eliot's final record of the scene in his play (its scenarios go

17

back to 1934–5)[35] gives more identity to the man and woman, as well as an explanation for their fading emotion. Two women are associated with the sunlit moment: Agatha, a middle-aged college teacher, and the virginal, waiting Mary, who is destined to become what Agatha is. Mary brings Harry "news" of a door that opens to "Sunlight and singing," but this is for Harry "only a moment." For Harry, the mystical rapport fulfills his craving for visionary communion, and the moment takes him past the woman who initiates it. In a revealing letter to the play's director, E. Martin Browne, Eliot explained that Harry's attraction to a particular woman wars with his general idea that all women are unclean creatures. The nightmare of his marriage has given him a horror of women; his solution is to find refuge in an "ambiguous relation."[36]

A similar ambiguity was to remain in Eliot's relation to Emily Hale over two more decades. When Vivienne died unexpectedly in 1947, Emily was confident that Eliot would marry her, but he withdrew in the puzzling manner she recounts in a moving letter to a friend, Lorraine Havens:

> with the Dorset Players
> Dorset. Vt.
> August 7 '47

Dearest Lorraine,

... I am going to tell you, dear friend, that what I confided to you long ago of a mutual affection he and I have had for each other has come to a strange impasse whether permanent or not, I do not know. Tom's wife died last winter very suddenly. I supposed he would then feel free to marry me as I believed he always intended to do. But such proves not to be the case. We met privately two or three times to try to sift the situation as thoroughly as possible – he loves me – I believe that wholly – but apparently not in the way usual to men less gifted i.e. with complete love thro' a married relationship. I have not completely given up hope that he may yet recover from this – to me – abnormal reaction, but on the other hand I cannot allow myself to hold on to anything so delicately uncertain. . . .

> Yours
> Emily Hale[37]

After waiting so long, Eliot felt that it was now too late. Instead, he cast Emily Hale as the source for the rejected woman, the noble, martyred Celia in his next play, *The Cocktail Party.* She found, rereading the play years later, "many a passage which *could* have hidden meaning for me and for him." For the first and last time in his career, Eliot created a woman who acts in her own right, not as foil or prop to a man's self-realization as artist, convert, or sinner. Celia is not a statue, a bodiless virgin, or a Lady of silence. With brave distinctness, she states her surprise at the defection of her lover, Edward, and is the focus for sympathy in the play. Never before had Eliot conceived so lovable a woman, at once assured and vulnerable. Two men have loved her: the middle-aged husband, with whom she has had a long affair, and the young film director, the artist, who has loved her platonically. Of the two, it is the artist, Peter, who has the clearer view of her distinction. She aroused not the usual desire for possession, but a strange feeling, at once more intense and more tranquil. Peter speaks of "moments in which we seemed to share some perception, / Some feeling, some indefinable experience / In which we were both unaware of ourselves."[38] Here, Eliot explores the rarefied moment that he owed to Emily Hale. Peter declares it to be his only experience of what he, like Eliot, calls "reality."

Celia answers this with her matching account of the "intensity of loving / In the spirit, a vibration of delight / Without desire, for desire is fulfilled / In the delight of loving."[39] It is an exaltation without the fret of desire that defies our usual categories of love and friendship. As Eliot strove to go *"beyond* poetry,"[40] so his tie with Emily Hale also defies definition. My guess is that she was a watcher of his destiny, that she replaced his mother as guardian of his search for perfection, and that the drama of his inward life – so different from his public performances – was the secret of her own life, too. As they grew old, she still watched him and let the association give shape and color to her own existence. Such a course of existence requires a climax, but nothing happened. The years ebbed. The story of Emily Hale was like a trailer that Eliot towed so far behind him that it was almost out of sight, bearing his frail hope of perfection. When that hope faded in the later forties and early fifties, the trailer was detached and the story of

Emily Hale put aside for a quite different story of forgiveness and marital fulfillment. Silenced in her lifetime, and further by Eliot's decision to burn her side of their long correspondence, she did regret, she owned, that she would not be here when Eliot's letters, sequestered until 2019, "burst upon the world."[41]

To Eliot, the "life of a man of genius, viewed in relation to his writing, comes to take a pattern of inevitability, and even his disabilities will seem to have stood him in good stead."[42] If we apply this theory to his own life, its inner coherence is obvious, particularly in his ties with women. It is curious how each was absorbed into what seems an almost predetermined pattern. Emily Hale prompted the sublime moments; Vivienne, the sense of sin, as well as providing, throughout the first marriage, the living martyrdom. Later, sensible, efficient Mary Trevelyan served her long stint as support during the years of penitence. For her their friendship was a commitment; for Eliot quite peripheral. His passion for immortality was so commanding that it allowed him to reject each of these women with a firmness that shattered their lives. At the same time, his poetry and plays transformed them as the material of art. As such, Emily and Vivienne became allegorical emblems of vision and horror that take his works to the frontiers of experience, and beyond.

## Notes

1  Described thus in a lecture at Scripps College (December 1932), reported in *The Scripture* (12 December 1932). I am indebted to the librarian, Judy Harvey Sahak, at the Ella Strong Denison Library, for the idea of looking at the backfiles of this college magazine.

2  *The Dry Salvages:* V, *Collected Poems 1909–62* (New York: Harcourt, 1963), 199. (All references to Eliot's poems are to this edition.)

3  Private paper, extracts from which are quoted by Valerie Eliot in her Introduction to *The Letters of T. S. Eliot,* vol. 1, *1898–1922,* edited by Valerie Eliot (New York: Harcourt, 1988), xvii.

4  *The Waste Land:* I.

5  *Ash Wednesday:* II.

6  "Cyril Tourneur," in T. S. Eliot, *Selected Essays* (1932; reprint, New York: Harcourt, 1960), 166.

7  Vivienne Eliot, in entry dated 13 April 1936 in Day Book (1935–6),

Bodleian Library. I am indebted to the late Maurice Haigh-Wood for permission, given in 1976, to quote. See Lyndall Gordon, *Eliot's New Life* (New York: Farrar, Straus, 1988), ch. 2.

8   "A Cooking Egg."

9   *The Diary of Virginia Woolf,* vol. 4 (10 September 1933), edited by Anne Olivier Bell (New York: Harcourt, 1982), 179.

10   "Conversation Galante."

11   Diary (2 October 1935), Bodeleian Library.

12   See "The Death of the Duchess," in Valerie Eliot, ed., *The Waste Land: A Facsimile and Transcript of the Original Drafts Including the Annotations of Ezra Pound* (New York: Harcourt, 1971), 104–7.

13   *The Waste Land:* II.

14   *The Waste Land:* I.

15   Reported by Mary Trevelyan in her unpublished memoir of her friendship with TSE, "The Pope of Russell Square." The typescript is owned by her nephew, the biographer, Humphrey Carpenter. See Gordon, *Eliot's New Life,* ch. 5.

16   *The Dry Salvages:* V.

17   Trevelyan, "The Pope of Russell Square."

18   *Little Gidding:* II.

19   *The Dry Salvages.* For full details of the relationship with Emily Hale, see Gordon, *Eliot's New Life,* chs. 1, 3, 4.

20   Catalogue 22, Glenn Horowitz, Bookseller, 141 East 44th Street, New York City (1990). I am grateful to Judy Harvey Sahak for this information.

21   Helen Gardner, *The Composition of* Four Quartets (London: Faber, 1978), 228.

22   *Shakespeare and the Stoicism of Seneca,* in, *Selected Essays,* 107–20. Published 22 September 1927.

23   *The Scripture* (15 May 1933).

24   Valerie Eliot, in her Introduction to the *Letters,* notes that they had exchanged some letters during Eliot's first year in England.

25   The draft is in Eliot's unpublished Notebook in the Berg Collection, New York Public Library. See Lyndall Gordon, *Eliot's Early Years* (1977; reprint, New York: Farrar, Straus, 1988), ch. 2.

26   These letters are sequestered at Princeton until October 2019. For fuller details on this correspondence, see Gordon, *Eliot's New Life,* ch. 4.

27   In a letter to Pound, dated 29 December 1929, Beinecke Library. Yale. In the Dante essay, he described the scene of meeting in detail. *Selected Essays.*

28 W. F. Stead, unpublished "Literary Reminiscences" (29 April 1940). Osborn Collection, Beinecke Library.

29 "Dante," *Selected Essays,* 234–5.

30 *The Dry Salvages:* V. See A. V. C. Schmidt, "Eliot's Intolerable Wrestle: Speech, Silence, Words and Voices," *UNISA English Studies* (Pretoria, 1983): 17–22, one of the outstanding articles on Eliot to be published in the 1980s.

31 "View and Reviews," *New English Weekly* 7 (6 June 1935): 152.

32 She recalled this date some years later in her Diary, Bodleian Library.

33 Included with the notes for *Murder in the Cathedral,* Houghton Library, Harvard University.

34 Six lines are quoted by E. Martin Browne, *The Making of Eliot's Plays* (Cambridge University Press, 1969), 44.

35 See Gordon, *Eliot's New Life,* ch. 2 and appendix 2.

36 The letter is quoted in full in Browne, *The Making of Eliot's Plays,* 107–8.

37 For a fuller quotation of this letter, see Gordon, *Eliot's New Life,* 170–1. I am greatly indebted to Mrs. Havens for a photocopy.

38 *The Cocktail Party,* act 1, scene 1.

39 Ibid., act 2.

40 "English Letter Writers," unpublished lecture delivered at Yale in the winter of 1933, quoted by F. O. Matthiessen, *The Achievement of T. S. Eliot,* (1935; 3d ed., reprint, New York: OUP, 1959), 90.

41 To Willard Thorp, The Thorp Papers, Princeton University. This important batch of letters gives some view of the relationship from Emily Hale's point of view. I am indebted to Professor Thorp for permission to quote.

42 "The Classics and the Man of Letters" (1942), in *To Criticize the Critic* (1965; reprint, New York: Noonday-Farrar, 1968), 147.

# Gender, Voice, and Figuration in Eliot's Early Poetry

CAROL CHRIST

It is a striking fact that three of the principal modernist poets –
Eliot, Pound, and Williams – each wrote a poem entitled "Portrait
of a Lady" within a few years of 1910.[1] The title, of course,
alludes to James's novel and, for Eliot and Pound, refers to the
Jamesian project of some of their early verse. Pound asserted that
*Hugh Selwyn Mauberley* was an attempt to condense the James
novel, and Eliot told Virginia Woolf that his early inclination was
to develop in the manner of Henry James.[2] Behind the model of
Henry James, however (indeed, behind James's *Portrait of a
Lady*), is a nineteenth-century poetic mode of female portraiture.
Tennyson, Browning, Rossetti, and Swinburne wrote portrait
poems – "Mariana," "The Gardener's Daughter," "Andrea del Sar-
to," "The Blessed Damozel," "The Portrait," and "Before the Mirror," to name just a few – that identify poetic style with the
portrait of a lady. These poems engage not just the subject of
woman but the gender of the poetical. Contemporary criticism

shows us that the gender of poetic style was an important matter of critical debate. Alfred Austin, for example, who was to succeed Tennyson as poet laureate, criticized both Tennyson and Swinburne for what he called their feminine muse. All the poets important in evolving the mellifluous erotic lyricism of the nineteenth century against which the modernists reacted – Shelley, Keats, Tennyson, the Pre-Raphaelites – were subject to the charge of feminizing poetry, often in those poems about women that define the characteristics of poetic vision and style. Thus the portrait of a lady in nineteenth-century poetry implies a debate about the gender of the poetical.[3]

The modern portrait of a lady likewise concerns the relationship of gender to poetic speech and figure. I will focus upon the case of T. S. Eliot, for his treatment of the feminine subject reveals much about the evolution of his poetic voice. Eliot's early poetry is, of course, full of women. In many ways, their predominance is not surprising. The poetic tradition with which he grew up, the strain of Romanticism that evolves through Tennyson and the Pre-Raphaelites, centers upon the lyric evocation of female subjects, and even a brief look at Eliot's early uncollected work shows powerful echoes of those voices. These lines from "The Portrait," for example, recall Rossetti's numerous sonnets on female portraits:

> Not like a tranquil goddess carved of stone
> But evanescent, as if one should meet
> A pensive lamia in some wood-retreat,
> An immaterial fancy of one's own.
>
> No mediations glad or ominous
> Disturb her lips, or move the slender hands;
> Her dark eyes keep their secrets hid from us,
> Beyond the circle of our thoughts she stands.[4]

Sandra Gilbert and Susan Gubar have shown echoes of Swinburne's *Lesbia Brandon* in "The Love Song of Saint Sebastian,"[5] and "Circe's Palace" also echoes Swinburne. Thus, when Eliot writes "Portrait of a Lady" or "The Love Song of J. Alfred Prufrock," he is revising a nineteenth-century mode of portraiture one sees in his early verse. In addition to the influence of this "feminized" poetic tradition, Eliot also felt the impact of what

Gilbert and Gubar describe as an increasingly feminized literary culture, in which women writers, editors, and patrons played important roles.[6] Finally, the strongest influence on Eliot's ambition to be a poet was probably his mother, who was a poet herself and who told her son that she hoped he would succeed in the literary vocation at which she had failed.[7] Thus in terms of literary tradition, literary culture, and personal biography, Eliot would define his voice in the context of a powerful female presence.

Eliot's early poetry is centrally concerned with the difficulties of defining a voice in the context of this presence. "Portrait of a Lady" represents the situation most explicitly. The poem is a contest of voices, a juxtaposition staged to determine who – or whose music –should "have the advantage, after all." Eliot structures the poem's three parts by pairing the voices of the Lady and the speaker. The speaker first presents the Lady's arrangements – the way she figures her room, the accents of her voice – and then searches for a voice and figuration of his own to separate himself from her. The predominant metaphor in this contest of voices is music; the Lady speaks through "attenuated tones of violins / Mingled with remote cornets," violins the speaker hears as broken and out of tune as he seeks to construct a prelude of his own, "capricious monotone."

The idiom in which the Lady expresses herself is a sentimental one that depends upon the stock figurations of a poetic sensibility – lilacs and hyacinths, gray and smoky afternoons, evenings that are yellow and rose. She projects the plot of an Arnoldian romance – friendship that provides the one secure value in an unfulfilling world, a buried life, hands that reach across a gulf, missed affinities. In addition to this resonance in imagery and theme with a conventional nineteenth-century idiom, the sections of the poem that the Lady arranges have the unity of atmosphere, setting, and dramatic situation that characterize the Victorian lyric. The Lady is seeking to construct a poem in the tradition of "Two in the Campagna," "To Marguerite – Continued," or Amours de Voyage.

Into the Lady's lyric the speaker introjects "false notes" in an attempt to assert the "tom-tom" of his own poetic identity. He strives for an urban, masculine vocabulary – tobacco, bocks, the comics and the sporting page, the late events, the public clocks.

He exploits the irony and the incongruous juxtaposition that mark him as modern:

> Particularly I remark
> An English countess goes upon the stage.
> A Greek was murdered at a Polish dance,
> Another bank defaulter has confessed.

Such a use of irony and disjunction, for all its veiled recognition of some of the psychological issues of the poem, sustains the speaker's sense of poetic command:

> I keep my countenance,
> I remain self-possessed. . . .

But this is a command, as Hugh Kenner says of Laforgue, whose virtuosity is "the debonair panic of a man whose strategy . . . is to hasten across abysses he has no taste for exploring."[8] The speaker displays an increasing anxiety in his search for poetic figures to maintain his poise, as he borrows "every changing shape to find expression."

The speaker ultimately seeks to allay his anxiety by imagining the death of the Lady, a death anticipated from the beginning of the poem, both in its epigraph and in the atmosphere of Juliet's tomb established in its opening lines. The poem thus comes to the end of its contest of voices, a contest it concedes to the Lady. By her death she achieves a certain advantage of realized expression – "This music is successful with a 'dying fall'" – that the speaker himself never attains. Even at the end he is "Doubtful, for a while / Not knowing what to feel or if I understand / Or whether wise or foolish, tardy or too soon . . ." But the speaker achieves a victory of sorts as well: by imagining her death, one might say by enacting the murderous fantasy of that death, he fixes her within the bounds of the portrait he has painted and thus reduces to manageable limits the discomfort she causes him. She thus joins the portrait gallery of dead literary ladies of the nineteenth century – Poe's "Oval Portrait," Tennyson's "Gardener's Daughter," Browning's "Last Duchess." These nineteenth-century portraits frequently identify the death of their subject with the appropriation of a literary mode identified as feminine. In the case of Eliot's poem, the device of the portrait not only allows the speaker to aestheticize and therefore distance an uncomfortable relationship, it allows Eliot to identify a fantasy of desertion and murder with issues of literary style. He thus constructs a drama whereby he separates himself from a feminized poetic idiom at the same time that he appropriates its effects through the ventriloquized voice of the Lady. Eliot imagines the literary past as a woman, whom he deserts, dishonors, even murders while he appropriates her voice. Indeed, Eliot's poetry gives reason to question the Bloomian paradigm of poetic influence, for, at least in his poetry, Eliot tends to cast safely distant voices of the literary tradition, with whom he wishes unabashedly to identify himself, as male, whereas he associates poetic effects of the nineteenth century, far closer to his poetic idiom, with a woman whom the poem in some way involves in a drama of betrayal and appropriation. He thus tends to imagine his relationship to the immediate literary past not as an Oedipal struggle but as a desertion or a rape. Eliot's gendering of this drama of betrayal – a gendering already implicit in the feminization of poetic idiom in the nineteenth century – allows him at once to enact and mask issues of poetic influence.[9]

Even when the woman is more ideally conceived than the woman in "Portrait of a Lady," Eliot connects her portrayal with similar issues of desertion and literary style. The other portrait poem in the "Prufrock" volume, for example, "La Figlia che Piange," also associates its female subject with a nineteenth-century style, in this case, Victorian sentimental narrative painting, which implies a domestic drama in the pose of its subject. Like "Portrait," the poem enacts a fantasy of desertion, whose reward, as it were, is an image that becomes the funerary monument to which the poem's title alludes. By composing his portrait of a lady, the lover/poet at once appropriates "a gesture and a pose" while he secures his separation from a woman whose actual presence threatens to overwhelm him.[10] In this way Eliot's speaker –both in this poem and in "Portrait of a Lady" – bears an uneasy similarity to that nineteenth-century commissioner of portraits, Browning's Duke. He changes himself from one who is the object of a discomforting female gaze to one who controls the look, who "puts by the curtain." By carefully composing an image, he secures himself from decomposure.

27

The prose poem "Hysteria" makes explicit the connection between the composition of a bodily intact image and the composure of the male subject. The poem relates a fantasy of being swallowed up in "the dark caverns" of a woman's throat, a fantasy that the title identifies as hysteria. The speaker's hysteria begins to rise when he becomes absorbed in the woman's voice: "As she laughed I was aware of becoming involved in her laughter and being part of it. . . ." He loses a sense of the visual integrity of her image, representing body parts by grotesquely anthropomorphized metaphors: "[H]er teeth were only accidental stars with a talent for squad-drill." He diverts himself from this fantasy of engulfment only by focusing on a visually discrete male image, the elderly waiter, who "with trembling hands was hurriedly spreading a pink and white checked cloth over the rusty green iron table." These trembling hands – for Eliot frequently the last determining site of human identity in moments of dehumanization and fragmentation – perform the one act in the poem described with clear boundaries and visual precision: the spreading of a pink and white checked cloth on a rusty green iron table. The patterning of the two adjectival phrases – "pink and white checked," "rusty green iron" – suggests that they function to anchor attention in visually discrete images that suppress the speaker's hysteria, much as they cover the table. The speaker then decides that if he can provide clearer boundaries to the female image by stilling the shaking of the woman's breasts, he can collect the fragments of the afternoon, and he concentrates his attention "with careful subtlety to this end."

"Hysteria" thus suggests the function of the stilled and bounded images of "Portrait" and "Figlia:" They keep the speaker from being engulfed by the woman – an engulfment that Eliot associates with absorption in her voice or her music – and allow him some security in maintaining his own voice. But this security is at a certain cost. Eliot associates the carefully composed whole woman of his poetry with a repressively genteel feminine society. The poems in which they appear also bear the closest affinity in Eliot's work to a nineteenth-century poetic idiom and structure, one he identifies as feminine. Eliot controls his images of women by staying within these poetic and social confines, but he portrays those confines as not allowing him an authentic identity.

In an essay on Pound's attitudes toward the visual arts in the *Cantos*, Michael Bernstein argues that Pound associated female sexuality with unbounded art, ungraspable imaginative dispersal that was opposite of his ideal of the firm and bounded line.[11] Pound's own portrait of a lady, "Portrait d'une Femme," supports Bernstein's thesis, for the Sargasso Sea of the lady's mind, her sea-hoard of deciduous things, represents an identity without a center, a collection of detail without a defining principal, a sensibility without boundaries, which is a negative image of Pound's poetic ideal. For Eliot, too, the boundedness of the female image is central to the evolution of his poetic idiom, but he works out the issue in a way very different from that of Pound. Eliot associates the bounded line with a feminized poetic idiom from which he seeks to distance himself, whereas he locates his strongest and most characteristic poetic voice through the imaginative dispersal of the female body.

In *Women in the Poetry of T. S. Eliot*, Tony Pinkney argues that Sweeney's lines, "Any man has to, needs to, wants to / Once in a lifetime, do a girl in," define the central impetus of Eliot's poetry.[12] I think that Pinkney's insight is only partially true, for among the most striking characteristics of Eliot's poetry is the way in which it fragments not just female bodies but all bodies, and frequently in a way that makes their gender ambiguous. I would say that the issue of corporeal intactness rather than aggression toward women dominates Eliot's poetry. The two are, of course, connected. If one were seeking to articulate a motivating psychology for Eliot's poetry, one might argue that difficulty in separating himself from woman leads, among other things, to various attempts to do her in. But such a mysogynistic reading would be at the cost of simplifying both the violence of his poetry and the ambiguity in its representation of gender. The murderous impulse toward the woman in Eliot is always connected to a concern with the intactness of the body, and violent fantasies of bodily dismemberment shift quite fluidly between the sexes, as in "The Love Song of Saint Sebastian," where Eliot follows a fantasy of flogging himself to death with one of mangling the woman to whom the poem is addressed. Eliot's concern with corporeal intactness is in turn closely connected with his constitution of poetic voice. When Eliot creates an intact image of a woman's body, as he does in the portrait poems, he represents the male as having difficulty locating his own voice, as we can see in the shifting figures of "Portrait of a Lady" or the split persona of "La Figlia che Piange." He tends to cast such poems as an iron-ized dialogue with a nineteenth-century idiom that he at once betrays and appropriates; in the process, however, he fails to define his own voice with any surety. In contrast, he locates his strongest voice not only by fragmenting the body but by making ambiguous its identification with both character and gender.[13] He places at the center of such poems a moment of vision that is deferred, evaded, or suppressed but whose bodily manifestations are displaced, ungendered, onto other elements of the poem. For Eliot, poetic representation of a powerful female presence created difficulty in embodying the male. In order to do so, Eliot avoids envisioning the female, indeed, avoids attaching gender to bodies.

We can see this process clearly in "The Love Song of J. Alfred Prufrock." The poem circles around not only an unarticulated question, as all readers agree, but also an unenvisioned center, the "one" whom Prufrock addresses. The poem never visualizes the woman with whom Prufrock imagines an encounter except in fragments and in plurals – eyes, arms, skirts – synecdoches we might well imagine as fetishistic replacements. But even these synecdochic replacements are not clearly engendered. The braceleted arms and the skirts are specifically feminine, but the faces, the hands, the voices, the eyes are not. As if to displace the central human object it does not visualize, the poem projects images of the body onto the landscape (the sky, the streets, the fog), but these images, for all their marked intimation of sexu-ality, also avoid the designation of gender (the muttering retreats of restless nights, the fog that rubs, licks, and lingers). The most visually precise images in the poem are those of Prufrock him-self, a Prufrock carefully composed – "My morning coat, my collar mounting firmly to the chin, / My necktie rich and modest, but asserted by a simple pin" – only to be decomposed by the watching eyes of another into thin arms and legs, a balding head brought in upon a platter. Moreover, the images associated with Prufrock are themselves, as Pinkney observes, terrifyingly unsta-ble, attributes constituting the identity of the subject at one moment only to be wielded by the objective the next, like the pin that centers his necktie and then pinions him to the wall or the arms that metamorphose into Prufrock's claws.[14] The poem, in these various ways, decomposes the body, making ambiguous its sexual identification. These scattered body parts at once imply and evade a central encounter the speaker cannot bring himself to confront, but in the pattern of their scattering they constitute the voice that Prufrock feels cannot exist in the gaze of the other.

For all of its brilliance as a poetic resolution of the difficulties in constituting a gendered self that mark Eliot's early poetry, "The Love Song of J. Alfred Prufrock" ends with a confession of the relational failure that is its cost. In *The Waste Land* Eliot, with a desperate virtuosity, presents various ways of constituting the male and female, as if in search of a poetic figuration and voice that place him beyond the conflicts that characterize his earlier poetic stances. The early sections of the poem, up to the entry of Tiresias, develop the strategy of "Portrait of a Lady." They juxtapose the meditations of a male voice with a number of female portraits: Mme. Sosostris, the wealthy woman and the working-class woman in "A Game of Chess," Marie, the hyacinth girl, and, in Eliot's rough draft of the poem, Fresca. In this collage Eliot gives the women of the poem the attributes of traditional literary character. They inhabit settings, they exist in dramatic situations, they have individual histories, and they have voices. They constitute most of the identified speakers in the first three sections of the poem, and they contain among them a number of figures for the poet: the sibyl of Cumae; Mme. Sosostris with her Tarot deck; Fresca, who "scribbles verse of such a gloomy tone / That cautious critics say, her style is quite her own"; and La Pia, who can connect "nothing with nothing." One might appropriately object that these are for the most part satiric portraits (indeed, some of them savagely satiric), but they are nonetheless the ways in which the poem locates both verbal fluency and prophetic authority.

In contrast, the male voice through which Eliot presents these women has none of the definitional attributes of conventionally centered identity. It resists location in time and space, it conveys emotion through literary quotation, and it portrays experience only through metaphoric figuration: the cruel April at the poem's beginning, the desert landscape, the rat's alley, where "dead men lost their bones." Eliot thus turns the shifting figuration that appears as unsurety in "Portrait of a Lady" to a poetic strength. The very lack of location and attribute seems to place the speaker beyond the dilemmas of personality, as if Eliot had succeeded in creating the objective voice of male tradition. But for all this voice seems to offer, the early parts of the poem imagine men as dead or dismembered: the drowned Phoenician sailor, whose eyes have been replaced by pearls, the one-eyed merchant, the fisher king, the hanged man, the corpse planted in the garden. Thus Eliot allows us to read the sublimation of body and personality that mark the poem's voice as a repression of them as well, an escape from dismemberment by removing the male body from the text.

The one place where Eliot attaches a specific historical experience to the speaking voice of the poem – the episode of the hyacinth girl – supports such a reading. The episode begins with the speaker's quoting a woman who addressed him, recalling a gift he gave her: "You gave me hyacinths first a year ago." The speaker then describes his own consciousness of that moment in their relationship. When they came back from the Hyacinth garden, her arms full and her hair wet, he could not speak and his eyes failed, he was neither living nor dead, and he knew nothing, "looking into the heart of light, the silence." Perhaps in recognition of the special status that this episode has by virtue of its attachment to the poet's "I," many critics have found in it the emotional center of the poem.[15] The moment offers some revelation of spiritual and erotic fullness ("the heart of light"), but the speaker portrays himself as unequal to it. Speech and vision fail him, and he ends the passage by borrowing the articulation of another poem (*"Oed' und leer das Meer"*), a ventriloquized voice that is not his own, that reveals him at a loss for words. We have here a Tiresias who, at the moment of sexual illumination, loses not only his sight but his voice as well, a seer who does not gain prophetic power from sexual knowledge. As in his early poetry, Eliot represents the moment of looking at a woman as one that decomposes his voice.

Eliot's use of visual imagery in "A Game of Chess" sustains this sense of a moment of vision evaded. For all the elaborate description of the woman's dressing table and chamber, the passage avoids picturing the woman herself, unlike its source in *Antony and Cleopatra*. The long opening sentence of the description – seventeen lines long – carefully directs the eye around what is presumably the woman sitting in the chair, but she only appears at the end of the passage, in the fiery points of her hair, which are instantly transformed into words. The passage thus finally gives the reader only a fetishistic replacement of the woman it never visualizes, a replacement for which he immediately substitutes a voice. A number of the images in "A Game of Chess" reinforce this concern with the desire to look and its repression – the golden Cupidon that peeps out while another hides his eyes behind his wing, the staring forms leaning out from the wall, the pearls that were eyes, the closed car, the pressing of lidless eyes, and in the second section, Albert's swearing he can't bear to look at Lil. All of the eyes that do not look in this section of the poem are juxtaposed to images of a deconstituted body, imagined alternately as male and as female: the change of Philomel, withered stumps of time, the rat's alley where dead men lost their bones, and the teeth and baby Lil must lose. As the men in the section resist looking, so they do not speak. Albert is gone, and the speaker cannot or will not answer the hysterical questions of the lady.

The poem changes its figuration of gender with the introduction of Tiresias. Eliot states in a note to the passage that "the two sexes meet in Tiresias. "What Tiresias *sees*, in fact, is the substance of the poem" – a declaration that critics have tended to view rather skeptically. But what Tiresias sees is the sight that the poem has heretofore evaded: the meeting of the sexes, a meeting that Tiresias experiences by identifying with the female. As the typist awaits her visitor, Tiresias asserts, " I too awaited the expected guest," and at the moment when the house agent's clerk "assaults" her, he states, "And I Tiresias have foresuffered all," a position assumed again in the lines spoken by La Pia. Paradoxically, when the poem assumes the position of the female, male character becomes far more prominent: in the satiric portrait of the house agent's clerk, which is the first extended satiric male portrait in the poem, in the image of the fishermen, and in the extended fisherman's narrative that originally began Part IV and concludes with the death of Phlebas. As if repeating the doubleness of identification that Tiresias represents, that death affords at once the definitive separation of male identity and a fantasy of its separation of male identity and a fantasy of its dissolution as "He passed the stages of his age and youth / Entering the whirlpool."

In the final section of the poem, Eliot changes its representation of gender dramatically. He drops the strategy of character that had been the principal way in which the poem had up to this point centered its emotion and develops a voice and figuration for the speaker that remains separate from categories of gender. He accomplishes this by using both specifically religious allusions and natural images that for the most part avoid anthropomorphization. He seeks to evoke a poise from natural elements, as in the water-dripping song, which he gives a religious rather than a sexual resonance. Through the song Eliot moves the power of articulation in the poem from character to nature. The hermit-thrush sings in the pine trees, and the sound of the water for which he yearns is finally realized in the last line of the section: "Drip drop drip drop drop drop drop." As if in recognition of its separation from gender, this temporary poise immediately issues in the appearance of the third figure, "who walks always beside you[,] . . . / . . . hooded / I do not know whether a man or woman. . . ."

When the sexual concerns of the poem return, in the next passage, they assume a very different form than they have heretofore. Eliot does not locate them in relation to particular female characters or voices, although the image of the woman who "drew her long black hair out tight" does recall the woman in "A Game of Chess"; he evokes them through a sexual fantasy that represents the collapse of civilization as an engulfment within an exhausted and blackened vagina, suggested in the images of empty cisterns, exhausted wells, and bats "with baby faces" crawling "head downward down a blackened wall." This passage develops the technique of "Prufrock" in displacing images of sexual anxiety onto elements of the poem's landscape, such that the world itself rather than the characters within it locates its sexual malaise. These feminized images now possess the power of music and song that had been given to the water and the thrush; the woman fiddles "whisper music" on the strings of her hair, the

34

bats whistle, and voices sing out of the cisterns and wells. Despite what would seem the movement of the power of articulation to the feminine, Eliot's figurative technique here opens the way both for the poem's resolution and for the transfer, through nature, of the power of music and song to the male poet. By shifting to a poetic mode that expresses emotion through landscape rather than through character, Eliot can achieve sexual potency in purely symbolic terms, as, in the decayed hole, the cock crows, and the damp gust comes, bringing rain. The very way in which these images resist, because of their natural simplicity and the literary allusions with which Eliot surrounds them, what would seem to be their obvious sexual symbolism is precisely their virtue, for they enable the poem to resolve its sexual conflict at the same time that it arrives at a figuration that places the poet beyond it. At the moment when the cock crows, Eliot transfers the power of articulation to the landscape, as the thunder speaks, giving the power of translation to the poet. When the poet interprets the commands of the thunder, he once again describes human situations, but he articulates them in abstract and ungendered terms, as if only a language free from the categories of gender allows him to imagine human fulfillment.

Such abstract and ungendered terms seemed necessary to Eliot to escape his concern with bodily intactness. Even in "Ash Wednesday," written after his conversion, Eliot links the appearance of the Lady of silences to the dismemberment of his own body. As the Lady is withdrawn, in a white gown, to contemplation, his bones sing, scattered and shining, after the three white leopards have fed on his legs, his heart, his liver, and what had been contained in the hollow round of his skull. In the second volume of her biography of Eliot, Lyndall Gordon calls this female figure the watcher or the guardian.[16] For Eliot, the gaze of this watcher, even when she is conceived in more ideal terms than "the eyes which fix you in a formulated phrase" from "The Love Song of J. Alfred Prufrock," leads to the dissolution of the male body. The voice of Eliot's early poetry issues from this dissolution. Like J. Alfred Prufrock, the bones sing, whereas the Lady is a Lady of silences.

Gordon writes of the way in which Eliot conceived of much of his poetry in connection with some female muse, whether the dark muse that Vivienne represented or the ideal guardian he found in Emily Hale.[17] These concerns – psychological and biographical as they are – had a base in certain elements of the nineteenth-century poetic tradition that Eliot reformed in his own work. Images of women were for him intimately connected with issues of voice and visualization. In his early poetry Eliot associates a carefully composed female image with an insufficiently articulated male voice. Eliot achieves a more successfully articulated voice, even in the context of his concern with its inadequacy, by scattering the body, by repressing and dislocating the visual. Indeed, he seems to embrace the psychological materials of a certain primal crisis in body definition as a way of breaking the visual integrity of the female subject that is at the center of the nineteenth-century tradition. But Eliot embraced these materials at considerable personal cost. He therefore increasingly seeks a poetic language that avoids the categories of body and gender, a language that we first find in the religious and natural figuration of the last section of *The Waste Land*. This is not androgyny, but a repression of sexual difference, a third, hooded figure one cannot recognize as man or woman. That is the language of *Four Quartets*, which in its abstraction, in its predominantly natural and religious imagery, avoids the issues of gender and body that dominate Eliot's early poetry.

## Notes

1  A. Walton Litz has pointed out to me that Williams moved the dating of his "Portrait of a Lady" back from 1920, when it was originally published, to 1913, presumably to establish a contemporaneity with Eliot's and Pound's poems. See *The Collected Poems of William Carlos Williams*, A. Walton Litz and Christopher Mac-Gowan, eds., vol. 1 (New York: New Directions, 1986).

2  *The Letters of Ezra Pound, 1907–1941*, edited by D. D. Page (London: Faber and Faber, 1951), 180; *The Diary of Virginia Woolf*, vol. 2, edited by Anne Oliver Bell (New York: Harcourt Brace, 1978), 68.

3  For a fuller development of these ideas, see Carol Christ, "The Feminine Subject in Victorian Poetry," *ELH* 54 (1987): 385–401.

4  T. S. Eliot, *Poems Written in Early Youth* (London: Faber and Faber, 1967), 27.

5 Sandra Gilbert and Susan Gubar, *No Man's Land: The Place of the Woman Writer in the Twentieth Century*, vol. 1 (New Haven: Yale University Press, 1988), 30–1.

6 Ibid., 125–62.

7 *The Letters of T. S. Eliot*, vol. 1, edited by Valerie Eliot (New York: Harcourt Brace Jovanovich), 13.

8 Hugh Kenner, *The Invisible Poet: T. S. Eliot* (New York: Citadel, 1959), 21.

9 In *No Man's Land* Gilbert and Gubar describe Eliot's construction of influence somewhat differently in arguing that Eliot's yearning for a golden age before the dissociation of sensibility set in was an attempt to erase the history associated with the entrance of women into the literary marketplace (p. 154).

10 Ronald Bush's treatment of the attempt of Eliot's speaker in "La Figlia" to keep the girl's image from becoming vivid and uncomfortable is particularly fine. See *T. S. Eliot: A Study in Character and Style* (New York: Oxford University Press, 1983), 11–14.

11 Michael Bernstein, "Image, Word, and Sign: The Visual Arts as Evidence in Ezra Pound's *Cantos*," *Critical Inquiry* 12 (1986): 347–64.

12 Tony Pinkney, *Women in the Poetry of T. S. Eliot* (London: Macmillan, 1984), 18.

13 Nancy J. Vickers argues that Petrarch allays the threat that the sight of the female carries to his own bodily integrity by transforming her visible totality to scattered words through which he composes his *Rime Sparse*. See "Diana Described: Scattered Women and Scattered Rhyme," in *Writing and Sexual Difference*, edited by Elizabeth Abel (Chicago: University of Chicago Press, 1982), 95–110. Vickers's paradigm is a suggestive one for Eliot, although his songs can hardly be seen as songs of praise, and Eliot does not merely scatter the female body but decomposes all bodies.

14 Pinkney, *Women in the Poetry of T. S. Eliot*, 44.

15 See Calvin Bedient, *He Do the Police in Different Voices: The Waste Land and Its Protagonist* (Chicago: University of Chicago Press, 1986), 28–35; Bush, *T. S. Eliot*, 64–6.

16 Lyndall Gordon, *Eliot's New Life* (New York: Farrar Straus Giroux, 1988), 61–2, 155–6, 188–9.

17 Ibid., 8–16, 54–7.

## PART TWO

# The Genesis and Transmission of The Waste Land and Its Associated Poems

# Ara Vos Prec:
## *Eliot's Negotiation of Satire and Suffering*

JAMES LONGENBACH

═══════════

The title was not one to beckon to a reading public, and even those who knew their Dante and their Provençal would have been thrown off the right track by a misprint on the title page (*vus* for *vos*). Eliot complained that critics found the work "learned & cold," but who could blame them? "The truth is I am neither," he told Virginia Woolf,[1] who surely knew Arnaut Daniel's words in the *Purgatorio*: "*Ara vos prec, per aquella valor / que vos guida al som de l'escalina, / sovegna vos a temps de ma dolor!*" (And so I pray you, by that Virtue which leads you to the topmost of the stair – be mindful in due time of my pain).[2]

*Ara Vos Prec* is a book about pain, pain in all its guises, psychological and physical, the pain of belonging and the pain of standing apart. Most of all, it is a book about the pain of sexuality, the pain of Arnaut Daniel, whose sin was lust. Still, even seventy years after the poems in quatrains were written, they remain strangely aloof. In the classroom, students move easily from

"Prufrock" to "Gerontion" to the intricacies of *The Waste Land,* but give them "Mr. Eliot's Sunday Morning Service," and all is lost. That poem almost seems the work of a different poet, the calculated diction at odds with the oracular resonance of the dramatic monologues that come before and after, and in recent years the critical consensus has seconded the classroom response. Since we discovered that bits of *The Waste Land* had been bubbling inside Eliot as early as 1910, the tendency has been to see the quatrain poems as a public ruse, the companion to the impersonal theory of poetry: "[I]n retrospect," says Lyndall Gordon in *Eliot's Early Years,* "the witty, satiric poems Eliot wrote between 1917 and 1919 seem like a digression from his poetic career."[3]

The vicissitudes of Eliot's reputation are forever bound with the fortunes of the mode of literary criticism he helped to propagate, so it's not surprising that an earlier generation of readers saw *The Waste Land* as a falling away from the quatrain poems (or that students once had trouble with "Prufrock"). It was *Ara Vos Prec,* after all, that led I. A. Richards to invite Eliot to teach at Cambridge, and when John Crowe Ransom read the long poem in 1922, he was forced to reconsider his high estimation of the quatrains.[4] Admirers of the passionate Eliot of "the awful daring of a moment's surrender" (CPP 49) don't read these poems very differently from the New Critics who initially admired their austere learning and self-conscious craft. But what of the Eliot who asks us to be mindful of his pain? By the 1930s, when *The Waste Land* had already accumulated more commentary than it could comfortably bear, Malcolm Cowley could describe Eliot's message as a "simple" one: "The past was dignified; the present is barren of emotion."[5] Eliot responded to the charge in a letter to Paul Elmer More: "I was not aware, and am not aware now, of having drawn a contrast between a contemporary world of slums, hysterics and riverside promiscuity etc. with any visibly more romantically lovely earlier world. I mean there is no nostalgia for the trappings of the past, so far as I can see, and no illusion about the world ever having been a pleasanter place to live in than it is now."[6]

That statement has the assurance that only a backward glance facilitates, but it nevertheless helps to dislodge *Ara Vos Prec* from the detour in Eliot's development to which it has recently been consigned. It's especially troubling that both admirers and revisers of the cold and learned Eliot have felt that the same poet could not write both *The Waste Land* and "Burbank with a Baedeker"; the confluence of opposing camps suggests that the revisers have aimed their sights more clearly upon the admirers than upon the poems. To come to terms with the quatrain poems is to make an important step toward seeing Eliot whole. Which is not to say that either *Ara Vos Prec* or Eliot's career at large is not reft by contradiction. Far from filling a cul-de-sac in his development, however, I think this volume reveals most clearly the opposing impulses that shaped Eliot's sensibility and fueled his future accomplishments. To write a book about pain and then title the book in a language no one speaks is a strategy both deliberate and desperate; Eliot chose the title, as he told his publisher, precisely because it was "unintelligible to most people" (L 338). The poems following that title force us to ask if wit and satire are incompatible with the sincere utterance we expect from a book of suffering. At times they are so, and "Lune de Miel" or "The Hippopotamus" betray a troubling lack of generosity – a facile cleverness and an easy nostalgia for an idealized past. Eliot could often see other people's pain more clearly than his own. But the process of composing the poems of *Ara Vos Prec* reveals the widening of Eliot's horizon and the crucial integration of satire and suffering. The arrangement of the volume, beginning in the depths of "Gerontion" and ending on the stair of "La Figlia che Piange," suggests a kind of purgatorial progression in itself, but "Gerontion" was the last poem to be written, whereas "La Figlia" (reprinted along with most of *Prufrock and Other Observations*) was among the first. The poems in French and the poems in quatrains stand between these achievements, and a chronological reading of the poems suggests a different progression: the contradictory impulses that make up Eliot's sensibility were not simply static but worked out over time.[7] And the final poems of *Ara Vos Prec*, poems that hover ambiguously between lyric utterance and dramatic monologue, approach the condition of a novel Eliot praised as both the work of "the satirist's satirist" and a triumph "of unrelieved horror": For Eliot at his best, one quality could not be achieved fully without the other.[8]

43

That novel was Edith Wharton's *Summer,* to which Eliot gave a brief but laudatory notice in January 1918. Something in that quintessentially American book made Eliot see himself, especially in the context of the Henry James in which he was then immersed. Eliot's remarks on *Summer* provide the clearest indication of the synthesis he was working to achieve in the quatrain poems, but the story of these poems begins ten months earlier, when Eliot began working in the Colonial and Foreign Department of Lloyds Bank. At that time the muse had not spoken to him for almost two years. His last poems ("The *Boston Evening Transcript,*" "Aunt Helen," "Cousin Nancy," "Mr. Apollinax") had come during his year at Oxford, before he married Vivienne Haigh-Wood in June 1915. That fall Eliot began teaching at High Wycomb Grammar School (and later at Highgate Junior School) while writing his dissertation and attending to his wife – a "nightmare of anxiety" (L 151). When the work on Bradley was complete, he began a simultaneous career as extension lecturer in modern English and French literature. The job at Lloyds soon offered a welcome but tedious security, and while speaking the language of money by day, Eliot began to write poems in French by night. "I have served my own apprenticeship in the City," he later recalled, ". . . have written (or compiled) articles on Foreign Exchange which occasionally met with approval from my superiors; and I was never convinced that the authorities upon whom I drew, or the expert public which I addressed, understood the matter any better than I did myself – which is not at all."[9] The poems in French sharpened the satiric impulse of the poems written at Oxford; having condemned American readers of the *Boston Evening Transcript,* Eliot now berated the British readers of the *Spectator* with an irony so raw that its success depends almost exclusively upon the music of French rhymes that some readers would not hear at all; translated into English, the final lines of "Le Directeur" tell us: "In a sewer a little pugnosed girl in rags regards the conservative editor of the *Spectator* and bursts with love."[10]

"Le Directeur" reveals the Eliot who told Lytton Strachey (not to be confused in this context with John St. Loe Strachey, who edited the *Spectator*) that his work in the bank made him "regard London with disdain, and divide mankind into supermen, termites, and wireworms. I am sojourning among the termites" (L 299). The American tourists of "Lune de Miel" lie in bed "*A l'aise entre deux draps, chez deux centaiens de punaises*" [at ease between two sheets with two hundred bedbugs] while the Byzantine perfection of Sant' Apollinaire in Classe slowly decays nearby, unnoticed (CPP 29).[11] When Pound first read these poems he told Joyce that Eliot had "burst out into scurrilous french," but more revealingly, he added that Eliot "is 'just as bad' as if he had been to Clongowes."[12] Pound knew that his friend felt the pressure of his Unitarian heritage as Stephen Dedalus carried his Jesuit training from Clongowes Wood, and he also understood that the blunt, externalized satire of the French poems was a kind of misplaced exorcism. The ironies of *A Portrait of the Artist as a Young Man* are not nearly so corrosive as Eliot's because Joyce allows us to see the humanity of his victim. Whereas Joyce dramatizes himself, Eliot stands aloof in these poems, and their ironies remain decidedly uncomplicated. Only in "Mélange Adultère de Tout" is Eliot's satire anything other than caustic, since for the first time he casts a cold eye on himself. The fool who is a philosopher in Germany, a banker in London, and a lecturer in Yorkshire is T. S. Eliot (who gave his University of London Extension lectures in Yorkshire); he would soon demand from poets a professional single-mindedness that he himself could not yet sustain: "The opposite of the professional, the enemy, is the man of mixed motives."[13]

Not inexplicably Eliot's critical standards hovered above his production, and just as he began writing in French he published his first important literary essay, "Reflections on *vers libre.*" Pound would remember how he and Eliot then set out to fulfill the essay's prescriptions: "[A]t a particular time, at a particular date in a particular room, two authors, neither engaged in picking the other's pocket, decided that the dilutation of *vers libre,* Amygism, Lee Masterism, general floppiness had gone too far and that some counter-current must be set going. . . . Remedy prescribed 'Emaux et Camees' (or the Bay State Hymn Book). Rhyme and regular strophes."[14] Gautier provided the model for the poems of both *Ara Vos Prec* and *Hugh Selwyn Mauberley,* but Pound sensed again that the shadow of the *Bay State Hymn Book* stood somewhere behind Eliot's desire to chastise the readers of

the *Boston Evening Transcript* and the *Spectator.* As if to stress
the thematic continuity of his formal experiments, Eliot turned
on the readers of the *Westminster Gazette* in an unpublished
quatrain poem titled "Airs of Palestine, No. 2." There, he explained that God told the *Gazette's* editors to smite the living
rock, and from the rock poured forth a continuous river of daily
editions, flooding London's streets and suburbs with print, con-
founding the sources of the Thames, and finally rising to the
gates of heaven, where the risen souls cleanse themselves in a
deluge of received opinion.[15]

Initially the very form of the quatrain encouraged rather than
complicated the dualist ironies of the French poems. In "The
Hippopotamus," the first quatrain poem Eliot published (July
1917), the quatrains tend to break in half, solidifying the simple
contrast of beast and church in an antiphonal exchange; once we
know that

> The hippopotamus's day
> Is passed in sleep; at night he hunts;

we can easily predict the fate of the church.

> God works in a mysterious way —
> The Church can sleep and feed at once. (CPP 30–1)

But these lines, like Eliot's comments to Strachey, reveal only
half of Eliot's sensibility. In the same letter to Strachey, Eliot
isolated exactly what is missing in poems like "Le Directeur" or
"The Hippopotamus": "Whether one writes a piece of work well
or not seems to me a matter of crystallization – the good sentence, the good word, is only the final stage of the process. One
can groan enough over the choice of a word, but there is something much more important to groan over first. It seems to me
just the same in poetry – the words come easily enough, in
comparison to the core of it" (L 298–9). That sounds a lot like the
Eliot who three decades later would describe the "demon" or
"embryo" (OPP 106) a poet must exorcise in his work. Almost
none of that dolor emanates from the earliest quatrain poems,
which seem to have no core at all; but Eliot had become an
aficionado of pain long before he wrote those poems. An early
version of "Prufrock" had Arnaut's lines as its epigraph before

Eliot realized that that poem's suffering was infernal rather than purgatorial. In 1914 he quoted Shelley's "Julian and Maddalo" ("They learn in suffering what they teach in song") in a letter to Conrad Aiken, explaining that although he did not feel that pain is necessary to poetic achievement, he did feel that "what is necessary is a *certain kind* (could one but catch it!) of *tranquility,* and *sometimes* pain does bring it" (L 42–3). Along with these remarks, Eliot sent the manuscript of "The Love Song of Saint Sebastian," in which the saint flogs himself in "hour on hour of prayer / And torture and delight" (L 46). This and other manuscript poems from 1914–15 push their explorations of pain to depths that transcend Shelley's *Cenci* or Swinburne's "Faustine," and the work suffers from an unfocused excess of the particular kind of groaning that "The Hippopotamus" lacks.

Eliot did not turn to apparently impersonal quatrains to disguise his nightmare of anxiety; rather, his effort was to find a form that would present that dolorous core convincingly, and in his earliest quatrains the effort became purely technical. When Eliot began writing French poems in the spring of 1917, he also tried his hand at prose fiction, another effort to jump-start the muse. "Eeldrop and Appleplex" reveals the continuing interest in pain and evil (along with the obsession with "do[ing] a girl in" [CPP 83]) that is absent from the early quatrains: "In Gopsum Street a man murders his mistress. The important fact is that for the man the act is eternal, and that for the brief space he has to live, he is already dead. He is already in a different world from ours. He has crossed the frontier. . . . [T]he medieval world, insisting on the eternity of punishment, expressed something closer to the truth."[16] Eliot tried to visualize the far side of that frontier in "Elegy," a quatrain poem that languished among the discarded drafts for *The Waste Land.* Crossing Beaumont and Fletcher's *The Maid's Tragedy* with Poe's "Ligeia," Eliot tried to convey the anxiety of the "always inconvenient" return of the dead woman:

> God, in a rolling ball of fire
> Pursues by day my errant feet.
> His flames of anger and desire
> Approach me with consuming heat. (WLF 117)[17]

In their own way these lines are as "over the mark" (to use the phrase Pound penciled beside certain lines of "The Fire Sermon") as "Airs of Palestine, No. 2," and each poem reveals what the other lacks. The horror of "Elegy" is maudlin rather than chilling; the satire of the *Westminster Gazette* turns tedious without an emotional core to give it weight. By the end of 1917 Eliot had returned to the impasse at which he had begun. "I have a lot of things to write about," he told his father, "if the time ever comes" (L 214).

That autumn, when Pound drew H. L. Mencken's attention to Eliot's new poems, he remarked once again that Eliot's "unitarian upbringing has not been wasted."[18] At the same time Eliot began a more self-conscious investigation of that upbringing, realizing that if he were to become more than the author of bloodless jeremiads, he would have to come to terms with his American roots. The result was a sequence of essays on American literature and sensibility that grew from his extension lectures on Emerson, Hawthorne, and Thoreau.[19] Eliot was attempting to expurgate his American self when he complained that Conrad Aiken "does not escape the fatal American introspectiveness"[20] and when he offered an even more ominous generalization about the "Puritan inheritance" Henry Adams epitomized: "They are usually sensitive people, and they want to do something great; dogged by the shadow of self-conscious incompetence, they are predestined failures."[21] This at the same time when Eliot was struggling to produce a book to show his parents "that I have not made a mess of my life, as they are inclined to believe" (L 266).

Adams also seemed to Eliot a victim of "the Boston doubt: a scepticism which is difficult to explain to those who are not born to it."[22] The author of "The Hippopotamus" and "Lune de Miel" knew it too well. The world valued by cultural observers like Adams and Eliot himself no longer existed by the time these poems were written, and what really troubled these men was not so much the ascendancy of an enervated Puritan past as the fact that their patrician heritage had been marginalized. Eliot recalled that in St. Louis his grandmother insisted on living in the house his grandfather William Greenleaf Eliot (Emerson's colleague) had built and his father, "from filial piety, did not wish to leave the house that he had built only a few steps away; and so it came to be that we lived in a neighborhood which had become shabby to a degree approaching slumminess."[23] Sojourning among the termites, Adams and Eliot were (in Jackson Lears's phrase) "anti-modern modernists": While groping for a new life in the future, they were doubled over by a belief that a legitimate order existed only in the past.[24] Wallace Stevens revealed the longings he shared with Eliot when he copied these sentences from a 1915 letter of Henry Adams into his commonplace book: "I need badly to find one man in history to admire. I am in near peril of turning Christian, and rolling in the mud in an agony of human mortification."[25]

Rather than the slightly later pieces on Jacobean drama and metaphysical poetry, the essays on American literature that Eliot wrote between 1917 and 1919 form the most harmonious descant to the quatrain poems. (That Eliot himself saw the contiguity of these two bodies of his work is suggested by the fact that what became *The Sacred Wood* was at one time planned as a collection of the American essays – and that as late as the summer of 1919 Eliot was hoping to publish the essays and poems together in one volume.[26]) The crucial essay "In Memory of Henry James" appeared in January 1918, but in the same issue of the *Egoist* was included Eliot's long-forgotten notice of Wharton's *Summer*. The novel seemed to him a victory over just the kind of sensibility that made his own work appear learned and cold. "Even Mrs. Wharton's parerga have importance," he began, "and this parergon, a very brief novel, offers interest as a work in a curious kind of satire which Mrs. Wharton has made her own; and just the kind of satire, it may be remarked, that her literary training and sympathies might have made most difficult for her." Though Edith Newbold Jones Wharton was a product of New York rather than Boston society, Eliot saw that she was exorcising a familiar ghost. "The book is, in fact – or should be – the death-blow to a kind of novel which has flourished in New England, the novel in which the wind whistles through the stunted firs and over the granite boulders into the white farmhouses where pale gaunt women sew rag carpets." Eliot himself had tried to sting this sensibility in "The *Boston Evening Transcript*," whose readers "Sway in the wind like a field of ripe corn," and in "Cousin Nancy," who breaks "The barren New England hills – / Riding to hounds / Over the cow-pasture" (CPP 16, 17). But Wharton's satire was possessed of a deeper core of feeling that made her parergon more powerful than Eliot's. His capsule description of *Summer* reads like a précis of his own "Portrait of a Lady": "The young man comes up from the city (Springfield), Charity gives him all she has, and the young man returns to marry Annabel Balch of Springfield. The scene of the county fair at Nettleton is one of unrelieved horror." Wharton's satire did not strip away the veneer from New England society in order to reveal a mere emptiness within; rather, it exposed the passion and the anguish disguised by that veneer. Eliot concluded that although *Summer* "should add to Mrs. Wharton's reputation as a novelist the distinction of being the satirist's satirist," the novel would "certainly be considered 'disgusting' in America."[27] That Eliot glimpsed his own ambition revealed in this novel is suggested by the remark he made about *Ara Vos Prec* in precisely the same terms: "[H]ere I am considered by the ordinary newspaper critic as a wit or satirist, and in America I suppose I shall be thought merely disgusting" (L 363).

Eliot probably recalled *Ethan Frome* when he praised Wharton's past parerga; that novella also reveals the sordid and poignant events hidden behind a trio of emotionally and physically crippled New Englanders, but *Summer* is more complicated. Initially based on a series of simple dualisms (the dark world of the mountain versus the village of North Dormer, the simplicity of the village versus the "refined civilization" of Nettleton), the novel works to break down those oppositions, and the county fair is (as Eliot suggests) a scene of unrelieved horror because it unveils the dark side of what seemed innocent. Charity Royall first visited Nettleton to hear an illustrated lecture on the Holy Land; her escort was the Reverend Miles, to whom she liked to fancy herself married. When Lucius Harney (the young man from Springfield) appears, Charity sees Miles revealed as a balding middle-aged man, but she does not see Harney as he truly is. The horror Eliot admired in this tale is not explicitly demonic or otherworldly; it is the kind of horror that led Conrad to tell Wharton that *Summer* was her masterpiece. Harney's seduction culminates in the trip to the Nettleton County Fair, where he takes

Charity to a dreary French restaurant ("It's the real thing," he explains) and then to a different sort of picture show:

> Mr. Miles's pictures had been shown in an austere Y.M.C.A. hall, with white walls and an organ; but Harney led Charity to a glittering place – everything she saw seemed to glitter – where they passed, between immense pictures of yellow-haired beauties stabbing villains in evening dress, into a velvet-curtained auditorium packed with spectators to the last limit of compression. After that, for a while, everything was merged in her brain in swimming circles of heat and blinding alternations of light and darkness. All the world has to show seemed to pass before her in a chaos of palms and minarets, charging cavalry regiments, roaring lions, comic policemen and scowling murderers; and the crowd around her, the hundreds of hot sallow candy-munching faces, young, old, middle-aged, but all kindled with the same contagious excitement, became part of the spectacle, and danced on the screen with the rest.[28]

The long, exquisitely modulated scene of the county fair builds to this passage; the entire experience is Charity's spectacle, a giant picture show, and the horror grows as we see the world behind the screen that Charity does not. The simple dualities, on which the novel seemed initially to be built, are revealed as the characters' illusions; their function is more properly dramatic than essential.

In the essay "In Memory of Henry James" Eliot remarks that the novelist's great strength is his "dramatic" sense, not so much his delineation of the mind as the "contact of mind with mind" and the "curious precipitates and explosive gases" that result: "it makes the reader, as well as the personae, uneasily the victim of a merciless clairvoyance."[29] A few months later Eliot would isolate this quality in "The Hawthorne Aspect" of James as an instinct for the "deeper psychology" (Eliot took the phrase from James's *Hawthorne*).[30] Wharton's *Summer* possessed some of the same qualities, but I think it was more useful to Eliot because it exposes the intensity not only of mind meeting mind but of body meeting body. *Summer* is Wharton's most openly passionate novel; Charity Royall's sexual awakening offers her a freedom she had never known in the village of North Dormer, despite

51

Harney's ultimate betrayal. But Eliot saw only the horror of sexuality in Charity's tale; as his plot summary suggests, he read *Summer* as a recipe for doing a girl in. For Eliot, the novel's power lay in its moments of horrific unveiling, such as the scene in which Charity, having discovered the wonder of her own body, confronts her mother's corpse: The woman "seemed to have fallen cross her squalid bed in a drunken sleep, and to have been left lying where she fell, in her ragged disordered clothes. One arm was flung above her head, one leg drawn up under a torn skirt that left the other bare to the knee: a swollen, glistening leg with a ragged stocking rolled down about the ankle." There was no sign "of anything human" in the mother's face; "she lay there like a dead dog in a ditch."[31] This was the world Wharton's satire laid bare, a world that the inhabitants of Boston would find merely disgusting, not recognizing it as their own. For Eliot, *Summer* exposed the dark side of the Boston doubt without acquiescing to an even thinner skepticism; it showed satire in the service of horror.

That quality distinguishes Eliot's earliest poems in French or in quatrains from the work he published in September 1918 (most of which was in manuscript by May): "Sweeney Among the Nightingales," "Whispers of Immortality," "Dans le Restaurant," and "Mr. Eliot's Sunday Morning Service."[32] The new French poem turns on the same dramatic intricacies as the country fair scene in *Summer*. Although "Dans le Restaurant" begins with an easy condemnation of the world's wireworms and termites, the judgment is now located in the mind portrayed by the poem (rather than a point of view external to the poem, as in "the Hippopotamus"). The gentleman in the restaurant condemns his interlocutor as "Le garçon délabré qui n'a rien à faire / Que de se gratter les doigts et se pencher sur mon épaule" (a scarecrow waiter with nothing better to do than scratch his knuckles and perch at my shoulder), but as the waiter tells his off-color tale of an early sexual experience (involving both a girl and a dog), this victim of the Boston doubt sees the spectacle as his own, and what begins as satire builds to the horror of recognition (CPP 31). Pound's free translation of "Dans le Restaurant" emphasizes the explosive contact of mind with mind:

Your head is not flealess
now at any rate, go scrape the cheese off your pate
and dig the slush out of your crowsfeet,
take sixpence and get washed, God damn
     what a fate
You crapulous vapulous relic, you ambulating offence
  To have had an experience
so nearly parallel, with,
    Go away!
I was about to say mine,
I shall dine
elsewhere in the future,
     to cleanse this suture.[33]

Eliot himself translated the poem's final stanza to make the "Death by Water" lyric in *The Waste Land,* and there, as in the French version, he offers a sympathetic warning instead of a detached condemnation, suggesting that the even more horrible recognition is the one experienced by the reader or the poet: "O you who turn the wheel and look to windward / Consider Phlebas, who was once handsome and tall as you" (CPP 47). This is the keynote of *Ara Vos Prec,* a volume named with the words of a poet who purged his sin of lust in fire rather than in water, saying, "Be mindful in due time of my pain."

Another poem written around the same time as "Dans le Restaurant," the "Ode on Independence Day, July 4th 1918," published only in *Ara Vos Prec* and never reprinted, presents a second sexual experience (this one in adulthood) and attempts a similar transfiguration in its final lines: "Indignant / At the cheap extinction of his taking-off. / Now lies he there / Tip to tip washed beneath Charles' Wagon."[34] These lines, which are the closest Eliot came to writing a French poem in English, lack both the satiric edge and dramatic structure that makes the pain of "Dans le Restaurant" more vivid; curiously, the "Ode" seems simultaneously an exercise burdened with learned reference and a confession little more than maudlin. In the quatrain poems of 1918 Eliot would more successfully reach the level of sustained horror he admired in *Summer.* At first, "Whispers of Immortality" seems as programmatic and simplistically ironic as "The Hippopotamus"; the poem breaks into two halves, and the contrast of the integrated sensibilities of Webster and Donne with the excessively fleshy Grishkin mirrors some of Eliot's more well-known critical formulations. But this quatrain poem is more like "Dans le Restaurant" than "The Hippopotamus." It is another rendering of the detached sensibility, a dramatic presentation of mind meeting (or more poignantly, not meeting) mind. The clipped quatrains make that sensibility seem considered and thoughtful, but the poem is wildly visionary – far more successfully so than the "Elegy" not included in *Ara Vos Prec:*

> And breastless creatures under ground
> Leaned backward with a lipless grin.
>
> Daffodil bulbs instead of balls
> Stared from the sockets of the eyes! (CPP 32)

In itself this is one of Eliot's best moments of visualized horror, but the more sustained psychological horror of "Whispers" unfolds as the speaker turns from this account of Webster to a consideration of Donne (who "I suppose, was such another," he says, belying his pedantry with egregious casualness) and then to a living human being instead of a book: "Grishkin is nice." That he can see only the "promise of pneumatic bliss" in her "friendly bust" and "feline smell" confirms not Grishkin's inadequacy but his own. Surely there is a skull beneath her skin, but unlike the Donne he understands so well, the speaker is unable to seize, clutch, or penetrate and find out. And though he describes Grishkin's empty form with a stylishly modern word ("pneumatic"), that word contains the "pneuma," the soul, which the speaker perceives in neither the word nor the body. "Whispers of Immortality" presents the world as Charity Royall saw it on the screen, and the horror is not so much the vision of the skull beneath the skin but the growing disparity between the vision and the reality, what Eliot would call, apropos of Flaubert and Stendhal, "the awful separation between potential passion and any actualization possible in life."[35]

Eliot drafted "Whispers of Immortality" early in the summer of 1918 while resting with his wife at a cottage in Marlow. "I have written several poems lately," he told his mother, adding that he had been "sitting out in a back garden all day writing about

Henry James and Hawthorne" (L 233–4). That essay is the companion piece to "Whispers," for it reveals what the sensibility of that poem (like Henry Adams and Eliot himself) lacked: that instinct for the "deeper psychology" that enables the deepest contact between minds. It was at Marlow, Eliot admitted many years later, that he first experienced the "state of dispossession" he would describe in *The Family Reunion* as "that sense of separation, / Of isolation unredeemable" (CPP 272).[36] At Marlow Eliot could diagnose the problem in American literature at large, but when he turned from books to the woman at his side, he was paralyzed. Unlike the earliest quatrains, "Whispers of Immortality" grew from the kind of groaning Eliot told Strachey was essential to poetry.

The secondary sort of groaning, the technical aspect of the poem, was also improved. In the poems of 1918 Eliot gained a much fuller control over the quatrains themselves, and the subtleties of internal rhyme and enjambment complicate rather than reinforce the ironies. Consequently, unlike the comparison of church and beast in "The Hippopotamus," the binary opposition of Webster (seventeenth-century male) and Grishkin (twentieth-century female) in "Whispers of Immortality" begins to disintegrate as soon as it is offered, enforcing Eliot's retrospective remark to More that he never meant to contrast a rich past with a deprived present. (Eliot might have been more honest if he'd said that he sometimes *had* wished to do so but knew he shouldn't.) The historical comparisons in the final quatrains of "Sweeney Among the Nightingales" are similarly complicated, and in "Mr. Eliot's Sunday Morning Service" the overtly sexual Sweeney, shifting "from ham to ham / Stirring the water in his bath," is not so much a vulgar counterpart to the baptised Christ as the embodiment of the Word that the "enervate" Origen and the "epicene" presbyters cannot reach (CPP 34). If anything, this poem teeters on the contrary mystification, idealizing the modern sensibility, freed from the legacy of a Puritan past, to rediscover its primitive energies.

Comparing Provençal, Trecento, and Renaissance sensibilities in his 1926 Clark Lectures, Eliot remarks that they "represent differences in the human spirit too wide for judgment, they belong to those differences which are reincarnated in different human beings every day, placing insuperable barriers between some of every handful of us."[37] That statement did not prevent Eliot from making judgments in the lectures, but it does help to clarify the historical sense of the later quatrain poems and *The Waste Land*. Their horror comes not from the contrast of past and present but from the contrast of sensibilities (Sweeney and the presbyters, Burbank and Bleistein, the "cooking egg" and Pipit) that condense historical difference into the small space of mind meeting mind. When Eliot wrote in "Sweeney Erect":

> The lengthened shadow of a man
>   Is history, said Emerson,
> Who had not seen the silhouette
>   Of Sweeney straddled in the sun. (CPP 26)

he was not disagreeing with the Emerson who wrote that "an institution is the lengthened shadow of a man" and that "all history resolves itself very easily into the biography of a few stout and earnest persons."[38] A few months after Eliot published "Sweeney Erect" he gave a lecture on modern poetry in which he said that the past would lose all its meaning – "even if it *could* continue to exist" – if we were "deprived of [our] personal present": "[T]he present only, keeps the past alive."[39] Like Emerson, Eliot knew that our knowledge of history is inextricably mingled with self-knowledge, but he wanted to point out that our knowledge of the past varies with the quality of our selves (something that, contrary to Eliot's judgment, Emerson knew very well).

The brief pamphlet of Eliot's *Poems* that the Woolfs' Hogarth Press produced in May 1919 included all the French and quatrain poems (excluding "Dans le Restaurant") that Eliot had published to date; the final quatrain poems, "A Cooking Egg," "Burbank with a Baedeker: Bleistein with a Cigar," and "Sweeney Erect," were published later that summer, when Eliot finally gave up the idea of a combined volume of poetry and prose and began planning *Ara Vos Prec* for John Rodker's Ovid Press.[40] The satire of these poems is even more finely honed than that of the previous year's crop; Eliot's dramatic sense was further refined. In "Burbank with a Baedeker," as Ronald Bush has aptly pointed out, Eliot presents not his own point of view but that of "an Adams-like compatriot [who] succumbs to the New Englander's inability

to understand either the beauty or the evil of the Old World."[41]
When Burbank turns from the pages of his Baedeker to Bleistein
(like the persona of "Whispers of Immortality" turning from Webster to Grishkin) the "lustreless protrusive eye" he sees is a reflection of his own, and his judgment of modern Venice ("The
smokey candle end of time / Declines") is the inevitable product
of a mind that retreats from the immediacy of experience to the
safety of Ruskin's laws (CPP 24).

"Burbank with a Baedeker" was first published side by side
with "Sweeney Erect," and that poem's epigraph from *The Maid's
Tragedy* would be equally appropriate to "Burbank." Lamenting
the loss of her lover, Beaumont and Fletcher's Aspatia sees her
grief mirrored in the image of the deserted Ariadne, which her
attendants are weaving into a tapestry. "Sweeney Erect" begins
by extending Aspatia's desire that she become the model for
Ariadne ("Paint me a cavernous waste shore" – "Paint me the
bold anfractuous rocks"), substituting the mythic grandeur of
Ariadne's loss for the actual loss she has experienced (CPP 25).
But this illusion cannot be sustained. When the scene shifts to
the tawdry reality of Sweeney and the epileptic in the house, it
naturally seems repugnant by comparison, just as the reality of
Venice disappoints a mind satured in literary ideas of Venice.

The crucial question to ask these poems is: Who makes the
comparison? That the answer is not always clear allows Eliot to
make these judgments of modern culture and leave to the readers
the more difficult question of whether the poet wants the judgments undermined or confirmed. The voice that speaks these
judgments in "Lune de Miel" or "The Hippopotamus" is the poet
who stands aloof; in contrast, the heightened ambiguity of the
later quatrain poems arises from the contrast of the artfully
turned quatrains themselves (which imply a controlling vision
outside the poem) and the dramatic rendering of a sensibility
(which implies that the point of authority rests within the poem).
But rather than dramatic monologues, Eliot's most sophisticated
quatrain poems resemble Henry James's idea of the "controlling
consciousness." If Burbank spoke his own mind (as does Prufrock), his judgments would appear more obviously flawed; if
Burbank's remarks were not located in a character (as in "The
Hippopotamus" or "Lune de Miel"), the judgments would be easi-

er to condemn as the author's. And even though Eliot placed his opinions or fears inside a dramatic frame in "Dans le Restaurant," "Whispers of Immortality," or "Burbank with a Baedeker," that layer of self-consciousness does not always save him from the implications of the anti-Semitism or antifeminism of the poems' personae. The dramatic irony undercuts the personae's beliefs, but it does not erase Eliot's presence in the poem; in fact, it is precisely that veil of irony itself that allows those otherwise unpalatable judgments to be made. Eliot remains a divided antimodern modernist in this work, but the balance has shifted subtly from the former to the latter.

Like "Prufrock" or even "Gerontion," "A Cooking Egg" is less radically ambiguous than "Burbank with a Baedeker" because Eliot gives this poem over to a dramatic speaker. The poem grew from a discarded final quatrain for "Whispers of Immortality" that (had Eliot retained it) would have clarified that poem's sensibility; in this stanza the speaker who was repulsed by Grishkin turns to the decidedly less threatening Pipit, with whom he is free to imagine himself mischievous and brave when he is neither. In "A Cooking Egg" the speaker goes one step further. He turns away from Pipit (who has abandoned her knitting and picture books to tend to him, though from "some distance") and enters a fantasy world where Sidney and Coriolanus are his companions – "heroes of *my* kidney," as an early draft had it (rather than "of *that* kidney"). With Lucretia Borgia as his wife and Piccarda de Donata (who led Dante into paradise) as his guide, he has no need of Pipit. When the fantasy is dispelled, his final questions are as inevitable as Burbank's disdain for Venice as it is: "But where is the penny world I bought / To eat with Pipit behind the screen?" he asks: "Where are the eagles and trumpets?" The question might have been asked by Charity Royall, and the answer is not a comment on the world behind the screen but merely the histrionic wail of a mind retracted to its limited potential.

> Buried beneath some snow-deep Alps.
> Over buttered scones and crumpets
>   Weeping, weeping multitudes
> Droop in a hundred A.B.C.'s. (CPP 27)

The step from these questions and answers to those offered in "Gerontion" is logical and short. "What will the spider do, / Suspend its operations, will the weevil / Delay?" Of course not. "After such knowledge, what forgiveness?" What knowledge is that? Like the sensibilities of "Burbank" or "A Cooking Egg," the voice of "Gerontion" is a self-satisfying dreamer, but unlike them, Gerontion seems to understand the problem even as he speaks: It's comforting to put the blame on "history," but a mind that's lost the power of "sight, smell, hearing, taste and touch" can offer only "Thoughts of a dry brain in a dry season" (CPP 22–3).

"Gerontion" was the last poem of *Ara Vos Prec* to be written. On 9 June 1919 Eliot told Rodker that the poem was nearly finished (L 312), and *Ara Vos Prec* was published the following February. *Poems*, the American edition, followed shortly, and *The Sacred Wood* (the more recent essays on Jacobean drama replacing those on American literature) came nine months later. A conversation Eliot had with Virginia Woolf in September 1920 recapitulates the development that had taken place between "Le Directeur" and "Gerontion": "He told me he was more interested in people than in anything," Woolf recorded in her diary. ". . . His turn is for caricature. In trying to define his meaning ('I don't mean satire') we foundered. He wants to write a verse play in which the 4 characters of Sweeney act the parts. A personal upheaval of some kind came after Prufrock, & turned him aside from his inclination – to develop in the manner of Henry James."[42] From satire to drama by way of Henry James: The Sweeney play would come later, but its principles were already in operation. That Eliot found his simple, undramatized satires of 1915–17 inadequate (wanting to think of his current work as "caricature" rather than "satire") is suggested further by his review of Pound's *Quia Pauper Amavi*. Singling out Pound's most simple and acerbic satires, "Moeurs Contemporaines," Eliot confessed that he was "not at all sure that . . . the modern satirical vein is of permanent importance."[43] These remarks came in October 1919, and the following month Eliot told John Quinn, "I am now at work on an article ordered by *The Times*, and when that is off I hope to get started on a poem that I have in mind" (L 344). The poem was *The Waste Land*. The article was "Ben Jonson," which, not coincidentally, explained this poet so often dismissed as the perpetrator of cold and learned (if not disgusting) satire, was up to something different: "The objection implies that the characters are purely the work of the intellect, or the result of superficial observation of a world which is faded or mildewed. It implies that the characters are lifeless. But if we dig beneath the theory, beneath the observation, beneath the deliberate drawing and the theatrical and dramatic elaboration, there is discovered a kind of power" (SW 117).

Along with a continuing interest in the quatrain form, however, some of the less powerful kind of satire is evident throughout the drafts of *The Waste Land*. And though Pound indulged in that mode himself, it is mostly due to his ear for Eliot's strengths and weaknesses that those passages were cut. "Knowing the manner of these crawling bugs / I too awaited the expected guest," says Tiresias of the typist and the young man carbuncular in "The Fire Sermon": "too easy," said Pound, canceling the first line and disrupting the symmetry of the original quatrains (WLF 45). But at its best, "The Fire Sermon" offers not satire revealing emptiness, but satire in the service of deeper emotion, and the sequence of quatrains that follows these lines details a seduction scene worthy of *Summer*. Pound touched nothing in the following eight lines, which might have been more appropriate to a book about pain than "The Hippopotamus" or "Lune de Miel":

> The time is now propitious, as he guesses,
> The meal is ended, she is bored and tired;
> Endeavours to engage her in caresses
> Which still are unreproved, if undesired.
>
> Flushed and decided, he assaults at once,
> Exploring hands encounter no defence;
> His vanity requires no response,
> And makes a welcome of indifference. (WLF 45–6; CPP 44)

The technical triumph of these lines is the result of four years of struggle with their form. ("Try to put into a sequence of simple quatrains the continuous syntactic variety of Gautier or Blake," challenged Eliot in 1918).[44] They are also a triumph of dramatic rendering. "And I Tiresias have foresuffered all," announces the following line, reminding us that this scene is filtered through a

sensibility like Burbank's or Gerontion's. In Tiresias Eliot epitomized the emotional center of *The Waste Land,* and the emotion
remained quintessentially American. Here is the detached observer, the victim of fatal introspectiveness and disintegrating
skepticism. But more important, here is a sensibility painfully
aware of that "deeper psychology" Eliot admired in Hawthorne
and James.

Neither the visionary poems of suffering from 1914 nor the
uncomplicated satires of 1915–17 alone can account for the development of "The Fire Sermon" in 1921. Nor can the apparent
continuity of "Prufrock" and "Gerontion." Eliot's negotiation of
satire, drama, and authority in the quatrain poems was the essential step. The problem of sorting out the intricacies of voice and
point of view in "Burbank with a Baedeker" is the problem (writ
small) of finding an organized reading for *The Waste Land.* If all
of *The Waste Land* were more clearly, like "Gerontion" or "A Cooking Egg," a dramatic monologue, the problem would be easier to
solve. Eliot thought of making "Gerontion" the preface to *The
Waste Land* when he feared that the dynamics of the long poem
were unclear. But instead of suggesting with "Gerontion" that the
whole of *The Waste Land* was a dramatic utterance, Eliot liter-
alized the poem's tensions in his notes, suggesting that all of the
characters, though discrete, merged in Tiresias. That note allowed some interpreters to read *The Waste Land* as a lyric utterance, equating Eliot with his "protagonist" and understanding
the heart of the poem as the contrast of a full past and a depleted
present. Such a reading reduces *The Waste Land* to satire like
"The Hippopotamus" or "Moeurs Contemporanies" (in which the
authority for the point of view is more clearly the author's, standing outside the poem); it ignores the poem's uneasy position
between lyric and drama – an ambiguity that allows *The Waste
Land* to seem simultaneously a poem of radical openness and of
closed authority. Whether we read it as leaning toward the first
alternative or the second may depend on the nature of our own
sensibilities. But either way, the story of Eliot's struggle with the
quatrain poems of *Ara Vos Prec* helps to isolate the contradictions
of *The Waste Land.* It would not be the final chapter in a book
about pain that Eliot continued to write for many years to come.

## Notes

1 *The Diary of Virginia Woolf,* vol. 2, edited by Anne Oliver Bell (New York: Harcourt Brace, 1978), 91.

2 This is Eliot's translation, as it appears in his 1929 essay on Dante; see *Selected Essays* (New York: Harcourt Brace, 1960), 217. Further references to Eliot's collected writings are made in the text using the following abbreviations:

    CPP  *The Complete Poems and Plays of T. S. Eliot 1909–1950* (New York: Harcourt Brace, 1962).

    L    *The Letters of T. S. Eliot,* vol. 1, edited by Valerie Eliot (New York: Harcourt Brace, 1988).

    OPP  *On Poetry and Poets* (New York: Noonday–Farrar, 1969).

    SE   *Selected Essays* (New York: Harcourt Brace, 1960).

    SW   *The Sacred Wood* (New York: Methuen, 1960).

    WLF Valerie Eliot, ed., *The Waste Land: A Facsimile and Transcript of the Original Drafts Including the Annotations of Ezra Pound* (New York: Harcourt Brace Jovanovich, 1971).

3 Lyndall Gordon, *Eliot's Early Years* (New York: Oxford University Press, 1977), 90–1.

4 See Ransom's review of *The Waste Land,* along with Allen Tate's response, in the *New York Evening Post Literary Review* (July–August 1923), reprinted in Michael Grant, ed., *T. S. Eliot: The Critical Heritage,* vol. 1 (London: Routledge and Kegan Paul, 1982), 172–82.

5 Malcolm Cowley, *Exile's Return,* 2d ed. (New York: Viking, 1951), 113.

6 Eliot to Paul Elmer More, 20 July 1934 (Princeton University Library).

7 I have constructed this chronology from the poems' dates of publication and from material in Pound's and Eliot's correspondence. Eliot dated his poems in a copy of his *Poems* (New York: Knopf, 1920) that he gave to Frank Morley and is now in the John Hayward Collection in King's College Library, Cambridge; however, I have not followed these dates because many of them contradict the publication record. The poems that appear in Pierre Leyris's translation of Eliot's *Poèmes 1910–1930* (Paris: Éditions du Seuil, 1947) were provided with dates by John Hayward, and these dates by and large confirm the publication record.

8 Eliot, "Short Reviews," *Egoist* 5, 1 (January 1918): 10.

9 Eliot, "A Commentary," *Criterion* 10, 39 (January 1931): 310.

10 "Le Directeur" appeared with "Lune de Miel," "Mélange Adultère

de Tout," and "The Hippopotamus" in *Little Review* 4, 3 (July 1917): 8–11.

11  William Arrowsmith, in "Eros in Terre Haute: T. S. Eliot's 'Lune de Miel,'" *New Criterion* 1, 2 (October 1982): 22–41, has offered a detailed reading of the poem as a sophisticated expression of Eliot's historical sense. Although his argument is compelling and certainly appropriate to Eliot's early work at large, I find that the range of historical reference woven into "Lune de Miel" does not override its disdain for the contemporary world. If Arrowsmith had placed "Gerontion" or *The Waste Land* at the center of his essay, I think his general description of Eliot's Bradleyan sense of the past would be unassailable.

12  Pound to Joyce, 19 April 1917; in Forrest Read, ed., *Pound/Joyce: The Letters of Ezra Pound to James Joyce* (New York: New Directions, 1967), 112. On 11 April 1917 Eliot told his mother, "I have been doing some writing – mostly in French" (L 175).

13  Eliot, "Professionalism, or . . . ," *Egoist* 5, 4 (April 1918): 61.

14  Ezra Pound, "Harold Monroe," *Criterion* 9, 45 (July 1932): 590.

15  The manuscript of "Airs of Palestine, No. 2" (and all other manuscripts and drafts of poem to which I shall refer) are part of Eliot's poetry notebook in the Berg Collection, New York Public Library. Although I have not been able to date "Airs of Palestine, No. 2" precisely, I suspect that Eliot wrote it in 1917 soon after he began writing in French. Late in 1916 he began reviewing for the *Westminster Gazette,* and though in his correspondence he remarks that he has written many reviews for the *Gazette* (L 143, 149, 152), only one appeared (of Durkheim's *The Elementary Forms of the Religious Life*). Eliot was in dire need of the income he derived from reviewing at this time, and "Airs of Palestine, No. 2" probably grew from his frustration with the *Gazette.* See Louis Menand and Sanford Schwartz, "T. S. Eliot on Durkheim: A New Attribution," *Modern Philology* 79 (February 1982): 309–15.

In November 1919 Eliot included two stanzas similar to those of "Airs of Palestine, No. 2" in a letter to Middleton Murry (L 345), but I doubt the poem dates from this time, since the stanzas are adapted to mock not the *Westminster Gazette* but J. C. Square, who at various times edited the *New Statesman,* the *London Mercury,* and *Land and Water,* and who was associated with the *Owl* and the *Westminster Gazette* (all of which are mentioned in this version of the poem).

16  Eliot, "Eeldrop and Appleplex," *Little Review* 4, 1 (May 1917): 9.

17  It has not yet been possible to date "Elegy" more precisely than

1917–19, though Lyndall Gordon suggests that it was probably written in 1918 or even as early as 1917; see Gordon, *Eliot's Early Years*, 144.

18  *The Selected Letters of Ezra Pound: 1907–1941*, edited by D. D. Paige (New York: New Directions, 1950), 114.

19  See Ronald Schuchard, "T. S. Eliot as Extention Lecturer, 1916–1919," *Review of English Studies* 25 (August 1974): 294. The first reading assignment for Eliot's new courses of lectures in Modern English Literature consisted of Emerson's essays, Thoreau's *Walden*, and Hawthorne's *The Scarlet Letter*, along with the appropriate chapters in *Great Writers of America*, by W. P. Trent and John Erskine (the two professors who would edit the Cambridge history of American literature). From this volume Eliot's students absorbed what was by 1917 the standard explanation of Hawthorne's "aloofness": "He is the extreme example of the reflective Puritan, re-inspired by Transcendentalism"; but although Hawthorne's ancestors indulged the habit of "conscientious self-scrutiny" but "half the time," Hawthorne "was contemplative all the time." Transcendentalism itself, said Trent and Erskine, was a "parochial" movement marred by "a somewhat amusing immaturity" (*Great Writers of America* [London: Williams and Norgate, 1912], 65–6, 111).

20  Eliot, "Reflections on Contemporary Poetry [IV]," *Egoist* 6, 3 (July 1919): 40.

21  Eliot, "A Sceptical Patrician," *Athenaeum* 4647 (23 May 1919): 361.

22  Ibid.

23  Eliot, "The Influence of Landscape upon the Poet," *Daedalus* 89 (Spring 1960): 421–2.

24  See Jackson Lears, *No Place of Grace: Antimodernism and the Transformation of American Culture, 1880–1920* (New York: Pantheon, 1981).

25  Milton Bates, ed., *Sur Plusieurs Beaux Sujets: Wallace Stevens' Commonplace Book* (Stanford: Stanford University Press, 1989), 71. Stevens quotes from a letter by Adams in R. P. Blackmur, "Henry Adams: Three Late Moments," *Kenyon Review* 2 (Winter 1940): 26.

26  See Linda Shires, "T. S. Eliot's Early Criticism and the Making of *The Sacred Wood*," *Prose Studies* 5 (September 1982): 229–38.

27  Eliot, "Shorter Reviews," 10.

28  Edith Wharton, *Summer* (New York: D. Appleton, 1917), 139.

29  Eliot, "In Memory of Henry James," *Egoist* 5, 1 (January 1918): 2.

30  Eliot, "The Hawthorne Aspect," *Little Review* 5, 4 (August 1918): 51.

31  Wharton, *Summer,* 248, 250. That Eliot could see only half of Char-

ity Royall's story, the horror of the body but none of its wonders, reveals the limitations of his own experience and sympathy. He could praise Wharton's work in these limited terms and simultaneously voice his objection to "the feminization of modern society" and his distrust "of the Feminine in literature" (L 198, 204). For a reading of the novel Eliot did not see in *Summer*, see Sandra Gilbert, "Life's Empty Pack: Notes Toward a Literary Daughteronomy," *Critical Inquiry* 11 (March 1985): 355–84.

32  These poems appeared in *Little Review* 5, 5 (September 1918): 10–14. Eliot told his mother that this material was written in the spring of 1918 (L 251), and on 23 May 1918 Pound told Edgar Jepson that he had "four new poems of Eliot's" (*Selected Letters*, 136).

33  Pound's translation of "Dans le Restaurant" is in the Pound Archive, Collection of American Literature, Beinecke Rare Book and Manuscript Library, Yale University.

34  Eliot, *Ara Vos Prec* (London: Ovid Press, 1920), 30.

35  Eliot, "Beyle and Balzac," *Athenaeum* 4648 (30 May 1919): 393. Eliot illustrated this thought with a favorite sentence from Flaubert's *Bouvard and Pécuchet*: "*Ainsi tout leur a craqué dans le main.*" Eliot quoted this line again in his essay on Marvell (SE 256), and he so fully absorbed its sensibility that he borrowed its syntactical pattern to describe his own thwarted effort to enlist in the army ("Everything turned to red tape in my hands" [L 254]) as well as the detached skepticism of Henry Adams ("[H]e could believe in nothing . . . and the pleasure of demolition turned to ashes in his mouth" ["A Sceptical Patrician," 361]). The horror of "Whispers of Immortality" was one that Eliot knew too well.

36  Ronald Schuchard has collected the evidence for this episode in "Eliot and the Horrific Moment," *Southern Review* 21 (October 1985): 1045–56. See also his "T. S. Eliot: The Savage Comedian and the Sweeney Myth," in *The Southern Review and Modern Literature 1935–1985*, edited by Lewis P. Simpson, James Olney, and Jo Gulledge (Baton Rouge: Louisiana State University Press, 1988), 207–20.

37  The typescript of Eliot's Clark Lectures, titled "On the Metaphysical Poetry of the Seventeenth Century with Special Reference to Donne, Crashaw, and Cowley," is part of the John Hayward Collection, King's College Library, Cambridge. This passage is taken from Lecture III, p. 2.

38  Stephen E. Whicher, ed., *Selections from Ralph Waldo Emerson* (Boston: Houghton Mifflin, 1957), 155.

39  Eliot, "Modern Tendencies in Poetry," *Shama'a* 1, 1 (Spring 1920):

12. This essay, an important companion piece to "Tradition and the Individual Talent," was delivered as a lecture to the Arts League of Service, London, on 28 October 1919.

40 "A Cooking Egg" appeared in *Coterie* 1 (May-Day 1919): 44–5; "Burbank with a Baedeker" and "Sweeney Erect" appeared in *Arts and Letters* 2, 3 (Summer 1919): 103–5.

41 Ronald Bush, *T. S. Eliot: A Study in Character and Style* (New York: Oxford University Press, 1984), 25.

42 Bell, *Diary of Virginia Woolf,* vol. 2, 68.

43 Eliot, "The Method of Mr. Pound," *Athenaeum* 4669 (24 October 1919): 1065.

44 Eliot, "Professionalism, or . . . ," 61.

# The Waste Land *and* Eliot's Poetry Notebook

### JOHN T. MAYER

One way in which we have tried to clarify what is at the heart of *The Waste Land* is to trace the origins of the poem and see what light these cast upon the finished version. Around fifteen years ago, Hugh Kenner located the "earliest continuous stretch" of *The Waste Land* in the London material of Part III; the poem originally was a city poem set in London about the urban apocalypse.[1] In 1977 Lyndall Gordon, emphasizing its personal elements, suggested that the poem "goes back to Eliot's fantasies of religious extravagance in 1914," especially "three visionary fragments" about revelation and the problems of conversion, or "turning": "[F]rom the beginning Eliot had in mind the traditional form of the spiritual journey from sin to salvation," against which *The Waste Land*'s more personal materials were to be shaped.[2] At Pound's urging Eliot played down the meditative voice of spiritual autobiography and "transferred the weight of the poem to Voices of Society," so in its published form there is "no longer a central figure . . . but a medley of voices which represent the weak human mass." More recently Ronald Bush has suggested that Eliot changed his original program for the poem, implied in the 1918 London fragment, from a spiritual analysis of empty lives in the modern city to a method of comment-free vignettes whose anxiety-charged content may best be understood through the theory of nightmare.[3]

My argument builds upon these insights, though with different emphases, and extends *The Waste Land*'s origins further back in time, to two projected poems, "An Agony in the Garret" of 1911 and "The Descent from the Cross" of 1914. Though these poems were never put together, their separate pieces have been secreted away for years in his poetry Notebook in the Berg Collection in New York[4]; recently, two parts of the "Descent" have appeared in print with the publication of the first volume of Eliot's *Letters*. The materials of both projected works show Eliot exploiting his experience of the city and his own anxiety-laden inner life in order to trade a kind of conversion experience, a quest for self-transformation and vocation. It was only in *The Waste Land* of 1922 that he undertook and completed the quest outlined in these earlier projects. In the meantime he had discovered that the shape of this internalized quest would fuse city and psyche, the horror and the boredom of the everyday world and the poet's "inner world of nightmare,"[5] with the result that the means of facing personal demons proved the way of articulating poetic and prophetic visions. Eliot's unpublished poetry helps to make clear that the heart of *The Waste Land* is not the wasteland myth but *The Waste Land*'s voices, for in this text, voices are vision.

Both of the projected poems may be said to exist in their parts because of Eliot's preference for composing poems out of existing poems and fragments, and the indications from Eliot's comments about the poems and from the evidence of their titles suggest that we have their basic materials in his poetry Notebook, which contains Eliot's unpublished poems and fragments from the period 1909–14, the time of the projected poems. Eliot carefully transcribed and dated the poetry he wrote into the Notebook, and these are the poems in which, under the influence of Jules Laforgue, he found his own poetic voice and developed the new form of "psychic" monologue through which to exploit his typical

material, the involutions of his own self-consciousness.[6] As we
know, Eliot often constructed his longer poems, such as *The
Waste Land* and "The Hollow Men," out of preexisting fragments
and short poems; the evidence in the Notebook shows that in
1911 he built his poem "Preludes" in this way and suggests that
he contemplated creating the "Agony in the Garret" in the same
way. In a letter to Aiken he reveals that the "Descent from the
Cross" was to be constructed this way, too, from "Oh little Voices"
and "Appearances, appearances he said," as well as from "The
Love Song of Saint Sebastian," copies of which he included with
the letter. The "Saint Sebastian" reflects, of course, Eliot's fascination at this time with psychotic behavior and bizarre martyr
saints. In Eliot's plan, a series of scenes would culminate in a
fool-house masquerade that the protagonist would attend in his
underwear as St. John the Divine.[7] The emphasis on role playing
and masquerade and the combination of vignettes and voices
irresistibly recall "Prufrock," which Eliot also assembled partly
from earlier fragments in 1911. Indeed, the choice of the model
figure of John the Divine, whom Eliot also originally intended to
make a significant voice in *The Waste Land*, suggests that *The
Waste Land* ultimately originated in the kind of identity and voca-
tional crisis rehearsed in "Prufrock" and more completely acted
out in Eliot's unpublished city poems of 1911, which were to form
the constituents of the projected "Agony in the Garrett." In these
poems of 1911 and of 1914, then, we find in outline what Bush
calls the "configuration" of *The Waste Land*. This configuration
will become clearer through demonstrating how the following
motifs developed in the Notebook relate to *The Waste Land*: (1)
the quest-journey as an interplay of city and psyche, (2) the role
of play, parody, and model figures, and finally (3) the transmuta-
tion of voices to vision.

The internalized quest played out in *The Waste Land* is em-
phatically predicted in the quest outlined in unpublished City
poems of the Notebook. We readily recognize that *The Waste
Land* is a quest poem, but despite our knowledge that the poem's
title and some of the incidental imagery associated with Jessie
Weston's book came late to the poem, many readers still connect
the poem's quest mainly with the traditions of medieval romance.
However, the quest enacted in *The Waste Land* reflects one Eliot

already rehearsed in his unpublished poems of 1911, a quest that has more to do with the Romantic poets' search for meaning and identity than with the Grail quest of medieval legend. As Harold Bloom points out, the romance quest had been transformed by the Romantics into an internalized quest concerned with the poet's imaginative life and vocation, and it is often enacted over a series of poems, "so that the entire rhythm of the quest is heard again in the movement of the poet himself from poem to poem."[8] In Eliot's case this movement of the poet himself is especially apparent in the series of unpublished city poems he wrote at Harvard and in Paris as a very young man. The quest in these poems, despite Eliot's well-known anti-Romantic stance in his criticism, is a modern version of the Romantic internalized quest to clarify the individual's vocation and destiny. Eliot's contribution to the type is to make the city rather than nature the landscape through which the quester journeys, in interaction with which he discovers his identity and destiny. The quest in *The Waste Land* is essentially that rehearsed in the city poems of 1911: The wasteland myth is a belated addition that deepens resonances and universalizes its import.

Some comments by the Spanish critic Ortega y Gasset shed light on why the modern version of the Romantic quest takes place not in nature but in the city, the industrial city of the late nineteenth-century naturalistic novel whose automaton city dwellers are moved by their environments rather than inspired by nature. For Ortega consciousness was the discovery of the Renaissance, and its discovery brought an end to the epic and "its aspiration to support a mythical world bordering on that of material phenomena but different from it." With the loss of this mythical world, Ortega notes, "the reality of the adventure" becomes solely psychological.[9] The Romantics had discovered in nature and the creative imagination a way of accessing this mythical world and thus recovered transcendental reality, the world of spirit. By the mid-nineteenth century, however, the motions of the inner life had been reduced to mechanistic formulas, imprisoned by Darwin within physical necessity. "Life," Ortega observes, was "reduced to mere matter. . . . The human organism, which seemed an independent unit, capable of acting by itself, is placed in its physical environment like a figure in a tapestry. It is no longer the organism that moves but the environment that is moving through it. Our actions are no more than reactions [to material stimuli]. . . . Darwin sweeps heroes off the face of the earth."[10]

Eliot's version of the inward quest adventure plays itself out according to Ortega's guidelines, as consciousness moves through a physical environment of matter in search of traces of the more-than-physical in the city environment now moving through the mind. The unpublished city poems in the poetry Notebook, begun at Harvard but written mainly in Paris, record the quest of the poems' common protagonist, who journeys the streets and interiors of the city, a restaurant, a garret, several bars, seeking the meaning of life and the meaning of his own life. The empirical world against which the Romantics revolted also challenges him, and he searches for evidence that life is more than matter and sensations. The squalid cityscapes and the mechanical lives of the city dwellers call to him to abandon his detachment and become the voice of the city, recording its pain in the role of the classical *vates*, the poet-prophet. Like Prufrock, the seeker moves through these poems vacillating between embracing and escaping this role, and like Prufrock he finally chooses not to act.

But unlike Prufrock, he gets another chance, and in *The Waste Land*, the protagonist of the city poems of 1911 again walks city streets and haunts city interiors – a boudoir and a pub in Part II, the typist's flat and a church in Part III, even a fortune teller's. Now he is not alone, however, for he walks with voices singing in his ears, familiar voices from life and literature and voices from sacred and profane works who utter what A. Walton Litz calls magical touchstones, filled with talismantic, occult power.[11] These voices sometimes haunt him as ghosts but often act as enabling model figures, self-fashioning voices through which he shapes his identity. In the city poems of 1911 the environment is Ortega's environment, moving through the mind and subjecting it to its matter; matter overcomes mind. In *The Waste Land* of 1922, however, these magical voices become the means through which, by what Shelley in "Mont Blanc" calls "an unremitting interchange / With the clear universe of things around" (which in *The Waste Land* is both an interchange between the city and the psyche and a dialectic of voices within the psyche), the seeker transforms a city that is both ghost-ridden personal world and cultural wasteland into the desert that is the testing ground of prophets. By listening to the voices he hears, and taking on their perspectives, he simultaneously takes on the prophet's role and utters his witness.[12] In *The Waste Land,* it is mind, and voices, over matter. In the 1911 city poems the seeker discovers in the streets and rooms of the city his poetic vocation, but he cannot embrace it until he traverses in *The Waste Land* the ghost-ridden landscape of his own life and recognizes the city of this world as Unreal.

It will be helpful to review in some detail the quest developed in the unpublished city poems to highlight elements that bear upon *The Waste Land.* The quest begins in two 1909 caprices set in North Cambridge, which establish the city as Ortega's City of Matter and the observer as a detached individual determined not to become a participant in what he observes. The city seems to contain nothing but matter, ugly objects that seem so much trash, but human pain is heard, especially in the voices of city children, who wail Blakean cries of woe. The observer sees Wordsworth's nature disfigured and hears the city dwellers' call for pity, but he shifts his eyes and stops his ears by conscious Laforguian acts of detachment, the "caprices" of the poems' titles, which may seem mere whims but suggest as well the observer's willfulness, his deliberate resistance. Another sign of his desire to escape is the suppression of the first-person singular and a preference for general references to "your," "us," and "our," as if to efface his individuality and its correlative, responsibility. This characteristic reappears in *The Waste Land* in the apparent absence of a central consciousness in a poem replete with "I"s, most of which seem to be the "I"s of others, rather than the awareness of the protagonist who focuses the poem's quest.

The domestic setting of the Eliot family summer home at Eastern Point on Cape Ann inspired "Mandarins" and "Goldfish," two major unpublished poems of 1910 that Eliot wrote after his graduation from Harvard.[13] Though not part of the city series, in their description of the social routines of bourgeois family life they confront the seeker with the same questions posed by the grimy details of city life, and the poet plays out the same ambivalent response, vacillating between detachment and engagement.

Here in this summer world the overwhelming question is the meaning of the quotidian, the daily life typified by the stultifying social routines of the privileged. The title "Mandarins" indicates one pole of response: One confronts meaninglessness from within by playing roles to imitate the model figures the poem sets forth and by assuming strategies of disengagement. This mandarin response suggests an Eastern and psychic response, a modification through attitude. It is the passive way, the way of the mind, the way of inwardness. Its antithesis is adumbrated by the title of the companion summer poem, "Goldfish," which sardonically equates the elegant world of veranda ceremonial with decorative but useless goldfish circling in little glass bowls. In the third part of "Goldfish," active revolt against such meaninglessness is posited but not enacted. Taken together, the two poems suggest the protagonist's – and Eliot's – dilemma: Aware that his continued participation in a meaningless life implicates him, he recognizes that he may have to act change his life rather than simply alter his attitude. Whether to change the mind or to change the world, arguably the overwhelming question posed in Eliot's early poetry, is also a main subtext of *The Waste Land.*

In Paris in 1910 Eliot resumed his city series with another unpublished caprice, set in Montparnasse, its observer journeying through streets he has never seen before but finds somehow familiar: This expression of déjà-vu shows that a decade before *The Waste Land* Eliot had recognized that all cities are really only one city in the modern world. *The Waste Land* deepens this recognition, adding a historical identity linking all cities – "Jerusalem, Athens, Alexandria, / Vienna, London" – in a common and inevitable fall. The Montparnasse poem also marks a milestone for the observer, who admits discomposure before the city scene, the first sign of his potential involvement in its world.

The next city poems leave city streets for city interiors – a supper club, a bar, the protagonist's garret – and more intense journeys, as if these interior spaces take the observer deeper within himself to confront more insistent questions. In "The smoke that gathers blue and sinks" (dated February 1911) he senses that the empiricist's world, the world of matter, may be the only world there is. A grand meal leads only to the deadening silence of matter going by itself, overfed to torpor, refueled with

alcohol: here is the emptiness of matter but no evidence of anything beyond it. In "Interlude: In a Bar" (dated February 1911) an
increasingly desperate search for such evidence begins in a
smoky bar whose scene takes on a visionary aura. This impression may be his own self-projection or simply the bar's smoke; as
evidence it is as ephemeral as the latter. We are far removed from
the visionary experiences of the Romantic poets, for an impression of the visionary is not the experience of vision, and it may be
something worse, a false hope. Still, the poem measures a change
in the consciousness common to these poems: The previously
uninvolved observer has clearly turned into a seeker.

"Inside the gloom" finds him in the private world of his own
garret, where on an August night he playfully engages the constellations about his questions. Some, like Cetus the Whale and
the Great Bear, overwhelm him with their hulking matter, but
there are intimations of alternative readings of the universe. The
constellations are said to take their stations, that is, their positions in the night sky, but also in a higher sense, in this "august"
sky, their places in the zodiac, the perennial patterns traced in
the movements of the stars. He burlesques these ancient patterns by trivializing them, associating them with his passing concerns of the moment. But as in *The Waste Land,* where a fortune
teller's Tarot reading yields valid signs despite the context of de-
based prophesy, here, too, we may see a more esoteric pattern.
The idea of zodiacal stations recalls another ancient pattern, that
of the Stations of the Cross, a series of meditations upon the
fourteen stages of Christ's Passion that coincide with fourteen
stations, or stopping places, along the Via Dolorosa, the Way of
the Cross. Representations of these stations are part of the typical
interior decor of Roman Catholic churches, and Eliot may have
known of them from his Irish nurse's Catholic church in St.
Louis or seen them in France in any church or cathedral, where
in March, when the poem was likely composed, they would have
been a popular Lenten devotion. In the Notebook, the poem is
deliberately set up as fourteen miniature stanzas, each of which
is carefully numbered (the rhyming dimeters could easily have
been written as a series of tetrameter couplets in a single stanza)
so that the poem seems a secular travesty of the Christian observance. Still, the stations remain a sign of the potentially transfor-

mative value of suffering, even of the little agonies of mental anguish that seekers play out in garrets.

Such a possibility is not as fanciful as it may sound. In "Preludes," the only city poem besides "Rhapsody on a Windy Night" that Eliot eventually published from the city poems in the Notebook, it is just such transformation through suffering that becomes a momentary vehicle of both vision and vocation. "Preludes" originates in four separate poems. The first two, originally set in Boston's Dorchester and Roxbury, evoke the modern daily grind that reduces people to robots, slaves of the Industrial City of Matter. The final two preludes, subtitled "Morgendämmerung" and "Abenddämmerung" ("Dawn" and "Twilight") in the Notebook, form a pair of "enlightenment" preludes dealing with privileged moments of awareness brought on by the stress of city life. In effect they find in the dehumanizing matter of the first two preludes the possibility of enlightenment through suffering. By fusing city and psyche, that is, by making the "matter" of the first two preludes the cause for and the material of the protagonist's vision in the third and fourth preludes, Eliot traces in small what he develops in the whole series of the fourteen city poems of the Notebook, the evolution of his prophetic quest out of the matter of the city.

As the observer figure of the first city poem, under the pressure of his need for meaning, turns into a seeker in a smoky bar, so a similar movement from detachment to involvement is the psychic subtext of the Preludes sequence. The Notebook's subtitles, emphasizing enlightenment, point up their essential theme: the protagonist's possible discovery of his destiny. A crucial stage in his personal quest occurs when, having remained detached in the first two preludes, he is drawn into the pain of the city in the third prelude by interpreting a streetwalker's dream-plagued sleep, that is, her suffering, as "a vision of the street." Seen in this light, her suffering is both a form of revelation that alters his perspective and a means of releasing her from blind enslavement to a life of mechanical sex. In the fourth prelude he himself suffers and experiences enlightenment as the cumulative impact of his preceding experiences release in him a vision that parallels the agony of the woman in the third prelude. He sees himself undergoing a kind of crucifixion – "his soul stretched tight across the skies" – as he becomes the street's "conscience." However, torn between assuming the city's pain and carrying burdens that may crucify him, he finally retreats and dismisses its challenge.

But this is not the final station on this protagonist's Via Dolorosa. The title of the last city poem in the Notebook is "The Little Passion," and although the overt Christian framework is belittled, it still helps to clarify Eliot's thinking in the series as a whole. We see that the journey has been a kind of "dark night of the soul," deliberately diminished as a "little passion" to suggest the lack of feeling, passion, and commitment in the seeker, as well as the meanness of the modern City of Matter. The important point, however, is that the poem's subtitle in the final version in the Notebook identifies it as "From 'An Agony in the Garret,' " an announcement of the longer poem to be developed out of the city series, which, if Eliot had used all the city poems in the Notebook, would have consisted of fourteen poems, fourteen stations of a modern, diminished Way of the Cross.[14] The seeker of these poems is not unlike the Quixote described by Ortega, "the sad parody of a more divine and serene Christ . . . torn by the modern anguish; a ridiculous Christ of our own neighborhood, created by a sorrowful imagination, which has lost its innocence and its will and is trying to replace them."[15] And like Quixote, the seeker "stands at the intersection where two worlds meet[,] . . . on the one hand, [the world] of poetic aspiration and spiritual adventure, and, on the other, of empirical reality, 'the anti-poetic per se' " of the late nineteenth-century City of Matter.[16]

Two versions of the poem exist in manuscript,[17] and the second, with its "Little Passion" title and derivation from "An Agony in the Garret," is the last poem entered into the poetry Notebook. By their titles the projected "Agony in the Garret" and "Descent from the Cross" are complementary, the latter in some way developing the former as Christ's crucifixion completed his agony in the garden.[18] In "The Little Passion" such a parody Christ figure torn by the modern anguish dominates the individual's thoughts. The speaker describes a figure whom he knows well, one compelled to walk the streets on hot August nights and, like the protagonist of "Rhapsody," to follow the sight lines set by the street lights and regard what they reveal; in other words, this figure is forced from within to seek enlightenment through the city's images. This neighborhood Christ is also tempted, like Christ in the garden before he endures the Via Dolorosa, to avoid his destiny by diving into dark retreats, which recall the earlier garret and its gloomy privacy but can also be taken in the religious sense of retreat, a place of withdrawal in which to seek illumination – here, regarding one's role in life. The idea of an agony in a garret, the garret of the seeker's mind, recalls Christ's agony in the garden, an act of suffering through which he commits himself to his role of suffering savior and thus defines his identity through an act of submission: "Not my will but thine be done."

Here the seeker follows the model of Christ and embraces the cross, the suffering to which the streets lead and upon which our souls, those of the seeker and the speaker, are pinned. The two quatrains that comprise "The Little Passion" in the manuscript may be a complete poem, but it seems equally possible that, as a revision of the second set of quatrains, which formed the octave of an Italian sonnet in the first draft, they are meant to connect to the sestet of that sonnet. If so, the observer would relate to the seeker far more intimately, for the sestet reveals that he has been watching the seeker in a bar – or rather, he has been watching his own image in the bar mirror – and puzzling out the meaning of the history of his seeking. He focuses at last on the unforgettable smile that the face of his seeker-self wears, and the poem ends.

If the series ends without the seeker's clear commitment to be the voice of the city, the unpublished poems nevertheless suggest a different conclusion to the city quest than can be inferred from Eliot's familiar published city poems "Rhapsody" and "Preludes"; in the latter, the seeker withdraws before the city's challenge, unwilling to become the conscience of the blackened street. However, the series as a whole, including published and unpublished poems, traces an arc of increasing involvement in the anguish of the quest, as the protagonist moves from detached observation to intense questioning of the adequacy of the materialist account of life, and finally, in "The Little Passion," to the acceptance of some kind of cross to bear. His smile bears the marks of an inherited, unconscious disgrace, that is, of something like original sin, the inherited fall of which the contemporary world is unaware. Yet this wan but compelling smile may signal the seeker's acceptance of the parody cross that modern history inflicts upon the modern consciousness.

The notion that the modern seeker may find that the end of all his seeking is but a parody cross and other grotesque forms of suffering leads us directly to "The Descent from the Cross" and to a consideration of its role in shaping *The Waste Land*. Though Eliot confessed to Aiken his dissatisfaction with the parts of the "Descent" he sent to him and suspected the "St. Sebastian" to be "morbid" and "forced," he felt that "the idea was right."[19] To realize his "idea" Eliot planned a multipart sequence whose variety and range of content, styles, and forms is a very persuasive precedent for the form of *The Waste Land*. It begins with "Oh little voices," a complaint both philosophical and poetic, in which the familiar seeker figure anguishes over the frustration of his search for meaning in a world of appearances, and his frustration as well in the world of song; in short, he sums up Eliot's current (1914) frustrations as seeker and poet. This evokes in "Appearances, appearances he said" an imagined exchange with an older, mentor figure modeled on Bradley, the philosopher of appearances; the resultant dialectic of voices and views brings a certain ambiguous and momentary resolution to troubled consciousness. The thinker dozes off, only to enter, in the section that follows, the nightmare world of "The Love Song of St. Sebastian" and its fantasies of sadomasochistic love and death. Twisted combinations of religious and sexual impulses first inspire self-inflicted excesses of self-flagellation and self-abasement before an idealized beloved and then a correlative fantasy of coolly deliberate, self-satisfied ritual strangulation. From this "love song" Eliot's plan calls for an insane section, a happier love song, a mystical section, and the concluding fool-house masquerade, which the speaker attends in his underwear as St. John among the Rocks.[20]

Here, Eliot thought to test the voice of John the Divine, the voice of revelation, as a strategy of innocent witness, and thus avoid the fate of the Baptist whose forthright witness brought his head in upon a platter. Who could accuse one who simply mimicked a voice in his masquerade role? In the desert and rocks of Patmos the John of Revelation speaks obliquely, in the language of symbol and vision. In 1911 Eliot had Prufrock think to disturb the universe by speaking out directly in the voice of John the Baptist. The lengthy "Pervigilium" that forms the very center of the original version of "Prufrock" recorded in the poetry Notebook, deleted by Eliot apparently on the advice of Aiken, who was working to get the poem published, makes clear that Prufrock is brought to the verge of madness and mental collapse by the meaninglessness of life that the streets of the city reveal. By deleting the "Pervigilium" Eliot decided not to stress the potential for madness in Prufrock's vision but to focus mainly on the emptiness of the drawing room's masquerade. But in 1914 in "The Descent from the Cross" Eliot restored madness to center stage, and once again, as in the "Pervigilium," this madness, in the form of the "Sebastian" fantasies that follow "Oh little voices," seems occasioned by the seeker's anguish before the meaninglessness of the everyday world developed in "Oh little voices." By 1921–2 the anguish of his own marriage and the conflicting demands of his own deeply divided temperament compelled Eliot to let his own inner world of nightmare play a significant role in shaping *The Waste Land.*

*The Waste Land*'s mode is indicated by Eliot's 1914 title "Descent from the Cross." The descent is in one sense from Christ's cross of overwhelming physical suffering that brings universal spiritual salvation to the little agonies of the modern seeker of individual self-enlightenment. Like Ortega's Quixote, a parody of both the questing hero of Romantic adventure and of Christ the divine redeemer, the modern agonist is a parody hero engaged in a parody quest, his movement no longer physical and outward over a landscape of monsters, but inward and psychic into the self and its nightmare world. The descent is from the transcendent world of the Grail romance into the Kurtzian retrospective vision of the self's ghosts and horrors that Eliot evoked in his original epigraph to *The Waste Land* from *Heart of Darkness:* "Did he live his life again in every detail of desire, temptation, and surrender during that supreme moment of complete knowledge. . . . 'the horror! the horror!' "

In this sense *The Waste Land* is a serious parody of Christ's descent from the cross to harrow hell in order to release the dead from the demons' grasp. As a modern descent from the cross, the poem crosses inner and outer, bodies and spirits, the city's matter and the psyche's memory, in a double descent. It descends into the city of this world, and especially into its world of the body and of sex. It also descends into the deeps of consciousness and memory in order to face, like the seeker in "The Little Passion," its own image scarred with disgrace. Only such a confrontation can release it from its hell of memory and desire. In *The Waste Land* the quester descends from the cross by moving from Christ and his cross, which brings salvation from outside the self, to an acceptance of a more Eastern approach in which salvation comes from within.

This is to say that behind the "Descent from the Cross" and several of the major poems of 1914, and of compelling importance in *The Waste Land*, are the perspectives that Eliot absorbed during his years of graduate work at Harvard between 1911 and 1914, when he plunged into a study of Indic traditions, aberrant forms of religious experience, and mysticism, all part of a concerted effort to discover and test the validity of forms of experience through which to overcome the limitations of empiricist and rationalist models of knowledge and reach beyond their world of appearances. The sensational materials of Eliot's saint poems should not obscure their final import as explorations of self-transformation through pain, self-violation, and even self-destruction. These poems develop out of the hypothesis Eliot first tested in the discarded "Pervigilium," that "madness" may express a sanity unmeasurable by science and unrecognizable to the conventional world. They prepare Eliot to accept the necessity of confronting the worst within the self in order to gain release.

The unpublished 1914 poems prepare for *The Waste Land* in other ways. In "So through the evening," the seeker moves out from the city at the violent hour between day and night to reach beyond the empiricist's world of sense in order to quest by means of the very images his journey releases, an important precedent for the method of *The Waste Land*. Its nightmare images of baby-faced bats and of women fiddling whisper music enter *The Waste Land* directly, as horrors of the desert of trial in "Part V"; its long-dead male figure comes from the first version of "The Little Passion," linking this quest, which is pursued in confusion and outward from the city, to the quest described in the city series. Like the protagonist of "So through the evening," the modern agonist quests by eventually moving out of the city of this world to enter the desert within and there confront the ghosts of the past and the specters of his own fears and loathings. Such self-confrontation suggests a relevant theme that Eliot develops in "The Death of St. Narcissus" (1915) and one that would become central to *The Waste Land*, the possibility of self-transformation through a change of attitude. Narcissus leaves from the city for the desert and there learns to dance before God, not by being other than himself but by transforming his attitude to himself. The Sibyl looks outward from her cage at those who mock her and yearns for death; in contrast, Kurtz looks inward, sees his life in a flash of memories, and by accepting their horrors, finds death and perhaps release. Eliot in his cage in the bank works to settle foreign debts, the debts of aliens; from the cage of his personal life in the City of Matter, the city of this world, he recognizes in *The Waste Land* that he is alien to life in this world and may have to die to it in order to live in it.

The movement in *The Waste Land* is from personal events, the personal city of the protagonist and his inner world of horrors in Parts I and II, to the impersonal and visionary, the desert of trial and release in Parts IV and V, with Part III as transitional stage, combining city and psyche, personal and impersonal. From the beginning this movement occurs through voices *and* visions – visions that do not come of themselves but through voices. Despite Eliot's yearning for vision, which he explored in the city poems and in "So through the evening," he seems not to have experienced the vision of the mystics, only privileged moments that, like the experience portrayed in the unpublished 1910 poem "Silence" and in *The Waste Land*'s Hyacinth Garden, are intensely ambiguous. By the time of *The Waste Land* Eliot accepted provisionally that the way to vision and prophetic utterance was not to be through vision itself but through voices, and it is voices that mainly shape *The Waste Land*.

The poem's quest originates not in the wasteland myth but in city streets (as the poem's original opening, a night scene on city streets, affirms). The poem is shaped by the internal quest played out in the unpublished city poems of 1911, through which the seeker confronts his own destiny in the City of Matter, and by the implied main point of the 1914 "Descent from the Cross," that the self's need is to journey through disguises and assumed voices over a ghost-strewn landscape of its own making. It is startling that in 1914, a full year before his marriage, Eliot forecast the psychic torture that awaited him in the symbiotic play of mutual destructiveness in which he and Vivienne would engage and to which the diaries of Vivienne Eliot would offer painful witness. This is a fool-house world whose horrors for the individual consciousness are its own images distorted by the mirrors of the mind. Only by encountering these horrors can the protagonist – and Eliot – enter the desert of final testing and possible release.

This internalized quest of self-confrontation is shaped especially through voices: For Eliot, a line from Shakespeare, a comment of Vivienne's, or a phrase from the Buddha's Fire Sermon are signatures of vast significances, and *The Waste Land* sounds through its voices the meanings out of which the protagonist constructs his own identity and experiences the quest. Once again, it is the unpublished poetry that shows how voice emerges as the encoder of meaning and eventually, through several voices in dialectic, as the means of reconciling the contradictions of experience. It was Laforgue who first taught Eliot to play with voices, especially as a way of expressing his own self-consciousness and feelings. The most important kind of play Eliot learned from Laforgue was the play of the mind itself. Laforgue showed him that his own inner life, especially his intense self-consciousness, was the stuff of art, and the practice pieces contained in the poetry Notebook show how Eliot adapted Laforgue's witty, improvisatory, and presentational style into a kind of modernist monologue, different from the Victorian dramatic monologue but recalling the introspective, meditative lyric of the Romantics. In this psychic monologue, the conflicting claims of experience are often heard as voices. "Prufrock" is an obvious exemplar from Eliot's familiar works, though the presence of voice goes well beyond the voices of "you" and "I" and the women "talking" of Michelangelo. The "voices from a farther room" express the boredom of the masquerade world; the eternal Footman snickers, the mermaids sing to each other but not to Prufrock; human voices drown us. Other, more subtle voices of vocation

call Prufrock to test possibilities through role play – as lover or
prophet, attendant lord or fool. He actually practices the voice of
Lazarus, but not that of John the Baptist, fearing his fate should
he disturb the universe; he flirts with the role of the Fool but
finally resigns himself to play Polonius and thinks in this voice to
dare to eat a peach.

"Prufrock" brilliantly exhibits Eliot's mastery of the theatrics of
self-consciousness inspired by Laforgue. The poetry Notebook
contains the trial pieces that led to such mastery. First, he portrayed the mind's play with its own constructs: In "Convictions" a
poet contemplates his own creations, the characters of his poems,
and hears them speak in their own voices. In the Harvard *Advo-
cate* poem "Humouresque" the mind thinks of a role to be played
as a marionette, and it immediately springs to life, speaking the
typical phrases of this voice, an obvious precedent for "Prufrock."
Play and role playing dominate the early poetry, and the unpublished "Suite Clownesque" particularly clarifies its function.
For Eliot role playing was a significant strategy through which to
guard the self and to gain self-mastery, especially by internalizing
the attitudes of model figures, such as this poem's Master of
Ceremonies, who controls his audience strictly through role playing. For the Master of Ceremonies a voice and a set of gestures
constitute self-empowerment. The poem plays out a series of
turns on a vaudeville stage; the observer may be attending a show
(as Eliot and Aiken often did in Boston) or, as seems more likely,
playing it out in his own mind, for the final turn is clearly his own
fantasy, with himself as star. The use of model figures to describe
desirable patterns of behavior is most clearly articulated in the
unpublished "Mandarins" in a series of figures who represent,
sometimes comically, various forms of mandarin behavior. The
first embodies a kind of psychic mandarinism, like that practiced
by the Master of Ceremonies in "Suite Clownesque"; the self
becomes the unmoved center of its world by relying solely upon
its inner resources and attitudes. Models of social and cultural
mandarinism are contemplated, and a myopic intellectual is
ridiculed. In offering positive and negative model figures, this
1910 poem is an important precedent for *The Waste Land.*

Then, in an important unpublished poem that Eliot wrote in
Paris in March 1911, "He said: This universe is very clear," voice

becomes a way of defining intellectual positions, not *as such,* but for the individual who absorbs them and constructs thereby a kind of self out of them. This poem ends with the recognition that the self is incomplete, for the individual has not yet finished the task of shaping his identity. Without such shaping the self may be only the sum of the positions it absorbs. Eliot's 1916 poem in French "Mélange Adultère de Tout" extends this to constitute the self out of the roles it has played in life; it is the various voices through which it has spoken. We have seen that voice as the carrier of particular, indeed, conflicting, points of view functions in the unpublished 1914 fragments "Oh little voices" and "Appearances appearances he said," with which Eliot thought to introduce the "Descent from the Cross." Here, the conflicting approaches to resolving the maze of appearances are set forth by different voices in dialectic (one urges persistence in the quest, the voice of Bradley recalls the contradictoriness of appearances); the separate voices are indicated only indirectly, through pronoun shifts, diction, and the content of their positions. These voices anticipate the masquerade of figures and voices with which the poem is to end.

By the time of *The Waste Land* Eliot's experience had confirmed the value of this unconventional approach to understanding how we construct our identities, and it became the basis for the quest conducted in *The Waste Land.* Its radical model of consciousness is an extension of that proposed in "He said: This universe is very clear" of 1911 and "Oh little voices" of 1914. However, in *The Waste Land* the voices are no longer little but insistent and powerful, for they, like the images that constitute the soul of the woman in the Third Prelude, carry the messages and meanings that constitute the soul in *The Waste Land.* However, they are so forceful as presences that they literally, or more precisely, vocally and aurally, inhabit the first two parts of the poem at the expense of the implicit consciousness they comprise, which does not itself emerge forcefully until the very center of the poem, in Part III, where it is often confused with the voice of Tiresias. In fact, the experiencing self of the poem is not the prophet Tiresias, but a would-be prophet who has been a recessive and dispersed presence in the poem from the outset: recessive because its experiences and memories take center stage, playing themselves out like the vaudeville turns in the "Suite Clownesque" of 1910, dispersed because it exists as the ground of its voices, the voices of the model figures through whose experience it conducts its quest.

As we have seen, Eliot had this very plan in mind for the 1914 projected poem "Descent from the Cross," which begins with the play of voices and ends with a masquerade, the protagonist attending as St. John the Divine. This plan – we recall that Eliot knew his "idea" for the poem was "right" – is the operational base of *The Waste Land,* and it actually surfaces in the original *Waste Land* manuscript, for in Part I, "The Burial of the Dead," the protagonist, having heard the voices of the modern fortune teller Madame Sosostris, and the voice of Dante (all these voices remain in the published version), then assumes the voice of John the Divine and addresses the city, "I John saw these things. . . .," but Pound canceled the line and thus removed this signature of the 1914 poem from the finished text.

Even without this clue to the 1914 plan, Part I shows us how voice works in *The Waste Land.* The protagonist uses some of the images given him by Madame Sosostris and then assumes as his own the voice of Dante, for he learns by means of her images and Dante's words to see the city through their eyes. By doing so, he is beginning to fashion a new self, different from the self at the outset trapped between memory and desire. If we think of the poem's different elements and tonalities (sometimes only a line long, or even a phrase or part of a word – "Tereu") not only as its different voices but as spoken by model figures whose perspectives the protagonist enters in the same way that we would play a role, we can see (or hear) how the protagonist takes on these voices and becomes their perspectives. He sees through their sayings. When in Part III he takes on the voice and perspective of Tiresias, he identifies so intimately with this blind prophet who experiences the world as both male and female that he becomes Tiresias, and this identification moves him to a new level of vision. The protagonist then confirms and intensifies his inner transformation at the end of Part II by recalling, identifying with, and thus making his own the voices and the perspectives of the Buddha and St. Augustine. Part III ends in a series of diminishing fragmented phrases that marks the gradual submergence of the protagonist's own self into the higher role of the prophet. "O Lord Thou pluckest *me* out / O *Lord* Thou pluckest / burning": The Lord plucks out his "me"; the protagonist then assents to the power that "the Lord" bestows, and as a result he becomes the burning vessel of the Lord, the inspired voice of the fiery Spirit, a fire sermon.

The quest played out in the city poems of 1911 is a quest for meaning and vocation, but it ends without the seeker embracing the prophet role or uttering his witness. The quest played out in *The Waste Land* enables the protagonist to make a prophetic statement through the very process of fashioning his identity. This fashioning of identity is simultaneously a discovery and acceptance of prophetic vocation and the uttering of his vision. How does this happen? As he hears the voices of other prophets we hear them too, and this makes his process of hearing and discovery our process of seeing his vision. "You! hypocrite lecteur! – mon semblable, – mon frère!" The voice of Baudelaire echoes in his mind, but it forces us into the poem, as hearers of his voices, and even of his burning fire sermon. When we see what the poem's words and voices articulate, what its "different voices" mean, we cease being uninvolved readers and we become the "semblable," the very double, of the protagonist. Inexorably we take on his experience, we hear his voices and his voice, and we see his vision.

## Notes

1  See Hugh Kenner, "The Urban Apocalypse," in *Eliot in His Time*, edited by A. Walton Litz (Princeton: Princeton University Press, 1973), 25.

2  Lyndall Gordon, *Eliot's Early Years* (Oxford: Oxford University Press, 1977), 86–7. The fragments are "After the turning," "I am the Resurrection," and "So through the evening." The quotations that follow appear on pp. 106–7.

3  Ronald Bush, *T. S. Eliot: A Study in Character and Style* (New York: Oxford University Press, 1983), 56–7, 63.

4  The Notebook was included in the gift that Eliot made to John Quinn of the manuscripts of *The Waste Land,* which on Quinn's death disappeared from view but remains in the Quinn family. In the early 1950s Quinn's niece discovered the manuscripts; they

were sold to the Berg Collection in 1958, but the acquisition remained a secret until late 1968, when the Library revealed the whereabouts of *The Waste Land* manuscripts in connection with the publication of B. L. Reid's biography of Quinn, *The Man from New York: John Quinn and His Friends* (see the Introduction to Valerie Eliot, ed., *The Waste Land: A Facsimile and Transcript of the Original Drafts Including the Annotations of Ezra Pound* (New York: Harcourt Brace Jovanovich, 1971), xxix). The Notebook, which Eliot entitled "Inventions of the March Hare," consists of handwritten entries of most of the poems that he wrote between 1909 and 1914 and carefully dated, with an awareness, it might seem, of posterity's interest. Several of the unpublished poems from this period were not entered into the Notebook, but they are included in a folder of miscellaneous poems in the collection. Because they are part of this body of work, my use of the term "Notebook" includes these as well.

5   Ronald Bush calls attention to this provocative phrase from Eliot's essay "Cyril Tourneur," *Selected Essays* (New York: Harcourt, Brace, 1950), 166. See Bush, *T. S. Eliot,* 52.

6.   For a detailed discussion of the characteristics of the form of the psychic monologue and its literary context, see John T. Mayer, *T. S. Eliot's Silent Voices* (New York: Oxford University Press, 1989), chap. 1. For the emergence of the form in the poetry Notebook, see chap. 3.

7   The McKeldin Library texts of "Oh little voices," "Appearances, appearances he said," and "The Love Song of St. Sebastian" appear in *Letters of T. S. Eliot,* vol. *1, 1905–1922,* edited by Valerie Eliot (New York: Harcourt Brace Jovanovich, 1988), 45–7, with variations from the Berg original typescripts noted. The couplet that Eliot quotes in his letter refers to St. John of the Rocks. Although this may evoke John the Baptist in the desert, Gordon suggests John the Divine (*Eliot's Early Years,* 65), and this seems reasonable, for rocks evoke John the Divine's isle of Patmos, where he composed his visionary Apocalypse, the Book of Revelation. The reference may be a conflation of both John the Baptist and John the Divine; both figures preoccupied Eliot at this time. For the full text of the letter, see T. S. Eliot to Conrad Aiken, 23 July 1914, *Letters,* vol. 1, 43–47.

8   Harold Bloom, "The Internalization of Quest-Romance," in *Romanticism and Consciousness,* edited by Harold Bloom (New York: Norton, 1970), 50.

9   José Ortega y Gasset, *Meditations on Quixote* translated from the Spanish by Evelyn Rugg and Diego Marin (New York: Norton,

1961), 138–9. Quoted in Joseph Campbell, *The Masks of God: Creative Mythology* (New York: Viking, 1968, reprinted by Penguin, 1982), 213.

10   Quoted by Campbell, *Masks of God* 214.

11   A. Walton Litz, "The Allusive Poet: Eliot and His Sources," see below, p. 143.

12   If I place particular emphasis here upon the voices through which the protagonist shapes his vocation, this is not to diminish the voices of his anguished personal experience; indeed, it is these personal voices that show him the horror of a world of personal betrayal and of love that leads only to destruction and death and thus dispose him to become a warning voice to the city of this world.

13   Each poem consists of four individual units, each of which may have been composed separately and then joined. The first poem in the Notebook clearly built up from separate units is "Easter: Sensations of April," a two-unit work that Eliot created by combining separately composed brief poems, the first dated April 1910, the second, May 1910. The first published poem constructed out of independent poems written at different times is "Preludes," whose four parts were composed between October 1910 and the fall of 1911. Eliot clearly was working in the assemblage format in 1910–11 and likely projected building "An Agony in the Garret" (1911) in the same way.

14   The fourteen poems are "First Caprice in North Cambridge" (November 1909), "Second Caprice in North Cambridge" (November 1909), "Fourth Caprice in Montparnasse" (December 1910) (there is no third caprice), "The smoke that gathers blue and sinks" (February 1911), "Interlude: In a Bar" (February 1911), "Inside the gloom" (undated, likely March 1911), "He said: This universe is very clear" (March 1911), "Rhapsody on a Windy Night" (March 1911), "Interlude in London" (April 1911), "First Prelude in Roxbury" (October 1910), Second Prelude in Roxbury (October 1910), "Third Prelude in Roxbury: Morgendämmerung" (July 1911), "[Fourth Prelude:] Abenddämmerung" (undated, likely October 1911), "The Little Passion" (undated and untitled, likely summer 1911; revised, titled and subtitled, likely 1914). The dates noted are Eliot's own.

15   Ortega y Gasset, *Meditations on Quixote*, 51; quoted in Campbell, *Masks of God*, 213.

16   Orgeta y Gasset, *Meditations on Quixote*, 136, quoted in Campbell, 213.

17   The first consists of five stanzas covering two pages, four quatrains

on the recto and a set of six lines on the verso, all written in what Gordon calls Eliot's "spiky Paris hand." This scratchy hand may reflect his use in Paris of a quill pen, perhaps the "calamus" referred to in the 1918 quatrain poem "Ode," which Eliot seems to associate with the "vatic" poetry of the poet-prophet, the poems he wrote in Paris. This version then would date from 1911. The later version, perhaps from 1914, in Eliot's post-Paris hand, is entitled "The Little Passion" and subtitled "From 'An Agony in the Garret'"; it is a slight revision of the second set of two quatrains. I take the two sets of quatrains to be alternative versions of the octave of an Italian sonnet, as the rhyme schemes bear out, and the six lines of the second page to be the sestet of this sonnet. It is unclear whether the two stanzas entitled "The Little Passion" are meant to stand alone as a poem (the rhyme scheme is that of an English sonnet) or to be a recasting of the Italian sonnet into an English sonnet, whose third quatrain and couplet close would be formed from the same six lines of the 1911 sestet (their somewhat irregular rhyme scheme would fit the Italian or English form). For me, "The Little Passion" gains in complexity if read as a sonnet rather than as a set of two quatrains.

18 The 1914 date seems reasonable, for Eliot's letters to Aiken from Germany that summer show him to be quite concerned that his poems of 1914 are not as good as his earlier work, his achievements of 1911, and very much interested in getting his best poetry published. As we know, as soon as he reached England and showed Pound "Prufrock" and "Portrait of a Lady," Pound immediately set to getting these poems in print, and Eliot presumably quickly assembled "Preludes" to provide Pound additional publishable works, along with the "Rhapsody." In one way it would make sense that Eliot was considering putting together the city poems for the longer "Agony in a Garret" in 1914 when he was also projecting the "Descent from the Cross" to be partly constructed from the recently written neurotic studies of 1914. Eliot seemed ready in the fall of 1914 to pursue his projected poems, for shortly after arriving in England he wondered, jocularly, in a letter to Aiken on 30 September 1914, whether he should not try to do something with the whole "March Hare," of which the city poems of "An Agony in a Garret" formed the most impressive sequence. See *Letters*, vol. 1, 59. Aiken had failed to get "Prufrock" published in 1912, and Pound was having some difficulty convincing Harriet Monroe to print it in *Poetry*, though eventually it appeared in 1915. Pound, a champion of his own form of intensely compact Imagism, may have dissuaded Eliot from pursuing longer constructions except those that could be

made from existing poems that were highly imagistic in character. The four "Preludes" fit this formula, as does the "Rhapsody," but except for the three caprices, the other poems in the city series would strike Pound as diffuse, a mix of reflections and images without intensity or complexity. Still, Pound submitted Eliot's "St. Narcissus" despite (apparently) disapproving of its "narcissism," to *Poetry*, and it was accepted; Eliot, however, withdrew it at the last minute. Had the "St. Narcissus" appeared, and had Eliot pursued the "Agony in the Garret" and the "Descent from the Cross," we would have a very different view of the early Eliot than the conventional one based on what Eliot actually published, poems such as "Prufrock," "Portrait of a Lady," and Boston satires like "Cousin Nancy."

19  Eliot to Conrad Aiken, 25 July 1914, *Letters* vol. 1, 44.
20  Ibid.

# The Price of Modernism: Publishing The Waste Land

### LAWRENCE RAINEY

"History is a nightmare," wrote Joyce. "History has cunning passages, contrived corridors / And issues," murmured T. S. Eliot. It characterizes the epic, declared Pound, in a transparent reference to his own life's work, *The Cantos*.[1] The modernists were obsessed with history. They mourned it and damned it, contested it as tenaciously as Jacob wrestling with the image of God: "I will not let thee go, except thou bless me." Yet if the deity of history had ever deigned to reply to them, it might have said: "Behold, I set before you this day a blessing and a curse." Modernism, scholars announced in 1965, had "passed into history." The comment appeared in the preface to a textbook; in part it was a historical description and in part a speech act enacting what it appeared to describe, a key moment in modernism's passage to academic respectability.[2] Today, of course, we confess that we live on the hither side of that moment. We take for granted modernism's place in the canon or even equate its progress among the professors with its trajectory through history. Yet in doing so, we forget that modernism flourished long before 1965, that it had erupted into the public consciousness at least forty years earlier, and that its status as a cultural resource had been secured by an array of institutions quite removed from the tepid confines of the academy. The event that epitomized this process was the publication of *The Waste Land* in late 1922, which announced modernism's unprecedented triumph. It generated an avalanche of publicity that marked a crucial moment in its critical fortunes, establishing the poem as a reference point for the assessment of modernism by a wider public. Long before textbooks about it were written, popular and critical understanding of modernism had already been configured by a specific dynamics of transmission that characterized modernism's productive processes and grounded its extraordinary success. The complex events that culminated in the 1922 publication of *The Waste Land* articulated both its essential features and its contradictions. It behooves us to reconsider that earlier, more fractured moment, to reconnoiter the problematic terrain suggested by the preposition *into* in the phrase *into history*. For *into* evokes transition, a liminal moment attended by the possibility of failure, a risk that modernism's passage through the "contrived corridors" might have miscarried.

A core of basic facts about the publication of *The Waste Land* has long been known. In October 1922 it received quasi-simultaneous publication in two journals: *The Criterion* in England, on 16 October, and *The Dial* in the United States, on around 20 October (though in the November issue). In December it appeared in a third form as an independent volume including Eliot's explanatory notes, published by the American firm of Boni and Liveright.[3] Together these constituted an event that has become a staple in the legend of modernism's emergence and triumph. Yet a reconsideration of this event might begin by exploring not where the poem was ultimately published, but where it was *not* published: the witty, sophisticated pages of *Vanity Fair* or the intransigent leaves of *The Little Review*. Though neither has been discussed in connection with the release of *The Waste Land*, both were considered as potential publishers at various points in

1922 as negotiations for the poem pursued a fragile, unpredictable course. And together these possibilities, with the untold stories that lie behind them, serve to register a spectrum of the possibilities of modernist publishing – a spectrum of how modernism negotiated its way among the "contrived corridors" of its own production.

One might begin by examining an unnoticed occasion in early August 1922, when John Peale Bishop visited the Paris studio of Ezra Pound. Two weeks earlier Bishop had resigned his post as managing editor of *Vanity Fair*, and ostensibly he was traveling on an extended honeymoon after his recent marriage. Unofficially, however, Bishop had come to visit the savage god of modern experimentalism – and to talk business.[4] The topic was the publication of *The Waste Land*, a work that Bishop had never read, but whose vicissitudes he had been following for five months. In early March, while still in New York and laboring for *Vanity Fair*, he had received an article from Aldous Huxley that reported the poem's composition and announced – mistakenly, it would subsequently turn out – its imminent publication in *The Dial*. An astute and conscientious editor, Bishop had phoned to confirm the report with his colleague and counterpart at *The Dial*, Gilbert Seldes. Seldes was puzzled, having heard nothing about the poem; on 6 March he cabled *The Dial* co-owner and chief editor, Scofield Thayer, who was then residing in Vienna:

Cable whether Eliot poetry coming Seldes

Three days later Thayer replied in French:

ELIOT REFUSA THAYER

Seldes immediately contacted Bishop and urged him to alter Huxley's article, which was to indicate that the poem's appearance in *The Dial* was, as Seldes expressed it, "problematical but probable."[5] More important, Bishop had now glimpsed the growing rift between Eliot and *The Dial*.

By late April 1922, in fact, relations between Eliot and Thayer had completely broken down; and in the wake of their collapse Pound had begun to intervene actively in the search for a publisher. On 6 May 1922 he wrote to Jeanne Foster, beloved companion of New York lawyer and patron John Quinn, a contributor to *Vanity Fair* and friend of Bishop.[6] Pound was soliciting an offer of publication for the poem in the bluntest possible terms:

> What wd. Vanity Fair pay Eliot for "Waste Land".
> Cd. yr. friend there [i.e., Bishop] get in touch with T.S.E., address 12 Wigmore St., London W.1.

By August, when he visited pound, Bishop was clearly apprised of the situation – indeed, was responding to a suggestion advanced by Pound himself. The two met on 3 August, and two days later Bishop reported their conversation to Edmund Wilson, his closest friend and his successor as managing editor at *Vanity Fair*:

> Pound I met the other afternoon. I found him extended on a bright green couch, swathed in a hieratic bathrobe made of a maiden-aunt-shit-brown blanket. His head is quite fine, but his voice is offensively soft, almost effeminate and [xxxx], and his body is rather disagreeably soft. However, he was quite gracious, and the twinkle of his eyes whenever he makes a point is worth something. He held forth for two hours on the intellectual moribundity of England – the old stuff. Here's the thing however – Eliot is starting a quarterly review: he is to run 'Waste Land,' the new series of lyrics in the first number: he and Thayer have split and *The Dial* will not publish it. Perhaps you might want to arrange for the American publication. Pound says they are as fine as anything written in English since 1900. I'm lunching with EP tomorrow [6 August] and will report further.

Whether Bishop wrote again to Wilson as he promised is unknown. On 7 August he left for Vienna, and by the time his letter could have reached Wilson in New York (around 16 August) and Wilson could have replied, his proposal had already been overtaken by events previously set in motion.[7] Yet the seriousness with which it was advanced by both Bishop and Pound should indicate that *Vanity Fair* was considered a serious contender to publish the poem. How serious, indeed, we shall see later.

Bishop's meeting in August also indicates the centrality of Pound's role in prompting and facilitating this abortive plan, recapitulating a story that grows increasingly familiar: Pound was the cultural impressario and entrepeneur who, precisely by virtue of these roles, occupied a critical position at the heart of modernism.[8] It is this position, in fact, that informs the rhetoric in which he articulated his advocacy of *The Waste Land*'s publication: "Pound says they are as fine as anything written in English since 1900," wrote Bishop, evidently quoting him verbatim. A month earlier Pound had written to Felix Schelling, his former professor at the University of Pennsylvania: "Eliot's *Waste Land* is I think the justification of the 'movement,' of our modern experiment, since 1900."[9] Bishop had clearly been subjected to a variant of the same argument: The poem was important precisely for its representative quality, and publishing it was not necessarily a matter of appreciating its quality or sympathizing with its substantive components – whatever those were – but of one's eagerness to position oneself as the spokesperson of a field of cultural production, the voice for an array of institutions ("the justification of the 'movement,' of our modern experiment, since 1900"). Indeed, how much this animated Bishop's interest in the poem is underscored by a curious anomaly in the nature of his enthusiasm, for Bishop was praising a poem that he had as yet not read, indeed, whose exact title was still a bit obscure to him ("'Waste Land,' the new series of lyrics").[10]

Bishop's imperfect knowledge was not unique. Indeed, insofar as he knew the title of the poem at all, he knew more than Horace Liveright had known when he first advanced his own offer of publication for the poem. The date was 3 January 1922, notable because it took place before the poem was completed, before it had even acquired its present title. Liveright's interest, like Bishop's, was not the consequence of an aesthetic encounter with a work he had read and admired, but an eagerness to buy a product that promised to meet a series of minimum conditions. But what were these conditions?

Liveright's access to Eliot's poem, like Bishop's, had been mediated by Pound. It was he who assumed the function of stage director cueing the characters in their parts: the shy reserved poet played by T. S. Eliot, the brash young publisher acted by Horace Liveright. Eliot had arrived on Paris on 2 January 1922 and would stay for two weeks, until 16 January. He had come from Lausanne, bearing the disorderly sheaf of manuscripts that he and Pound began to edit and revise, producing a quasi-final

version of *The Waste Land*.[11] His arrival coincided with the visit
of Liveright, the partner who was guiding editorial policy at Boni
and Liveright. Liveright was touring Europe to acquire new
works of literature, and his visit to Pound was designed to set
their relations on firmer grounds. In 1919 he had published his
*Instigations*, in 1920 he had undertaken *Poems 1918–1921*, a
volume released only three weeks before his arrival in Paris, and
in the summer of 1921 he had paid Pound for a translation of
Remy de Gourmont's *Physique de l'amour*, an engagement that
had helped Pound avert financial disaster. Now Liveright hoped
to establish more stable relations; he trusted Pound's capacity to
recognize new talent, saw him as a valuable link to other authors
whose work interested him, and even entertained the idea that
Pound's work might prove commercially viable at some point in
the future.[12] In turn, Pound thought that he might turn Liveright
into the principal publisher of modernism and hoped to secure a
long-term agreement guaranteeing financial security and time
for work.

Poet and publisher courted one another actively. During the
six days of Liveright's stay in Paris (30 December 1921–4 January 1922), they saw each other daily.[13] Pound treated Liveright to
visits with Paul Morand and Constantin Brancusi, and the young
publisher left "a good impression" on Pound, who felt that he was
"going toward the light[,] not from it." He was "much more of a
man than publishers usually are" and, indeed, "perhaps the only
man in the business."[14] He was "a pearl among publishers."[15]
The masculine publisher had arrived at an opportune moment.
Joyce was looking for an American publisher of *Ulysses*, and Eliot
would need a publisher for his unfinished poem. On 3 January
1922, Liveright had an extraordinary dinner with Joyce, Eliot,
and Pound to discuss a milestone publishing program. The encounter was productive. With Joyce he agreed to publish *Ulysses*
and to advance $1,000 against royalties. To Pound he offered a
contract guaranteeing $500 annually for two years in addition to
translator's fees for any work from French agreed upon by both
parties. To Eliot he offered a $150 advance against 15 percent
royalties and promised publication in the fall list. Liveright was
nervous only about its length; in a brief note dated 11 January, a
week before Eliot had left Paris, he expressed his concern that

the poem might not be long enough. "I'm disappointed that Eliot's material is as short. Can't he add anything?" he pleaded with Pound.[16]

Pound, it is clear, was eager to gather under one roof the principal works and authors of modernism, including Yeats, whom he encouraged to abandon a longstanding contract with Macmillan in favor of Liveright.[17] At stake in these efforts was an effort to present modernist writings as the articulation of an idiom, a serviceable language that was shared (and in this sense collective in character) yet amenable to a high degree of individuation: the voice of the "'movement,' of our modern experiment since 1900." In short, his activity was characterized by programmatic ambitions and a coherent sense of their interaction with market conditions.

These traits also appear in every stage of his dealings with Thayer, the editor of *The Dial* who was eventually to purchase *The Waste Land*. Pound lobbied forcefully for the poem's publication from the outset, invoking a rhetoric by now familiar. On 18 February 1922, when Thayer and Eliot were still at a preliminary stage of discussion, Pound wrote to Thayer: "Eliot's poem is very important, almost enough to make everyone else shut up shop." When Thayer replied (5 March) that he could not comment on the poem's merits, since Eliot had not yet sent him the text, Pound persisted:

> His poem is as good in its way as Ulysses in its way, and there is so DAMN little genius, so DAMN little work that one can take hold of and say, "This at any rate stands, makes a definite part of literature".

*The Waste Land* was represented as a verse equivalent of *Ulysses*, a work that epitomized not just the experiences of an individual, whether author or protagonist, but the modernist claim to a hegemonic position in the institution of "literature," an ambiguous entity that was distinct yet inseparable from the commercial production of reading matter and discourse. Its merits did not reside in a specific set of words or text, but in its capacity to articulate this collective aspiration of an elite.

Pound's letter of 9–10 March also outlined practical suggestions that would prove pivotal both for *The Waste Land* and for subsequent literature: "I wish to Christ he had had the December award," he hinted. But other solutions were also available. Eliot might be granted "a professorship," as Frost had recently been. Or he might be given a job on *The Century* or *The Atlantic*, since "he is not an alarming revolutionary, and he don't, as I at moments, get mistaken for a labour-leader or bolshy bomb-thrower."[18] Yet it was the hint of "the December award," the Dial Award for services in the cause of letters (granted for the first time four months earlier), that would bear fruit both for Eliot and for modernism.

Pound's suggestions were advanced precisely when communications between Eliot and Thayer were breaking down. On 8 March Eliot had telegraphed Thayer that he could not accept less than £50 (or $250). Unfortunately, the message was distorted in transmission, and Thayer had received a shocking request for an unprecedented sum:

cannot accept under !8!56 pounds = eliot +[sic]

In reply, on 12 March Thayer reiterated his offer of $150 for the poem, a figure that was advanced without sight of the manuscript and was 25 percent higher than the $110 to $120 he would normally have paid.[19] (One should recall that the national income per capita in the United States at this time was about $750 per annum. By contrast, the 1986 national income per capita was $14,166. Viewed as a percentage of national income per capita, Thayer's offer is the equivalent of roughly $2,850 in 1986 dollars.)[20] Not unreasonably, Thayer also asked to receive a copy of the manuscript. In addition, he pointed out the staggering deficits *The Dial* was incurring and argued that it could not alter its policy of "pay[ing] all contributors famous and unknown at the same rates." In a reply on 16 March Eliot was curt and frankly insulting, and he proceeded to withdraw the poem entirely:

Please excuse my not replying sooner to your letter, except by my wire; but I have had a good deal of trouble over letting my flat furnished and moving here, where I shall be till the 20th June. In addition, there have been engrossing personal affairs, and I have been prevented from dealing with any correspondence.

I also took some days to think about your offer, during which time I happened to hear on good authority that you paid £.100 [sic]

98

to George Moore for a short story, and I must confess that this influenced me in declining $150 for a poem which has taken me a year to write and which is my biggest work. To have it published in a journal was not in any case the way I should choose for bringing it out; and certainly if I am to be offered only 30 to 35 pounds for such a publication it is out of the question.

I have written to Ezra Pound to explain my reasons for refusing to dispose of the poem to the Dial at that price and he concurs with me.

[Paragraph omitted.]

You have asked me several times to give you the right of first refusal of any new work of mine, and I gave you the first refusal of this poem.

Opposite Eliot's charge about George Moore, Thayer noted in pencil: "novellette length / serially." At the bottom of the letter he also commented:

> Seen Moore work
> exception for him
> and because review had
> offended
> Moore had already sacrificed several hundred
> dollars

True, *The Dial* had paid Moore a higher than usual fee, but in part this was because of the work's length, in part because *The Dial* had been remiss in fulfilling earlier obligations to Moore ("had offended"), thereby forcing him to sacrifice "several hundred dollars," for which the larger payment had been a form of compensation. But more important was Thayer's remark opposite Eliot's last sentence, withdrawing the offer to publish. Thayer vented his tart indignation: "Not submitted."[21]

Eliot's allegations about Moore appeared to invoke a principle of equal pay for all contributors. In fact, it was precisely the opposite principle that interested him, as he had explained a few days earlier to Pound:

> I think these people should learn to recognize Merit instead of Senility, and I think it is an outrage that we should be paid less merely because Thayer thinks we will take less and be thankful for it, and I thought that somebody ought to take steps to point this out.

At first sight Eliot's argument may strike us as sympathetic, if only because it seems so familiar.[22] But the issues were rather more complicated: In an important sense the question of aesthetic value is inseparable from commercial success in a market economy, a difficulty that has beset every argument for the intrinsic merit of literary modernism. By 1922 literary modernism desperately required a financial-critical success that would seem comparable to the stunning achievement of modernist painting, yet every step in this direction was hampered by market constraints less amenable to the kinds of pressures from elite patronage and investment that had secured the fortunes of Cubism and modern painting. The legal definition of intellectual property – which continued to belong to the author after its purchase by the consumer, in contrast to a painting or statue, which became the property of the purchaser – posed a series of intractable dilemmas. Patronage could nurture literary modernism only to the threshold of its confrontation with a wider public; beyond that point it would require commercial success to ratify its viability as a significant idiom. That was the question that permeated discussion about publication of *The Waste Land:* Assuming that the poem epitomized the investment of twenty years in the creation of a collective idiom – "our modern experiment, since 1900" – the protagonists were obliged to find a return on their investment in modernity.

Thayer was shocked and insulted by Eliot's letter of 16 March, and refused to engage in further communications with him. Instead he turned to Pound, who was more vulnerable to the threat of losing his job with *The Dial* and might be reproached for having encouraged Eliot's intransigence. On 10 April Thayer demanded that he explain himself: "Perhaps you will be able to enlighten me as to why you concur with Eliot in his refusal to let The Dial have his poem. . . ."[23] In reply, Pound rehearsed the same charge (which Eliot had communicated to him), that George Moore was "getting special rates from The Dial (also Sherwood Anderson)," and he concluded:

> That being the case I can hardly reprove Eliot – if you have put the thin on a commercial basis, for holding out for as high a price as he can get. [Added in autograph in margin:] (*i.e. if The Dial is a*

*business house, it gets business treatment. If The Dial is a patron of literature T. contends it should not pay extra rates for "mere senility", all of which is extreme theory-ism, perhaps, on his part.)*

But in passing, Pound added another point. He could hardly attest to the veracity of Eliot's or Thayer's claims, but in general he preferred that the poem be published in *The Dial:*

> I shd. perhaps prefer one good review to several less good ones. I have, as I think you know, always wanted to see a concentration of the authors I believe in, in one review. The Dial perhaps looks better to me than it does to Eliot. (Life in general does.)

As always, Pound displayed a keen understanding of the nexus between cultural ambitions and their institutional actualization.[24] Implicit in his remarks to Thayer was his view that literary modernism could best present itself as a shared language through a centralization suggesting the coherence of its ambitions – the same project that animated his endeavor to unite the works of Joyce, Eliot, Yeats, and himself under the umbrella of a single publisher. Such a project would facilitate the perception of modernism as an idiom both collective and capable of individuation: an identifiable, distinctive, and serviceable language. Yet with equal acuteness Pound also articulated a central dilemma that characterized *The Dial* and the role it might play in any such project. Was *The Dial* a form of patronage, or was it a commercial venture? Unlike the traditional journals that were organs of publishing houses, *The Dial* could shun the increasing diversity and heterogeneity that typified the ordinary journals, presenting itself as a benign and disinterested patron. Its owners, on the other hand, were actively engaged in purchasing works of modern painting and sculpture and in this sense were investors in a market commodity whose value was rapidly rising, in part through the efforts of the publicity apparatus that they themselves owned and controlled. Literary modernism, by analogy, was now courting the risk of becoming "smart art," an investment that would pay and pay big if successful in an expanding market. But pay whom?

The contradictions were irreconcilable. Driven by conflicting imperatives, the participants muddled through the summer of 1922. On 30 April Thayer summarized the state of his relations with Eliot: "We now correspond only through Pound with whom my relations are also strained, but who seems to desire to keep his job." Pound himself was more cavalier. On 6 May, while traveling through Italy, he paused to send Thayer a postcard:

My present impression of the case is "Oh you two Bostonians."

The surface gaiety, however, was a pose.[25] The same day he also posted his letter inquiring about the price that might be offered by *Vanity Fair*.

Discussions remained stalled throughout the rest of May and June as the participants reconsidered their strategies. On 2 June Pound and Eliot met in Verona, a meeting recorded a few weeks later by Pound in a series of drafts and draft fragments suggesting the substance of their conversations. One of these (later incorporated into *The Cantos*) makes clear that they considered the editorial program of Eliot's new review (still untitled, but soon to be named *The Criterion*), a topic that probably led to another: where to publish *The Waste Land*.[26] From the outset of his undertaking *The Criterion*, Eliot had entertained the idea that it might collaborate with American reviews in simultaneous publication; his first letter announcing the new journal to Pound, written on 12 March, had proposed exactly this:

I also see no reason why some things should not appear in this and in the Little Review concurrently.

The timing of this suggestion should be noted: it was four days after Eliot had sent his provocative telegram to Thayer and four days before he withdrew his offer of publication to *The Dial*.[27] It was a curious proposal; Eliot had not published in *The Little Review* since 1918 and had never evinced particular interest in its fortunes. Yet if Eliot was already assuming that *The Waste Land* would be published by his own journal in England, then his 12 March reference to *The Little Review* – addressed to Pound, a primary force behind its editorial activity – was probably an effort to suggest a replacement for *The Dial*. The same idea, we may suppose, arose in their discussions at Verona. And quite naturally so, since the editors of *The Little Review* were now in Paris and often in touch with Pound, who had recently assembled a special Brancusi number for them. Like *Vanity Fair*, *The Little Review* was also a possible candidate for what had now become a project of simultaneous publication.

In the wake of the Verona meeting, the decisive episodes in the story occurred. Pound returned to Paris on 2 July 1922 and two weeks later received a personal visit from James Sibley Watson, Jr., the co-owner and co-editor of *The Dial,* and the partner of Thayer. Two days later Pound reported the meeting to his wife Dorothy:

> Usual flood [of people visiting]: Lunch with Watson of Dial, on Wed. [19 July], amiable [ . . .] wants T's poem for Dial, etc.

The report leaves no doubt about the purpose of Watson's visit: he had come to purchase *The Waste Land.*[28] Influenced by the assumption that the poem vindicated the project of modern experimentalism since 1900, Watson was seized with anxiety that *The Dial* would suffer an ignominious defeat in its effort to position itself as *the* representative of advanced cultural life. What if the poem were published in *The Little Review* or even *Vanity Fair?* The day after his meeting with Pound, Watson flew to Berlin and met with Thayer.[29] Among other matters, they discussed *The Waste Land* and *The Dial*'s prospects for publishing it. Now, increasingly fearful and excited, the two editors reached an unprecedented decision: They would offer Eliot the second annual Dial Award in confidence as the price for the poem, whereas officially they would pay only the $150 that had been their original offer.[30] Literary history records few spectacles so curious or so touching, i.e., two editors of a major review offering a figure nearly three times the national income per capita – in 1986 terms, the same ratio yields over $40,000 – for a poem that neither had seen or read. What they had decided to purchase was less a specific poem, more a bid for discursive hegemony. Moreover, their strategy for reaching their goal was exquisitely self-fulfilling: Since news of the Dial Award would attract media attention, it would augment the sales of the work and further redound to the credit of *The Dial.*

Seven days after his encounter with Thayer, Watson returned to Paris and met with Pound a second time. Two accounts of the meeting survive, one by Pound addressed to his wife Dorothy:

Watson in Thursday [27 July] with Cummings [. . .] Wat. troubled at not having T.S.'s poem for Dial.[31]

More revealing is Watson's account, addressed to Thayer:

Pound has written a ⟨very⟩ veiled hint to Eliot. He took me to see Brancusi, who [xxxx] appears very anxious not to be reproduced anymore. I gather this is mostly a pose. Such chittering and apologizing and kowtowing as Pound indulged in I have never before seen. It was disgusting. I pointed out several things I thought you would like, but no, I must take what the master will give. "You win the victory," says Brancusi, as though I had been beseeching him for a week. A dam' Pyrrhic victory, by me! [. . .] He will, of course, be furious if we don't take any; and Pound will say that we have destroyed his only remaining Parisian friendship. I hope you will write Brancusi rather than have me to go see him again; if I go, I shan't take Pound, that's sure. [. . .] Pound looks pretty unhealthy. He handed me two lemons which he recommends very highly and which I send to you on the [canceled: hope] chance you may like one of them.[32]

Pound's letter to Eliot, which has not survived, was written immediately after Watson's visit on 27 July. And while his "hint" had been "⟨very⟩ veiled" when issued from Paris, a certain rendering evidently took place as it crossed the channel. Eliot understood fully the implications of his request for a typescript:

I will let you have a copy of the Waste Land for confidential use as soon as I can make one. [. . .] I infer from your remarks that Watson is at present in Paris. I have no objection to either his or Thayer's seeing the manuscript.[33]

Evidently it took Eliot some two weeks to arrange (or type himself) a copy of the typescript, and it was not until 12 or 13 August that he sent it to Watson in Paris. When it arrived, Watson hastily read it and reported the news to Thayer in Vienna:

In response to Pound's letter Eliot has assumed a more conciliatory attitude and has sent on a copy of Wasteland for our perusal. I am forwarding it to you. . . . Anyway I wrote him more plainly about the prize and await his answer. I found the poem disappointing on first reading but after a third shot I think it up to his usual — all the styles are there, somewhat toned down in language

[autograph addition:] ⟨*adjectives!*⟩ and theatricalized in sentiment
– at least I thought.[34]

Here, too, one is struck by the discrepancy between Watson's initial assessment of the poem and views of it later enshrined in criticism. "On first reading" Watson found the poem "disappointing," and after perusing it three times he considered it merely "up to [Eliot's] usual." Indeed, in some respects it was below his usual: The diction seemed flat ("somewhat toned down"), and the tone was "theatricalized." Yet all this makes only more remarkable his decision to advance a publication proposal that entailed an unprecedented scale of payment, presented in his letter of 13 or 14 August to Eliot.

Eliot responded on 15 August:

> Subject to Mr. Liveright's consent I would let the *Dial* publish the poem for $150, not before November 1st. In this event I would forego the $150 advance from Mr. Liveright, and he would delay publication as a book until the new year. Possibly he would be glad to do this, on the possibility of the book's getting the prize, which might increase the sales.

His proposal reached Watson late in the afternoon of 16 August.[35] The next day, however, he was seized with panic at the audacity of his own proposal, and sent a telegram reporting that he could not make up his mind. On 19 August Watson reported both events to Thayer:

> Got a letter from Eliot [received 16 August] regretting his haste in thinking we were trying to rob him, and offering us the right of publishing his poem simultaneously in Dial with its pub. in the Criterion. I find from Pound that Bel Esprit hasn't enough yet for one year, that it goes to Eliot only when he leaves his bank and engages in writing exclusively. He gets only a nominal salary from Lady Rothermere. In other words I don't see why we shouldn't be doing something moderately popular in giving him the award. But the next day [17 August] I got a [canceled: cable] telegram saying ["]don't act till you receive a second letter." Haven't received it yet, though it may come on board tonight when we touch at Plymouth. So the matter is still in the air. Please don't do anything definitive without letting me know first. I reach New York probably August 26, and there is also the telegraphie sans fil.[36]

Pound had clearly informed him about the difficult state of Eliot's personal finances. Watson, in turn, hoped that this might be exploited to the advantage of *The Dial*, that it might be viewed as "doing something moderately popular in giving him the award." Eliot's actual services to letters (the ostensible justification for the award) and the merits of *The Waste Land* were issues that never appeared in his discussion of the Dial Award. Instead, Watson cheerily admitted his view that the proposal was a device intended to garner goodwill for *The Dial* or a tactic in its struggle to consolidate its position as the dominant journal of advanced culture.

Meanwhile, on 21 August Eliot sent his own letter to Quinn, apprising him of the recent developments and leaving open the possibility for action:

> A few days ago I had an attractive proposal from Mr. Watson of the *Dial* who are very anxious to publish the poem. [. . .] They suggest getting Liveright to postpone the date of publication as a book, but I have written to them to say that it seemed to me too late to be proper to make any change now and that I should not care to trouble either Mr. Liveright or yourself with any questions of alterations in the contract.[37]

Nine days later Eliot wrote to Pound and reported his letters to Watson and to Quinn:

> I received a letter from your friend Watson most amiable in tone [. . .] offering $150 for the "Waste Land" (not "Waste Land", please, but "*The* Waste Land"), and (in the strictest confidence) the award for virtue also. Unfortunately, it seemed considerably too late, as I had the preceding day [14 August] got contract, signed by Liveright and Quinn, [(]book to be out by Nov. 1st, etc.) I can't bother Quinn any more about it, I don't see why Liveright should find it to his advantage to postpone publication in order to let the Dial kill the sale by printing it first, and there has been so much fluster and business about this contract that I don't want to start the whole thing up again, so I see nothing but to hope that the Dial will be more businesslike with other people. Watson's manner was charming, if Thayer had behaved in the same way the Dial might have published it long ago, instead of pretending that I had given him the lie as if he was *ehrenfähig* anyhow. Anyway, it's

my loss, I suppose; if Watson wants to try to fix it up with Liveright I suppose he can, that's his affair. I suppose the move was entirely due to your beneficent and pacific efforts, which are appreciated. Dam but [why] don't they give the prize to you? More presently.[38]

Notwithstanding the disingenuous demur by Eliot, the issue was already all but settled. The suggestion which he had advanced – that *The Dial* undertake to arrange terms with Liveright – was rapidly realized through the agency of Watson. On 29 August his ship arrived in New York; the next day he received Eliot's letter of 21 August, broaching the new arrangement. He set to work immediately, as Seldes duly reported to Thayer: "Watson has just come back and the Eliot affair is taking up much of our time."[39] A week later he and Seldes met with Liveright in the office of the New York lawyer John Quinn, and there the deal was concluded. Liveright required that *The Dial* purchase 350 copies of the volume at standard discounts, assuring himself an advance sale and adding $315 to *The Dial*'s costs for procuring the poem. But *The Dial* had achieved its victory, and the outcome was a remarkable success.

Liveright reported on the later events in a letter to Pound written on 5 February 1923, eleven weeks after the poem's publication in *The Dial*, seven weeks after his own release of the book-cum-notes:

> God bless you and Cantos IX to XII. If we can get as much publicity from them as The Waste Land has received, you will be a millionaire. The Waste Land has sold 1000 copies to date and who knows, it may go up to 2000 or 3000 copies. Just think, Eliot may make almost $500 on the book rights of this poem. And Gene Stratton Porter makes $40,000.000 to $60,000 a year out of her books. Well, it's all in a life time, so who cares.[40]

Liveright's sales estimate was remarkably accurate. Yet more important was the tenor of his comments, insofar as it tended to echo Watson's rationale in urging Thayer to take on the poem, his argument that *The Dial* would "be doing something moderately popular in giving him the award." Liveright's stress on how much publicity the award-and-publication package received is telling. For by now it is clear that the publication of *The Waste Land* marked the crucial moment in the transition of modernism from a minority culture to one supported by an important institutional and financial apparatus.

The contours of this transition can best be understood by a rapid survey of the three journals that were considered for simultaneous publication in the United States – *The Little Review, The Dial,* and *Vanity Fair.* Each represented a moment in the growth and triumph of modernism. When Eliot suggested in March 1922 that *The Criterion* engage in simultaneous publication with *The Little Review,* his proposal looked back to the world of modernism's past, to its origins in a *literature de cénacle,* to the heady days of 1917–18 when his poems and articles had appeared in the rebellious journal. When Pound suggested in May and August that the Poem be published by *Vanity Fair,* his proposal looked forward to modernism's future, to the ease and speed with which a market economy could purchase, assimilate, commodify, and reclaim as its own the works of a literature whose ideological premises were bitterly inimical toward its ethos and cultural operations. These distinct moments were mediated by what, in the early 1920s, was modernism's present: the sensibility epitomized by *The Dial,* a form of production supported by massive and unprecedented patronage that facilitated modernism's transition from a literature of an exiguous elite to a position of prestigious dominance.

The velocity of this process is illustrated by the fate of Eliot's own work shortly after the publication of *The Waste Land.* Only seven months later, in June 1923, *Vanity Fair* devoted an entire page to reprinting earlier poems by Eliot; among them were "Sweeney Among the Nightingales" (first published in *The Little Review* in 1918), "A Cooking Egg" (first published in the tiny journal *Coterie* in 1919), and "Burbank with a Baedeker" (first published in the short-lived *Art and Letters* in 1919). Linking the poems was an editorial box in the center of the page, presumably composed by managing editor Edmund Wilson, that articulated the journal's assumptions and aims with remarkable lucidity:

> Since the publication of *The Waste Land,* Mr. T. S. Eliot has become the most hotly contested issue in American poetry. He has been frequently attacked for his unconventional form and what

many readers consider his obscurity. But if one has read Mr. Eliot's earlier poems . . . from which the present selection is made, one gets the key to both his technique and his ideas. . . .

In subsequent months *Vanity Fair* conducted an intense campaign, printing articles by Eliot in July and November 1923 and in February 1924, and in September 1923 it published a study of Eliot's work by Clive Bell. Eliot had indeed become "the most hotly contested issue in American poetry" – in part, because *The Dial* and *Vanity Fair* had said so themselves.[41]

It was a long way from the world of *The Little Review*, a distance that can be measured more accurately if we recall some of that journal's principal features. (As information on *The Little Review* is notoriously sparse, I shall also use data from *The Egoist*, which Eliot edited during 1918 and which occupied a similar position within the economic structure of modernism.[42]) The *Little Review* had existed in a special space that was isolated from the direct demands of larger market structures by the beneficent hand of a modest yet influential patronage (e.g., the syndicate organized by Quinn or Harriet Weaver's support of *The Egoist*). The scale of such operations was tiny; circulation of *The Little Review* was roughly three thousand, and circulation of *The Egoist* typically hovered near two hundred.[43] Both maintained a low ratio of advertising to circulation revenues, something like 1:10, indicating that they survived by a direct rapport with a restricted group of readers.[44] They rejected the strategy of the mass-circulation journals that had been the dominant market force since the early 1900s and instead returned to the kind of direct relationship with readers that had typified literary magazines in the genteel tradition. This relationship was also reflected in their form of sales; neither enjoyed newsstand sales (distributing agencies were not interested), and both were associated with a meager set of specific outlets (the Washington Square Bookshop and Brentano's for *The Little Review* in New York; the stores of Friedrich Neumaier, Elkin Mathews, and Harold Monro for *The Egoist* in London). At its height *The Egoist* sold only 132 copies to readers who were not already subscribers, *The Little Review* only 600 (19.4 percent of total circulation).

*The Dial* operated quite differently. Its subscription list was

2.5 times larger than *The Little Review*'s: 6,374 in 1922 (compared to 2,500 for *The Little Review* in 1917). Its ratio of advertising to circulation revenues was not 1:10, but 1:3 (specifically $9,200 to $31,400) – to be sure, much lower than that of more commercial journals, but much higher than those of *The Little Review* or *The Egoist*. But above all, *The Dial* was supported by massive patronage: its deficits for the three years from 1920 to 1922 were, respectively, $100,000, $54,000, and $65,000, a cumulative deficit of $220,000 that was paid for directly by Thayer and Watson at the rate of $4,000 per month from each.[45] Nothing is more revealing than comparable figures for *The Little Review*, which in 1918 was supported by a syndicate of four donors whose contributions totalled $2,350 per year, or for *The Egoist*, which from 1917 to 1920 was supported by donations from Harriet Weaver that averaged £253 per year, or $1,265.[46]

How *The Dial* mediated a transition between *The Little Review* and *Vanity Fair* is also apparent in its editorial practices. *The Dial*, for example, repeatedly published material that had previously appeared in *The Little Review*, such as Wyndham Lewis's painting "Starry Sky" or a photo of Ossip Zadkine's sculpture "Holy Family."[47] Indeed, at times all three journals were publishing the same material: The spring 1922 issue of *The Little Review* was devoted to works by Brancusi, the May number of *Vanity Fair* showed photographs of the same works, and the November issue of *The Dial* reproduced Brancusi's *Golden Bird* for a third time in the same year. Its mediating role was also apparent in editorial policy. *The Little Review* boasted its intransigent aestheticism on the masthead: It would brook "no compromise with the public taste." But *The Dial* was more cautious; in a letter of November 1922 Thayer told his managing editor that he wished to publish works that "have *aesthetic value* and are not *commercially suicidal*" (author's italics).[48] The litotes ("not commercially suicidal") is noteworthy; translated into ordinary prose it means *might be successful*. Its official policy was also a compromise; it invoked an uneasy translation of Crocean idealism to justify eclectic aestheticism, a tone of patrician urbanity, and the conviction that "one must confine one's self to works of art" independent of social or moral considerations.[49] *The Dial*, in other words, differed from *The Little Review* and *Vanity Fair* in its tone of high seriousness and gravity, not in substantive ideology.

Yet *The Dial* did not just borrow from *The Little Review;* in some respects it strove to imitate *Vanity Fair.* Editorially it copied *Vanity Fair's* practice of offering a regular "London Letter" and a "Paris Letter," and it imitated *Vanity Fair's* institution of so-called service departments that offered advice and arrangements for the purchase of books and travel. Its layout and design were also conspicuously similar, and by 1922 *The Dial* was even sharing the same printing operations. It also attempted to integrate editorial and advertising functions in ways reminiscent of *Vanity Fair:* Its monthly listing of gallery exhibitions took pains to praise its own advertisers. And like *Vanity Fair,* too, its management stressed publicity, advertising revenues, and street sales (as opposed to subscriptions). It developed displays to be set up at newsstands, and it aggressively cultivated a larger metropolitan public. When its editors contemplated penetrating the British market in 1921, Eliot urged them to pursue the same course abroad: "[Y]ou must have your future manager here arrange for the paper to be visible and handy on every bookstall, at every tube station."[50] Again, when *The Dial* published *The Waste Land* and announced its award, Thayer ordered the staff to keep a minute record of every reference to these events in the press, an early form of market testing.[51] Above all, *The Dial* imitated the central principle that lay behind the success of *Vanity Fair* and its sister journal *Vogue:* In an era when most publishers were attempting magazines aimed at a mass market, Condé Nast and *The Dial* deliberately appealed to a select, restricted audience.[52]

Indeed, *The Dial* was acutely conscious of its competition with *Vanity Fair,* a theme that recurs in letter after letter by Thayer. On 16 December 1922 he complained to his mother that contributors and staff members of *The Dial* were frequently writing for *Vanity Fair.* Ten days later he lamented to Seldes: "If we have no aesthetic standards whatever in what respect are we superior to Vanity Fair which in other respects gives more for the money?" A month later he urged Seldes to hasten the printing of a new photograph "lest 'Vanity Fair' get ahead of us on this point too." And four months later he ordered him to secure rights to a new painting by Picasso: "Otherwise Vanity Fair will be getting it." How closely the market for the two journals overlapped became clear when *The Dial* issued its special art folio in June 1923. Desperate to stimulate sales, Thayer begged Seldes to intervene: "Cannot you get Rosenfeld to write the thing up for Vanity Fair, which is our most important selling possibility?"[53]

To be sure, *The Dial* and *Vanity Fair* were not twins. By comparison *The Dial* was a modest operation. Its $9,120 in advertising revenues was tiny when compared to the $500,000 per annum generated by *Vanity Fair*. Paid advertising occupied less space; in the November 1922 issue that printed *The Waste Land*, 27.5 of 156 pages (or 18 percent) were taken up by advertising. Compare this with July 1923 issue of *Vanity Fair*, which contained Eliot's poems: Out of 140 pages, 76 were devoted to paid advertising (54 percent), and many articles offered fashion and automobile reviews that were advertising thinly disguised. In 1922 *The Dial*'s circulation stood at 9,000 copies per month; in the same year *Vanity Fair*'s reached 92,000.[54]

Still, much can be learned from the interaction between the three journals and their common role as potential publishers of *The Waste Land*. For these journals, it is clear, are best viewed not as antagonists who represented alien or incompatible ideologies, but as protagonists who shared a common terrain, whose fields of activity overlapped and converged at crucial points within a shared spectrum of marketing and consumption. Their activity suggests that there was no single or essential feature that distinguished the avant-garde from modernism. These were not irreconcilable poles of a dichotomy, as has been argued by scholars like Peter Bürger, Andreas Huyssen, or Marjorie Perloff, who have urged that a set of formal devices (e.g., montage) constituted a vague yet potent ideology that challenged dominant cultural norms, assaulted the bourgeois concept of art, or anticipated the concerns of postmodernism.[55] Such arguments are sustained only by confining one's attention to formal values viewed in isolation from their social actualization. When seen in institutional terms, the avant-garde was neither more nor less than a structural feature in the institutional configuration of modernism. It played no special role by virtue solely of its form, and it possessed no ideological privilege; instead, it was constituted by a specific array of marketing and publicity structures that were integrated in varying degrees with the larger economic apparatus of its time. Its typical endeavor was to develop an idiom, and that, indeed, is how the editors who purchased *The Waste Land* perceived it: They were buying "the justification of the 'movement,' of our modern experiment, since 1900." They were purchasing a work whose scope and pretensions could vindicate an emerging idiom – vindication that could, in a market economy, be ratified only in the conspicuous expenditure of money. Whence the Dial Award with its lavish expenditure for a single poem. Whence Liveright's decision to double his normal per-copy expenditure on advertising for *The Waste Land*.[56] Whence Thayer's concern to register every reference to *The Dial*'s announcement of the Award and publication of the poem. They were organizing an event that might be "moderately popular" (Watson), an occasion to generate "much publicity" (Liveright) – itself the surest commodity of the modernist economy.

The three journals that were considered as candidates for *The Waste Land* formed a tripartite structure within the productive apparatus of modernism. But a similar structure, with analogous kinds of relations, also informed modernism's larger productive economy. In particular, a modernist work was typically published in three forms: first, in a little review or journal; second, in a limited edition of recently collected poems (or as an individual volume if the work was large enough); and third, in a more frankly commercial or public edition issued by a mainstream publisher and addressed to a wider audience. Especially important were the two forms of book publication, the limited and public editions. These were part of a practice that had become normative in the course of a complex fusion of heterogeneous and to some degree conflicting traditions of publishing. On the one hand, there was the program of multiple publication itself, with its origins in practices that had been developed by Tennyson as part of his effort to be a truly national poet: In 1878, to cite only one instance, Tennyson had issued his collected works in both a thirteen-volume Shilling Edition and a single-volume Crown Edition printed in three bindings (plain, gilt, and Roxburgh), a program that effectively addressed a diverse and heterogeneous audience (first-year sales of roughly thirty thousand and roughly sixty thousand respectively).[57] On the other hand, there was the limited edition, with its origins in the publishing practices of William Morris and the Kelmscott Press. Originally the limited edition had realized a programmatic rejection of the capitalist production of texts. In its production, for example, the role of the publisher was minimized and authorial control was maximized, the standardized design and formatting that had become publishing norms were replaced with special typography and layout, and the altered author–publisher relations were embodied in differing contractual arrangements; instead of a small advance against 15 percent royalties, the author usually received a guaranteed advance against 50 percent profits and a right to republish in another (more commercial) form within a specified amount of time. But the rebellious impulses of the Morris enterprise were Janus-faced: Though Morris had at first intended to produce books solely for his own interest, the sheer cost of his experiments had obliged him to issue them as limited editions that might recoup at least a share of the expenses. The limited editions, in turn, had been rapidly assimilated by the rare and antiquarian book markets that had matured in the nineteenth century, turning them into commodities and potential investments. Thus, although the book increasingly resembled the work of art (as indeed its producers hoped), the work of art itself had already become subject to a commodity economy. Inevitably the limited edition was rapidly appropriated by other constituencies that were not merely indifferent, but even hostile to the socialist impulses that had animated Morris.

One constituency was represented by William Butler Yeats, whose sisters founded the Dun Emer (later the Cuala) Press in 1902 with advice and help in typographical design from Emery Walker, a close associate of Morris at the Kelmscott Press.[58] Beginning with *In the Seven Woods* in 1903, all of Yeats's works were published first in a limited edition at the Dun Emer/Cuala, then in a public/commercial edition with Macmillan. In turn, through Yeats's influence on his young admirer Ezra Pound, the practice of publishing books in two forms was adopted by the emerging English avant-garde, for which it was an indispensable instrument. The limited edition established a kind of special productive space insulated from the harsh exigencies of the larger marketplace. It bypassed a broad public receptive to standardized products and suspicious of novelty (e.g., the 6 *s.* novel), and instead it addressed a prosperous minority with a luxury good that emphasized innovation and was produced in small quantities (though with high profit margins per sale). It enacted, in other words, a return to an essentially precapitalist economic structure, an artisanal economy producing luxury goods in limited quantities for aristocratic consumption. By the early 1920s it had become a routine step in a tripartite publishing program – journal, limited edition, and public or commercial edition – that was now normative for the avant-garde.

Yeats did not represent the only constituency that appropriated and adapted the heritage of Morris. In the United States, for example, similar forms of book production were soon adopted by the ensemble of figures and institutions often labeled the genteel tradition and associated with Boston and Harvard. The entire process is epitomized in the career of the typographer Bruce Rogers.[59] After working briefly in Indianapolis for a journal called *Modern Art*, Rogers moved to Boston in 1895, where he was soon frequenting circles that evinced a growing interest in fine books and the experiments of Morris. In 1884 the Grollier Club had been founded; in 1892 *The Knight Errant* had appeared, a review that devoted extensive discussion to William Morris, and in the same year the Tavern Club had been founded, headed by Professor Charles Eliot Norton and devoted to fine books. From 1895 to 1912 Rogers worked for the Riverside Press, which acted as the printer to Harvard University, during which time he assimilated Morris's interest in the well-made book to an anachronistic and classicizing style of typography. After several other jobs, Rogers settled down. Between 1920 and 1928 he was serving as typographical adviser to Cambridge University Press and working for the printing firm of William Edwin Rudge, for which he issued a series of limited editions being published by Maurice Firuski, owner of the Cambridge, Massachusetts, bookstore known as Dunster House. And that, of course, brings us back to T. S. Eliot.

*The Waste Land*, as is well known, was not published in book form solely by Horace Liveright; nearly ten months later (12 September 1923) it also appeared a second time, issued by Virginia Woolf's Hogarth Press in a limited edition of about 460 copies. The date suggests a tardy afterthought, as if Eliot were seeking to retrace a missed step in the normal process of avant-garde publishing. Yet the idea of a limited edition was anything but tardy. Eliot had begun to worry about the precarious implications of his agreement with Liveright almost immediately after their encounter in January 1922. It was a precipitous move that bypassed the normal rhythms of avant-garde production, in which a work was transmitted from a small elite to an ever wider yet presumably less discriminating audience, and therefore a move that threatened the status of his work. Like anyone who works within a specific institution, Eliot had internalized an array of unwritten procedures and practices considered normal and appropriate. No sooner had he completed the poem in its final version (probably in the first week of February 1922) than he began to seek a publisher who would issue a limited edition. On 14 February he lunched with Conrad Aiken and discussed his dilemma. Aiken, the next day, reported their conversation to Maurice Firuski, who was issuing Aiken's own book of poetry, *The Pool of Priapus*:

> Brief is this note, and chiefly occasioned by a talk with Tom Eliot at lunch yesterday. He has a poem, 450 lines long, wh. I haven't seen. He seeks a publisher who will produce it nicely, and in America, and in a small edition. Firuski! cried I, and there you are. When I elucidated, mentioning [Bruce] Rogers and 450 copies and two years exclusive right and a possible hundred dollars and a beautifully produced book, his eyes glowed with a tawny golden light like fierce doubloons, his hands took on singularly the aspect of claws, his nails tore the table-cloth, and he took your address. . . . . . As I say, I have not seen the poem. It may or may not be good, or intelligible. But, reflect: Eliot has a real reputation; a poem of that length by him will be a real curiosity, even perhaps an event; and he assumes that you will have, of course, the English as well as the American market. He may have to get Knopf's permission, as I did, to make the arrangement: he doesn't remember how his contract stands. But that, I fancy, will present no difficulty, for the book is too small for Knopf, and besides Knopf doesn't regard Eliot as a golconda. . . . . . Address: 9 Clarence Gate Gardens, London, W. W. 1.[60]

Eleven days later, on 26 February, Eliot himself also wrote to Firuski, pursuing the same question more fully in a letter that has not previously been published:

116

Dear Sir,

Your name has been given me by Mr. Conrad Aiken, who has also shown me a volume of poems by Mr. John Freeman, recently published by you, with the appearance of which I was very much pleased.

I have now ready a poem for which that form of publication seems to me the most suitable. I understand that you issue these books in limited editions, and that for the volumes you take for this series you give a sum in advance royalty.

My poem is of 435 lines; with certain spacings essential to the sense, 475 book lines; furthermore, it consists of five parts, which would increase the space necessary; and with title pages, some notes that I propose to add, etc., I guess that it would run to from 28 to 32 pages.

I have had a good offer for the publication of it in a periodical. But it is, I think, much the best poem I have ever written, and I think it would make a much more distinct impression and attract much more attention if published as a book.

If you are interested in this, I should be glad to hear from you what terms you would be prepared to offer for it, at your earliest convenience, as the other offers for it cannot be held in suspence very long.

I am,

yours faithfully,

[Signature]

Eliot's letter, of course, is fascinating.[61] Among other things, it affects the long-standing debate about the poem's notes, suggesting that they were not merely a late and arbitrary addition imposed by the publishing exigencies of Horace Liveright, as often argued, but an integral part of the work as Eliot himself wished to have it published – a nod, perhaps, to the eighteenth-century tradition of poetry (e.g., Pope's notes to *The Dunciad*) that had so informed some of the poem's earliest drafts. But more important for our purpose, the letter demonstrates how fully Eliot understood the normative rhythms of avant-garde publishing, as well as how easily those procedures could be assimilated to features already long established in a genteel tradition of private and limited editions. The book of poems by John Freeman (1880–1929) that Eliot had seen and admired was *The Red Path, a narrative, and the Wounded Bird*, a slender volume of poems issued in 425 copies that was printed for Firuski's Dunster House at the Press of William Edwin Rudge, its design executed by Bruce Rogers. The volume was handsome and, like all of Rogers' work, inspired by rather classical models of typography and design; it suggested a tone of genteel decorum, a distinctly Harvardian note, and yet sounded that tone with even greater subtlety, as if to hint at an elite within the elite, or select and more reflective minority with discriminating taste, a minority lodged within the wider elite that unreflectively assumed its privileges solely on the basis of class, money, and inherited status.

Despite the fact that Eliot had already received "a good offer" of $150 for the poem from Thayer and *The Dial* and despite his preliminary agreement with Liveright in Paris, Eliot preferred to see the work issued in a limited edition: "I think it would make a much more distinct impression and attract much more attention if published as a book." To be sure, Liveright had also offered to publish the poem as a book, but as a different kind of book: a public and more commercial edition that would directly address a wider audience, not preceded by the limited edition typical of the avant-garde. That proposal violated the institutional logic of avant-garde production, so much so that Eliot instinctively sought a form of publication that would set matters right. Firuski, however, was slow to respond. Moreover, by 12 March (only two weeks after his letter to Firuski), Eliot had received another note from Liveright reaffirming his interest in publishing the poem. As Eliot promptly informed Pound: "Liveright wrote to say he wanted it, and I have written asking what he wants to give and telling him the exact length," adding cryptically, "and I have other plans also if Thayer doesn't cough out."[62] The other plans, of course, were those with Firuski, presented as an acceptable alternative to publication in *The Dial*. The plans underscore a common structure of publication: Just as *The Dial* occupied the middle position in the tripartite structure of journal publication (*The Little Review, The Dial,* and *Vanity Fair*), so the limited edition occupied the middle position within the larger tripartite structure of avant-garde and modernist publishing (journal, limited edition, and commercial edition). Indeed, it was the violation of this logic that distinguished the actual publication of *The Waste Land*, its first appearance in book form being the commercial edition by

Liveright, and it was a late and retrospective effort to "correct" this anomaly that prompted Eliot to issue a limited edition with the Hogarth Press in 1923.

Eliot, it is clear, wanted his poem to be successful, yet not too successful. For the prospect of immediate publication by a commercial firm raised prospects that were largely unimaginable within the logic of modernism. And similar considerations must also have influenced the discussions concerning *Vanity Fair* as a possible venue for the poem. Pound, after raising the issue on 6 May 1922, presumably reported his action to Eliot during their meeting in Verona a month later, though how the two men viewed this prospect cannot be stated with any degree of certainty. Still, it is clear enough not only that Pound and Eliot considered *Vanity Fair* a potential publisher, but also that *Vanity Fair* considered itself a serious candidate. The journal not only sent John Peale Bishop to discuss the project with Pound in Paris, but even advanced an explicit offer of publication. The proposal appeared in a letter written by Edmund Wilson to Eliot on 1 August 1922. Eliot, in a letter that has also not been previously published, replied on 14 August:

> Thank you for your letter of the 1st inst., I should be very glad to do for you such an article as you suggest. For the next two months I shall be far too busy to attempt such a thing, but I think that I should be able to provide one during October or November if that is satisfactory to you. As for a poem, I am afraid that is quite impossible at present as I have only one for which I have already contracted.[63]

Eliot, plainly, was not being straightforward; as yet he had not "contracted" for *The Waste Land* in a journal at all. Only a day or two prior to his letter to Wilson, in fact, Eliot had sent off the typescript of *The Waste Land* to Pound and James Sibley Watson, Jr., in Paris, and only the day *after* his letter to Wilson did he write to Watson announcing his terms for the poem: the Dial Award plus $150, providing the poem were published not much before the book issued by Liveright. Eliot, it is clear, did not reject the offer from *Vanity Fair* solely because he had "already contracted" for its serial publication, but because *Vanity Fair* represented a degree of commercial success and popular acceptance that would have undermined the very status of the work that he was trying to establish. That status, however, was not simply intrinsic or implanted in the poem's text, but a function of the institutional structures that had informed its production at every step in the poem's life.

In retrospect, we can see that the proposal for a limited edition by Firuski not only looked back to the Cambridge and Harvard environment of Eliot's college days, but also looked to modernism's future, to the moment when Eliot would make his triumphant return to Harvard in 1932 and seal the fateful association between modernism and the academy. Yet that association, which has been so much commented on, did not occur naturally or without relations to other changes in the wider culture. By the early 1930s, in fact, all the magazines that Eliot had once considered for *The Waste Land* were dead or dying. *The Little Review* and *The Dial* had both closed in 1929, and *Vanity Fair* would expire in 1936. The Great Depression, it is clear, effectively eliminated the structures of private patronage that had sustained modernism's growth and its emergence as a significant idiom within the languages of the twentieth century. Thereafter, modernism would be slowly but inexorably absorbed into the university, as it had also been appropriated by the marketing and publicity apparatus of *Vanity Fair*.

The price of modernism, in this sense, was a double one. In part, it was a specific and concrete figure epitomized in the sums paid to Eliot for publication of *The Waste Land:* $150 as the price of the poem proper, $2,000 for The Dial Award, a subsequent $580.28 in royalties on the sales of the Liveright edition, and perhaps another £20 from the Hogarth Press edition – altogether about $2,800, a figure that in modern terms would surely be somewhere between $45,000 and $55,000. (It was 2.5 times the $1,150 per annum earned by the executive secretary to the editor of *Vanity Fair*.)[64] But hidden among such figures was another price that was more important: an obscuring of a determinate productive space, the elision of boundaries between specific institutions and wider zones of cultural activity, the illusion that "art" or "the poem" or "the text" had been the central concern of participants whose decisions were consistently made when as yet they had not read a word of the work in question. And not without reason, for the text was largely irrelevant. When *The Waste Land* was published, it did not enter a conduit of transmission that received and reproduced a neutral image of its original, but a multiplicity of social structures driven by conflicting imperatives: It became part of a social event in a discontinuous yet coherent process, an unprecedented effort to affirm the output of a specific marketing-publicity apparatus through the enactment of a triumphal and triumphant occasion. It was not simply the institutions that were the vehicle of the poem, but the poem that was the vehicle of the institutions. The poem, like any cultural work, was more than a sum of meanings implanted or intended by its author; it was inseparable, finally, from the contradictory network of utilizations that constituted it historically.

If nothing else, reconsidering the publication history of *The Waste Land* might prompt us to question the dominant methodology of modern literary studies since roughly the end of World War II. Generations of students have been exhorted to look closely at the poem, to examine only the text, to indulge in a scholastic scrutiny of linguistic minutiae. Yet if we were to consider more fully the experience of the figures who actually engaged in modern textual production, assuming the case of *The Waste Land* tells us anything, we might elect a rather different procedure. Indeed, if we named it in their honor, we could call it the modernist principle of reading and formulate it thus: The best reading of a work is often one that does not read it at all. Such an extreme formulation would, no doubt, be misleading. Yet it might at least remind us that close reading is itself a historical form of activity that appears at a precise moment in the development of professional literary studies and that other kinds of reading are and have been practiced, not least among them, the not-reading that was practiced by the editors of *The Dial,* itself a trenchant "reading" of *The Waste Land*'s place in the structural logic and development of literary modernism. We might learn from them. For reading as we do, instead of as they did, we leave the ambiguous heritage of modernism in history just as desocialized, unexplored, and unexplorable as it was before. History may be a nightmare, as the modernists often claimed, but when they entered the "contrived corridors" of its making, at least they remembered to "protract the profit of their chilled delirium."

## Notes

References to libraries and their collections are made with the following abbreviations:

BLUI, *PM.1*  Bloomington, Lilly Library, University of Indiana, Pound Mss. 1

BLUI, *PM.2*  Bloomington, Lilly Library, University of Indiana, Pound Mss. 2

BLUI, *PM.3*  Bloomington, Lilly Library, University of Indiana, Pound Mss. 3

CHH  Cambridge, Houghton Library, Harvard University

NHBY, *DP*  New Haven, Beinecke Library, Yale University, *Dial Papers*

NHBY, *BP*  New Haven, Beinecke Library, Yale University, Bird Papers

NYPL, *JQP*  New York Public Library, John Quinn Papers

After the reference to the library and collection, further reference is made to (1) the catalogue or archival series, if relevant, (2) the box, if relevant, and (3) folder number or title, if relevant.

References to names of correspondents are abbreviated as follows:

TSE  T. S. Eliot, residing in London

HL  Horace Liveright, residing in New York; in Paris from 29 December 1921 to 4 January 1922, in London 5 to 28 January 1922

DSP  Dorothy Shakespear Pound, residing in Paris, but visiting in London from 13 July to late October

EP  Ezra Pound, residing in Paris; traveling in Italy from 27 March to 2 July 1922

JQ  John Quinn, lawyer in New York

GS  Gilbert Seldes, managing editor of *The Dial,* in New York

ST  Scofield Thayer, editor and co-owner of *The Dial,* in Vienna

JSW  James Sibley Watson, Jr., co-owner of the *The Dial,* resident in New York but traveling in Europe (Paris, Berlin, Paris) in July–August, 1922

The abbreviation *LOTSE 1* is used to cite: T. S. Eliot, *Letters of T. S. Eliot,* vol. 1, *1898–1922,* edited by Valerie Eliot (New York: Harcourt, Brace, Jovanovich, 1988). I wish to thank Patricia Willis, Curator for American Literature at the Beinecke Rare Book and Manuscript Library, for her assistance in facilitating consultation of the *Dial Papers,* and especially Diane Ducharmes for her help in locating specific materials.

The following conventions are used for the transcription of letters and documents. All editorial interventions are placed between square brackets, [thus]. An illegible word is represented by a series of $x$'s approximating the number of letters in the word, and is placed between square brackets, [xxxx]. Authorial additions to a document are presented in angled brackets, with the additional words placed in italics, ⟨*thus*⟩.

1   The quotations are from Joyce's *Ulysses*, Eliot's "Gerontion," and Pound's *Guide to Kulchur*.

2   Richard Ellmann and Charles Feidelson, Jr., eds., *The Modern Tradition: Backgrounds of Modern Literature* (New York: Oxford, 1965), vi. For helpful comments and suggestions about an earlier version of this paper, I wish to thank Ronald Bush, A. Walton Litz, Michael North, James Longenbach, Lyndall Gordon, and Jerome J. McGann.

3   For the English publication, see TSE to Henry Ware Eliot, 11 October 1922: "The *Criterion* is due to appear next Monday," or 16 October, in *LOTSE 1*, 580. See also TSE to Richard Cobden-Sanderson, 16 October 1922, in *LOTSE 1*, 582. The exact date of the American publication in *The Dial* is less clear. "We are to publish the text of the poem, without the notes, in the November Dial, which will be published about October 20th": copy of GS to HL, 7 September 1922. With a delay of perhaps one or two days, *The Dial* apparently met its schedule: Burton Rascoe reported that he received his copy of the November issue on Thursday, 26 October 1922. (See Burton Rascoe, "A Bookman's Day Book," *The New York Tribune*, 5 November 1922, section V, 8.) More mystery surrounds the exact date of the Liveright release. In a letter to Seldes of 12 September, Liveright confirmed that his firm was "not to publish The Waste Land prior to its appearance in The Dial," and speculated, "I don't think that we'll publish it before January." (Both in NHBY, *DP*, series 4, box 40, 1922.) However, it is clear that the book had already been typeset in August, for Eliot had received and corrected the proofs by 15 September (see *LOTSE 1*, 570), and by late October the volume must have needed only binding. Apparently Liveright hastened to release it on 15 December in order to capitalize on the publicity generated by the announcement of the Dial Award in its December issue (presumably released around 20 November). For the date, see Donald Gallup, *T. S. Eliot. A Bibliography* (London: Faber and Faber, 1969), A6, 29–32. For an earlier study on *The Waste Land*'s publication, see Daniel Woodward, "Notes on the Publishing History and Text of *The Waste Land*," *Papers of the Bibliographical Society of America* 58 (1964): 252–69.

4   On Bishop, see Elizabeth Carroll Spindler, *John Peale Bishop* (Morganton: West Virginia University Library, 1980), chs. 5–7. How-

ever, it should be noted that the work often errs on points of detail, especially in transcribing letters. See below, n. 7, for examples.

5  GS to ST, cable 6 March 1922, ST to GS, cable 9 March 1922; GS to ST, letter 11 March 1922. All are NHBY, *DP*, series 4, box 40, 1922.

6  EP to Jeanne Foster, 6 May 1922; CHH, bMS Am 1635. On Foster and Quinn, see B. L. Reid, *The Man from New York* (Oxford: Oxford University, 1968), 313, 367 (her background and their meeting in 1918), 464–6, 579 (her poetry), 549 (her work for *Vanity Fair*). On Quinn's own work for *Vanity Fair* and his relations with its editor, Frank Crowninshield, see Reid, 276–7, 302–4, 373. For a Foster contribution to *Vanity Fair* that was inspired by Pound, see "New Sculptures by Constantin Brancusi," *Vanity Fair* 18 (May 1922): 68. On her relations with Bishop, see EP to Jeanne Foster, [20 April] 1922; CHH, bMS Am 1635.

7  John Peale Bishop to Edmund Wilson, 5 August 1922; NHBY, Edmund Wilson Papers, series 2. The letter is reported by Spindler, *John Peale Bishop*, 68–9, though with numerous errors. Whereas Bishop states that he met Pound extended on a "bright green couch swathed in a hieratic bathrobe," Spindler reports him on "a *high* green couch swathed in a *heraldric* bathrobe" – curious garb indeed. And whereas Bishop describes the bathrobe as "made of a maiden aunt's shit-brown blanket," Spindler fabricates "a maiden aunt's *shirt*-brown blanket" (p. 68; all italics mine). Spindler also omits the three sentences from "Here's the thing . . ." to ". . . written in English since 1900." It is important to note that Bishop was apparently acting in collaboration with Edmund Wilson in his effort to purchase *The Waste Land,* a point elaborated below.

8  Pound himself was conscious of the dilemma presented by his role as impresario and its effects on his literary reputation. Consider his remarks to Margaret Anderson in 1921: "Point I never can seem to get you to take is that I have done more log rolling and attending to other people's affairs, Joyce, Lewis, Gaudier, etc. (don't regret it). But I am in my own small way, a writer myself, and as before stated I shd. like (and won't in any case get) the chance of being considered as the author of my own poems rather than as literary politician and a very active stage manager of rising talent." See EP to Margaret Anderson, [June 1921]; Milwaukee, University of Wisconsin at Milwaukee.

9  EP to Felix Schelling, 8–9 July 1922; in Ezra Pound, *Selected Letters 1907–1941,* edited by D. D. Paige (New York: New Directions, 1971), 180.

10  It should be stressed that Pound did not at this time have a copy of

the manuscript and so could not lend it to Bishop. One week before their meeting of 3 August, on 27 July, Pound had written to Eliot requesting a copy of the manuscript precisely because he had none available to show Watson, who was then visiting Pound and wished to read it. This can be inferred from Eliot's reply of 28 July, when he stated that he had only one copy to hand but would make another and send it as soon as he could (see *LOTSE 1*, 552). Equally important, the typescript did not arrive until 14 August, or seven days after Bishop's departure, as reported by Watson to Thayer when he sends it on to him in Vienna (JSW to ST, 16 August 1922, NHBY, *DP*, series 4, box 44, Watson 1922).

11   The dates of Eliot's arrival and departure are inferred from Vivienne Eliot to Mary Hutchinson, 12 January 1922; in *LOTSE 1*, 501. Vivienne reports that "Tom has been here ten days," implying that he arrived on 2 January, and states that "he will be back [in London] on Monday," or 17 January 1922, suggesting that he would leave the day before, or 16 January. The new dates also make clear that all of Pound's editorial interventions occurred between 2 and 16 January 1922. Further, as scholars have previously suspected, these consisted principally of two editorial sessions. This hypothesis is confirmed by Eliot's letter of 20 January 1922 to Scofield Thayer, in which he reports that his poem "will have been three times through the sieve by Pound as well as myself" (*LOTSE 1*, 503). In other words, in addition to the two times that Pound had already gone over the poem while the two men were in Paris, Eliot was planning to send it to him yet again, for a third time. Eliot probably sent the poem to Pound on 19 or 20 January, at roughly the same time as he was writing to Thayer, and in response to this Pound wrote his letter dated "24 Saturnus" or 24 January 1922 (mistakenly assigned to 24 December 1921 by Valerie Eliot and printed in *LOTSE 1*, 497–8).

12   On *Instigations*, see Donald Gallup, *Ezra Pound: A Bibliography* (Charlottesville: University of Virginia, 1985), A18. For Liveright's acceptance of *Poems 1918–1921*, see HL to EP, 13 September 1920; BLUI, *PM.2*, Liveright. For his helpful role in Pound's personal finances in 1921, see Lawrence S. Rainey, *Ezra Pound and the Monument of Culture* (Chicago: University of Chicago, 1991).

13   Copy of HL to JQ, 24 March 1922; BLUI, *PM.1*, Quinn:

I am attaching to this letter a card which James Joyce gave me in Paris one evening when I had dinner with him. [. . .] Ezra Pound and T. S. Eliot had dinner with us that night and as I am publishing

Ezra Pound, and I'm about to publish Eliot, providing that Knopf has no legal claim on his next book, I think Joyce belongs in the Boni and Liveright fold.

I saw Pound each day during the six days I was in Paris, and I made a little arrangement with him that will take care of his rent over there for the next two years anyhow.

Liveright's contract with Pound is dated 4 January 1922, which is also the date on which he apparently left Paris. He refers to his departure in a postcard from London to EP, dated 11 January 1922, where he reports that he met May Sinclair "last Thursday," which is to say 5 January 1922; presumably, therefore, he left Paris on 4 January. If so, and if he stayed "six days in Paris" (as he reports), then he must have arrived there on 29 or 30 December 1921. Since Eliot himself did not arrive in Paris until 2 January, the dinner could have occurred only on the evenings of 2 or 3 January. The latter date is more likely, as Eliot would have been tired after arriving from Lausanne on 2 January and as some time must be allowed for plans to have been formulated and accepted by all the parties. There are also three other references to the dinner. Eliot reports on his offer from Liveright in a letter to Alfred A. Knopf, dated 3 April 1922, in which he explains that "Mr. Liveright, whom I met in Paris," has made an offer for the poem; see *LOTSE 1,* 519. Pound also refers to the dinner in a letter to Jeanne Foster, dated 5 April 1922: "Liveright saw the right people in Paris [. . .]. He saw Joyce and Eliot with me [. . .]"; see EP to Jeanne Foster, 5 April 1922; CHH, bMS Am 1635. Finally, Eliot reports the meeting again in a letter to John Quinn, dated 25 June: "Pound introduced me to Liveright in Paris, and Liveright made me the offer [. . .]." See *LOTSE 1,* 530.

14 EP to Jeanne Foster, 5 April 1922.

15 EP to JQ, 20 June 1920; NYPL, *JQP,* box 34, folder 4.

16 HL to EP, 11 January 1922; NHBY, *BP,* folder 23. It is Liveright's concern with the length of the poem that explains Eliot's repeated proposals designed to make the book longer: (1) that he retain three minor pieces as prefatory matter for the poem, a suggestion that Pound rejected on 24 January, (2) that he reprint "Gerontion" as a preface to *The Waste Land,* advanced to Pound in his letter of around 26 January (assigned to [24? January] by Valerie Eliot), and (3) that he use one or two poems by Pound as prefatory matter to the poem, also advanced in the same letter of around 26 January to Pound. In addition, however, Liveright was nervous about its publication in periodical form and whether it would be printed in a

single issue: "And does it *all* appear in *one* issue of the Dial – please let me know." This concern prompted Eliot to worry about the same question, as emerges in his letter offering the poem to *The Dial* (20 January 1922): "It could easily go into 4 issues if you like, but not more." Liveright may have communicated his concerns directly to Eliot after he arrived in London on 17 January, for Liveright did not depart for the United States until 28 January and could easily have met or contacted the poet until then. Surely this explains Eliot's anxiety in his letters to Thayer (20 January) and Pound (around 26 January) on precisely those matters raised earlier in Liveright's note of 11 January to Pound.

17   See HL to EP, 12 October 1922; NHBY, *BP*, folder 23: "It doesn't seem that we've found the right thing yet, does it? [. . .] And if Yeats insists on sticking to Macmillan, and I firmly believe that Yeats has more to do with it than Watt [his agent] because I did have a long talk with Watt and he seemed inclined to let me have a look-in, – well, all the worse for Yeats."

18   EP to ST, 18 February 1922; ST to EP, 5 March 1922; EP to ST, 9–10 March 1922: NHBY, *DP*, series 4, box 38, 1922.

19   Thayer's marginalia on Eliot's letter of 20 January 1922 record his diligent calculations of the poem's price at normal rates: If typeset at thirty-five lines per page, the poem would come to slightly under twelve pages, yielding a price of $120; if typeset at forty lines per page, it would come to 11.25 pages, yielding a price of slightly over $110. Summarizing his results, Thayer firmly concludes: "12 pp. $120." His offer of $150, then, was already 25 percent higher than normal rates.

20   It must be stressed that there is no simple or straightforward procedure that enables us to establish an exact value in current dollars for a specific income figure from 1922. One can, for example, make an estimate based on the consumer price index (BLS), which has risen 5.79 times between 1922 and 1986. However, this may produce misleading figures insofar as it fails to indicate the relative position of a given income within the larger economy. If, for example, we assume that the average per capita income was $735 in 1922 and we multiply this by 5.79, it yields a 1986 average per capita income of $4,343. However, in reality the national income per capita in 1986 was more than three times as high: $14,166. The reason for this discrepancy is that the average person enjoys more wealth today than he did in 1922, a fact that must also be taken into account when attempting to estimate an equivalent income figure. A better approach, then, is to take the given sum as a percentage of

national income per capita. In that case, the offer of $150 was 20 percent of the national income per capita of $750 (hereafter the figure of $735 is rounded to $750), and the equivalent figure in 1986 dollars would be $2,833.20. Again, these figures are offered as rough estimates, not precise equivalents. It is impossible to be more exact because it was not until the 1940s that the minimum income requirement for annual tax returns was lowered enough to facilitate accurate nationwide estimates of income distribution for families and individuals. Prior to then, higher minimums meant that information was available for only a small fraction of the upper-income population. For various estimates of national income per capita, see National Bureau of Research (Wesley C. Mitchell, Willford I. King, Frederick R. Macaulay), *Income in the United States: Its Amount and Distribution, 1909–1919* (New York: Harcourt, Brace, 1921), with relevant figures on pp. 13, 76, 144–7, concluding that the national income per capita in 1918 and 1919 totaled $586 and $629, respectively. See also *Historical Statistics of the United States: Colonial Times to 1970, Part 1* (Washington, D.C.: Department of Commerce, 1976), 166–7, 284 ff., reporting that the average annual earnings of employees in the educational services in 1922 were $1,109. See also Robert F. Martin, *National Income in the United States, 1799–1938* (New York: National Industrial Conference Board, 1941), 7; Simon Kuznets, *National Income and Its Composition, 1919–1938*, vol. 1 (New York: National Bureau of Economic Research, 1941), passim. For help in considering these economic questions, I am grateful to Lance Davis.

21  TSE to ST, 16 March 1922; in NHBY, *DP*, series 4, box 31, 1922.
22  TSE to EP, 12 March 1922; in *LOTSE 1*, 507.
23  Thayer visited Pound for the first time on 12 July 1921. Pound's initial contract to serve as writer and talent scout for *The Dial* had expired twelve days earlier, and Thayer had advised him that it would not be renewed. However, when the two met for a second time on 13 July the contract was renewed, though only in part: Pound would continue to write for *The Dial* but not serve as talent scout, and he would receive roughly half his former salary. These meetings were only part of a series that continued throughout the month: 12 July, 13 July around 20 July, 26 July, and 28 July. For the meetings, see EP to DSP 12 July, 14 July, 21 July, 26 July, 30 July 1921; BLUI, *PM.3*, 1921. On the contracts, negotiations, and the economic background to Pound's finances, see Lawrence S. Rainey, "The Earliest Manuscripts of the Malatesta Cantos by Ezra Pound,"

Dissertation, University of Chicago, 1986, 25–51, especially 43–6. Hereafter cited as Rainey.

24 EP to ST, 23 April 1922; NHBY, *DP*, series 4, box 38, 1922.

25 EP to ST, 6 May 1922; NHBY, *DP*, series 4, box 38, 1922.

26 The visit is mentioned in TSE to Sidney Schiff, attributed to "[Early June 1922]" by Valerie Eliot in *LOTSE*, 528: "I also went to Verona and saw Pound." On Pound's travels in 1922, see Rainey, 70–91, especially 85–8. His meeting with Eliot is rehearsed in Draft B, lines 3–4, transcribed in Rainey, 406–7; Draft C1, lines 82–5, transcribed in Rainey, pp. 482–8; Draft C3, lines 61–100, transcribed in Rainey, 566–71, with annotations for specific passages. For Pound's later reminiscences, see *The Cantos of Ezra Pound*, Cantos 29 and 78.

27 TSE to EP, 12 March 1922; in *LOTSE 1*, 508. Eliot mentions *The Little Review* only twice in his correspondence for 1922, and both times in letters to Pound. Clearly he considered the journal to be largely Pound's.

28 EP to DSP, 21 July 1922; BLUI, *PM.3*, 1922.

29 ST to GS, 20 July 1922; NHBY, *DP*, series 4, box 40, 1922. Thayer reports that Watson "is present as I dictate," leaving no doubt that Watson departed within hours of his meeting with Pound on 19 July (date of meeting from EP to DSP, 21 July 1922).

30 ST to TSE, 5 October 1922; NHBY, *DP*, series 4, box 31, 1922: "I have been very glad to learn from New York that *the suggestion I made to Mr. Watson while he was with me in Berlin last July* has borne fruit and that we are despite your asperity to have the pleasure of recognizing publicly your contribution to contemporary letters." (Italics added.)

31 EP to DSP, 29 July 1922; BLUI, *PM.3*.

32 JSW to ST, 29 July 1922; NHBY, *DP*, series 4, box 44, 1922.

33 TSE to EP, 28 July 1922, in *LOTSE*, 552.

34 JSW to ST, 16 August 1922; NHBY, *DP*, series 4, box 44, 1922.

35 TSE to JSW, 15 August 1922; in *LOTSE*, 560.

36 JSW to ST, 19 August 1922; NHBY, *DP*, series 4, box 44, 1922.

37 TSE to JQ, 21 August 1922, in *LOTSE 1*, 564. Also cited in Valerie Eliot, ed., *T. S. Eliot, The Waste Land. A Facsimile* (New York: Harcourt, Brace, 1971), xxiv.

38 TSE to EP, 30 August 1922, in *LOTSE 1*, 567; punctuation here reproduces the original.

39 TSE to JSW, 21 August 1922, in *LOTSE 1*, 564–5. GS to ST, 31 August 1922; NHBY, *DP*, series 4, box 40, 1922.

40 HL to EP, 5 February 1922; BLUI, *PM.1*, Liveright.

41　"A Group of Poems by T. S. Eliot: A Selection from the Dramatic Lyrics of a Much Discussed American Poet," in *Vanity Fair* 20 (June 1923): 67. The publication is not mentioned by Gallup because his policy is to exclude reprints of poems that have previously appeared in book form. The other articles by Eliot appeared in *Vanity Fair* 20 (July 1923): 51, 98; 21 (November 1923): 44, 118; 21 (February 1924): 29, 98.

42　On *The Egoist*, see Jane Lidderdale and Mary Nicholson, *Dear Miss Weaver: Harriet Shaw Weaver 1876–1961* (London: Faber and Faber, 1970). Hereafter cited as Lidderdale.

43　On *The Little Review*, see Frank Luther Mott, *A History of American Magazines*, vol. 5, *Sketches of 21 Magazines 1905–1930* (Cambridge: Harvard University Press, 1968), 166–78, who considers it "unlikely that the circulation ever rose to much over a thousand" (p. 171). His figure is offered as a correction to the earlier estimate of two thousand given by Frederick J. Hoffman, Charles Allen, and Carolyn S. Ulrich, *The Little Magazine: A History and Bibliography* (Princeton: Princeton University, 1946), 57. My figures are from EP to JQ, 8 February 1917; NYPL, JQP. For *The Eqoist*, see Lidderdale, 460, who reports that its largest circulation was 400 copies per issue, with about 268 by subscription, during the first six months of its life (1913). "Then it went into a long decline, with a sharp drop in November 1916 when the long-term subscriptions ran out; and the circulation never rose again above 200."

44　In the second half of 1915 *The Egoist* earned £37 in sales and subscriptions, and one surmises that its advertising revenues were around £5 (see Lidderdale, 99). Mott estimates that advertising revenues for *The Little Review* "seldom or never exceeded $500 a year" (p. 171); sales and subscriptions, on the other hand, probably earned $4,000 in 1917, according to my estimate.

45　All figures are from the annual financial reports of *The Dial*, in NHBY, DP, series 2, box 9, folders 327–32.

46　For *The Little Review* figure, see Mott, *A History of American Magazines*, Reid, *The Man from New York*, 343. The four donors were John Quinn, Otto Kahn, Mrs. James Byrne, and Quinn himself. Quinn's patronage included a standing subsidy of $750 per year, in addition to his $400 gift as part of the syndicate. For *The Egoist*, see Lidderdale, 459. Weaver's contributions were, respectively, £251, £342, £234, and £185.

47　Lewis appeared in *The Little Review* of November 1918 and in the

*The Dial* of August 1921. Zadkine appeared in *The Little Review* of December 1918, and in *The Dial* of October 1921.

48  ST to GS, 28 November 1922; NHBY, *DP*, series 4, box 40, 1922.

49  See [Scofield Thayer], "Comment," *The Dial* 73 (July 1922): 119. Springarn's major essays are collected in Joel Springarn, *Creative Criticism: Essays on the Unity of Genius and Taste* (New York: Henry Holt and Company, 1917). The book is dedicated to "my friend Benedetto Croce, the most original of all modern thinkers on Art," and it reports that the central essay, "The New Criticism," was originally delivered as a lecture at Columbia University in 1910 (p. [iii]). For Springarn's influence on *The Dial*, see William Wasserstrom, *The Time of* The Dial (Syracuse: University of Syracuse Press, 1963), pp. 17–19. Also on *The Dial*, see Nicholas Joost, *Scofield Thayer and* The Dial (Carbondale: Southern Illinois University Press, 1964); The Dial *1912–1920* (Barre, Mass.: Barre, 1967).

50  TSE to ST, 1 January 1921; in *LOTSE*, 429.

51  ST to GS, 12 October 1922; NHBY, *DP*, series 4, box 40, 1922. The practice was a regular one at *The Dial*, and newspaper clippings for 1920–29 fill three boxes; NHBY, *DP*, series 2, boxes 16, 17, 18.

52  On *Vanity Fair*, see Martha Cohn Cooper, "Frank Crowninshield and *Vanity Fair*," Dissertation, University of North Carolina at Chapel Hill, 1976; Kitty Hoffman, "A History of *Vanity Fair*; A Modernist Journal in America," Dissertation, University of Toronto, 1980; Cynthia L. Ward, "*Vanity Fair* Magazine and the Modern Style, 1914–1936 (New York City)," Dissertation, State University of New York at Stony Brook, 1983. Also useful is Caroline Seebohm, *The Man Who Was* Vogue: *The Life and Times of Condé Nast* (New York: Viking, 1982). For a useful survey of the magazine market and industry, see Theodore Petersons, *Magazines in the Twentieth Century* (Urbana: University of Illinois Press, 1964). For Nast's strategy of market segmentation, see Cohn Cooper, 38.

53  "I was recently sent a copy of Vanity Fair and was interested to see how many of my friends are now writing for that paper. In the number for December I find the names of Kenneth MacGowan, Henry McBride, Kenneth Burke, Gilbert Seldes and of my acquaintance Miss Millay." ST to Mrs. Edward D. Thayer, 16 December 1922; NHBY, *DP*, series 4, box 43, 1922. ST to GS 26 December 1922; NHBY, *DP*, series 4, box 40, 1922; in this letter Thayer also complains that "Mr. Burke's review [in *The Dial*] interested me, but I do not find it so good as his recent article developing more or less

the same theme in Vanity Fair." ST to GS 18 January, 28 May, and 8 June 1923; NHBY, *DP*, series 4, box 40, 1923.

54 For the advertising revenues of *Vanity Fair,* see Petersen, *Magazines in the Twentieth Century,* 271. For the circulation figures, see *N. W. Ayer & Son's American Newspaper Annual and Directory* (Philadelphia: N. W. Ayer & Son's, 1922), 1225, reporting figures from the Audit Bureau of Circulation. On advertising as "an integral part of the magazine," see Cohn Cooper, 42.

55 See Peter Bürger, *Theory of the Avant-Garde,* translated by Michael Shaw (Minneapolis: University of Minnesota Press, 1984); Andreas Huyssen, *After the Great Divide* (Bloomington: Indiana University Press, 1986); Marjorie Perloff, *The Poetics of Indeterminacy* (Evanston: Northwestern University Press, 1983; 1st ed., Princeton University Press, 1981). See also Charles Russell, *Poets, Prophets, and Revolutionaries: The Literary Avant-Garde from Rimbaud through Postmodernism* (Oxford: Oxford University Press, 1985).

56 See Walker Gilmore, *Horace Liveright: Publisher of the Twenties* (New York: David Lewis, 1970), 38. A normal budget would have been twelve to fifteen cents per copy, while Liveright spent twenty-five cents per copy. Gilmore draws his information from interviews with Manual Komroff, a former Liveright employee.

57 On the multiple collected editions of Tennyson, see June Steffensen Hagen, *Tennyson and His Publishers* (University Park: Pennsylvania State University Press, 1979), 149–50. See also her entire study on the emergence of this practice and Tennyson's use of it throughout his later career.

58 See Liam Miller, *The Dun Emer Press, Later the Cuala Press* (Dublin: Dolmen Press, 1973).

59 See John Dreyfus, *Bruce Rogers and American Typography* (Cambridge: Cambridge University, 1959).

60 Conrad Aiken to Maurice Firuski, 15 February 1922, Chapin Library, Williams College, T. S. Eliot Collection. I wish to thank Robert L. Volz, Rare Book Custodian, for his kindness in drawing this letter to my attention.

61 T. S. Eliot to Maurice Firuski, 26 February 1922, Chapin Library, Williams College, T. S. Eliot Collection. Mention of this letter is made by Valerie Eliot in *LOTSE* 1, 515, n. 1. I am grateful to Mrs. Eliot for permission to quote from this letter in its entirety and to her kindness in responding to my inquiries. The letter from T. S. Eliot to Edmund Wilson quoted below is also printed by permission of Mrs. Eliot, and both are copyrighted by her.

62 T. S. Eliot to Ezra Pound, 12 March 1922, in *LOTSE* 1, 507.

63  T. S. Eliot to Edmund Wilson, 14 August 1922; NHBYU, Edmund Wilson Papers.

64  For the wages of Jeanne Ballot, executive secretary to Frank Crowninshield, who earned $22 per week, or $1,144 per year, see Cohn Cooper, 48. Needless to say, the $2,000 paid to Eliot in the form of the Dial Award was a remarkable figure: The highest sum that *Vanity Fair* ever paid was given in 1925 to F. Scott Fitzgerald for a short story, and it was $100.

PART THREE

# Eliot and the Practice of Twentieth-Century Poetry

# The Allusive Poet: Eliot and His Sources

A. WALTON LITZ

Out of the window perilously spread
Her drying combinations touched by the sun's last rays,
On the divan are piled (at night her bed)
Stockings, slippers, camisoles, and stays.

Listening to these lines from the description of the typist's flat in
Part III of *The Waste Land*, our ear may be caught by the distinguished word "perilously," which stands apart from the catalogue of domestic details. And we may find ourselves remembering or murmuring

Charmed magic casements, opening on the foam
Of perilous seas, in faery lands forlorn.

Did Eliot consciously intend an allusion to Keats's "Ode to a
Nightingale," or have we supplied it as we join enthusiastically in
his obsessive counterpointing of past and present? All of us who

137

write or read have the habit of thinking and feeling through literature. Even William Carlos Williams, in a work that tries to reject all connections with the past, cannot escape familiar echoes. One of the autumnal poems from *The Descent of Winter* ("10/22"), aimed at recording the "actual things" of the present, suddenly veers into an unmistakable recall of Shakespeare's Sonnet 73:

> and a white birch
> with yellow leaves
> and few
> and loosely hung

Having begun his poetic career with weak imitations of Keats and the Shakespeare of the sonnets, Williams cannot free himself from his own past. The difference between the two poets is that with Williams we can be reasonably sure the allusion was not intended (in fact, he would have rejected it), whereas with Eliot the question is more open, and our experience of the earlier poems and the rest of *The Waste Land* could argue for conscious placement.

When we look at the poetic development of Eliot (and of Pound) between roughly 1915 and 1920, one of the most striking aspects is the thickening of conscious, orchestrated allusions. In his September 1918 "A Note on Ezra Pound" Eliot reflects on the method; he has been discussing the fusion of past and present, of literary, historical, and personal references, in Pound's "Near Perigord":

> This effect is all the more peculiar because of the deliberateness. James Joyce, another very learned literary artist, uses allusions suddenly and with great speed, part of the effect being the extent of the vista opened to the imagination by the very lightest touch. Pound's recent unfinished epic, three cantos of which appear in the American edition of "Lustra," proceeds by a very different method than that of Joyce in "Ulysses." In appearance, it is a ragbag of Mr. Pound's reading in various languages, from which one fragment after another is dragged to light, and illuminated by the beauty of his phrase. . . .[There is] apparently no continuity. And yet the thing has, after one has read it once or twice, a positive coherence; it is an objective and reticent autobiography.[1]

Ronald Bush has claimed that Eliot learned a great deal about the systematic use of allusions from Joyce (he could have seen the first six episodes of *Ulysses* in their *Little Review* form by the time he wrote this "Note") and that Pound in turn was exposed to the method when he carefully revised Eliot's quatrain poems.[2] I agree with this general argument, which accounts in part for the differences between the "rag-bag" *Three Cantos* of 1917 and *Hugh Selwyn Mauberley* or the cantos written after 1918. As we discover more about the precise chronology of the period, we shall be able to refine our understanding of the virtual collaboration between Pound and Eliot that took place while *Ulysses* was appearing episode by episode. In general, I think it is safe to say that Pound and Eliot were from the beginning drawn by temperament and training to the art of local allusion and that *Ulysses* showed them how it could serve larger structural and thematic purposes. But they were moving toward the Joycean orchestration before the first chapter of *Ulysses* crossed their desks. "Near Perigord" (1915) itself is an example of Pound's extensive use of allusions before he had encountered *Ulysses,* and the last line of Eliot's "Cousin Nancy" (also 1915) is precisely the sort of allusion that he praised in Joyce: the Miltonic line from George Meredith ("The army of unalterable law") opens a new vista to the imagination "suddenly and with great speed."

Although there is no question that *Ulysses* provided a supreme example of the allusive method in action, deployed on a breathtaking scale, Eliot's almost insatiable appetite for allusion sprang from other sources as well. Partly it was a way of enforcing his critical arguments about past and present, of demonstrating how the contemporary scene could be defined by surrounding it with voices and actions from other cultures: In his "Note on Ezra Pound" Eliot's remarks on allusion follow a passage on the "historical sense" that anticipates "Tradition and the Individual Talent." Allusion was also "an objective and reticent" way of handling the emotions, of avoiding the direct exposure of personal feelings that was the natural tendency of Eliot's poetry. If we compare the suppressed "Death of Saint Narcissus" (1915) with the never-reprinted "Ode" of *Ara Vos Prec* (1920), this becomes clearly apparent. The subjects of the two poems are much the same, springing from the agony of Eliot's private life, but the allusive method of "Ode" enables him to shy away from direct confession, although the present-day reader fresh from a performance of *Tom and Viv* might find "Ode" even more harrowing than "The Death of Saint Narcissus."

Another classic example of displaced personality would be "Burbank with a Baedeker: Bleistein with a Cigar," where the allusions are so concentrated that they almost constitute a parody of the method. The attitudes of this poem strike me as quintessentially Eliot's, but by using Burbank as a Jamesian center of consciousness and attaching the allusions to *his* sensibility, Eliot is able to play a double game. The poem is simultaneously an anatomy of cultural decline, of a "falling off" reflected in the movement of the taut quatrains, *and* a critique of the paralyzed modern sensibility that can only think and feel through allusion. In its own way "Burbank" is "objective and reticent autobiography."

Beyond this desire for "impersonality" and the need to establish a complicated transaction between past and present, the passion for allusion must have been driven by the actual events of 1915–19. Like almost everything else in early modern writing, the method was an indirect response to the chaos and despair of the Great War. Traditionally, the art of allusion depends upon two things: first, "an established literary tradition as a source of value," and second, "an audience sharing the tradition with the poet."[3] At a time when these circumstances were conspicuously lacking and their vestiges threatened by historical events, the use of allusion was a desperate attempt to affirm what was absent, to assert that there was a tradition, even if it was available only to a very few.

This project of creating an audience was complicated, especially in the case of Pound, by the attitude of "isolated superiority" that developed as the war made the artistic departures of 1912–14 seem more and more irrelevant. James Longenbach has shown how Pound and Yeats, during their three winters at Stone Cottage, moved toward the idea of modernism as a "secret society,"[4] and in *'Noh' or Accomplishment* (1916) Pound relishes the fact that the "art of allusion," which lies at the heart of the Noh drama, is inherently elitist: "These plays, or eclogues, were made only for the few; for the nobles; for those trained to catch the allusion."[5] Like the troubadour obsessed by the *trobar clus,* or the Noh artist addressing a select audience, Pound delighted in the obscurity of his allusions. Perhaps the most telling example of this is "Villanelle: The Psychological Hour," which contains a tag from Yeats's "The People" ("Between the night and the morning") even though it was published before Yeats's poem reached print. Stone Cottage, where the two poems were written, was the only world that mattered.

I said earlier that all of us who read or write have a tendency to think and feel through literature, but in Eliot this tendency was so highly developed that it reached a different dimension and became the keystone of his poetic life. Peter Ackroyd, in an unusually perceptive section of his biography that deals with Pound's work on the *Waste Land* manuscript, says that Pound cut through Eliot's loose dramatic schema and "rescued the poetry":

> Eliot's most significant feelings, as opposed to his conscious intentions, are attached to a certain kind of rhythm derived from his earliest reading . . . and to certain literary texts which have been transformed in memory. His feelings cluster around literary cadences; the images and themes of *The Waste Land* are both his own and not his own, a continual oscillation between what is remembered and what is introduced, the movement of other poets' words just beneath the surface of his own.[6]

Ackroyd's comments, which square with my own experience of the poetry, point to a distinction between two kinds of allusion, what we might call "conscious" allusions (the sort we have been discussing so far) and "subliminal" allusions. This distinction does not lie entirely in Eliot's intentions, although we often can uncover unshakable evidence of conscious reference. The notes to *The Waste Land,* the passages quoted in the criticism that also find a place in the poetry, the record of his reading – all enable us to say in many instances that an allusion was meant to be recognized. As Eliot remarked in his late lecture "What Dante Means to Me":

> Readers of my *Waste Land* will perhaps remember that the vision of my city clerks trooping over London Bridge from the railway station to their offices evoked the reflection 'I had not thought

> death had undone so many'. . . . I gave the references in my notes,
> in order to make the reader who recognized the allusion, know that
> I meant him to recognize it, and know that he would have missed
> the point if he did not recognize it.[7]

The key to this sort of allusion is that both the poet and the reader are acutely – intellectually – aware of the interplay between texts. The critical faculty is brought into action, and we are drawn into thought and judgment at the same time that we are moved by the music of the words.

The dividing line between these conscious allusions and the more subliminal references is never clear-cut, and Keats's "perilous seas" probably lies on that shadow-line. Better examples of the truly subliminal would be those passages where our metrical expectations are subtly thwarted. The last fourteen lines of the set-piece describing the typist, beginning, "The time is now propitious, as he guesses," were originally sixteen lines cast – as was the whole passage – in quatrains. Pound cut the last two lines:

> And at the corner where the stable is,
> Delays only to urinate, and spit.

with the comment "proba[b]ly over the mark." Eliot accepted the cut, substituting an ellipsis, and merged the quatrains into a continuous verse-paragraph. Whether consciously intended or not, the result is that the last fourteen lines build toward a complete Shakespearean sonnet, and we begin to respond unconsciously to the familiar pattern, rocking to its rhythms, only to have them broken when the unrhymed last two lines ("kiss . . . unlit") replace the anticipated clinching couplet. The result is a vague feeling of disease exactly appropriate to the scene, but that feeling is not the result of the conscious process I have just rehearsed; it springs from our physical, reflexive response to familiar cadences.

Similarly, few readers of *The Waste Land* are conscious that the pathetic songs of the three Thames maidens introduced later in Part III form a ruined Petrarchan sonnet that comes to rest on the despairing Shakespearean "Nothing." Nor can we be sure that Eliot was conscious of the effect he had achieved, which fits perfectly the mood and theme of the passage. It seems quite possible that the poet and his more accomplished readers are operating more from instinct than from conscious intention or recognition.

Whatever the nature of the allusions in Eliot's early poetry, they are marked by a concentration and intensity beyond anything found in Pound's early poetry or even in *Hugh Selwyn Mauberley*. Pound aims at a kind of restless inclusiveness, a complete record of his poetic life, whereas Eliot focuses on lines or phrases that have become almost magical touchstones. Like the early critical essays, which tease out the implications of a few luminous passages, *Poems 1920* and *The Waste Land* turn on borrowed lines or phrases that Eliot has pondered so deeply as to make them part of his personality. The poet who believed that two lines could sum up the significance of Baudelaire (and by implication the significance of his own vision of the urban landscape) was possessed by a talismanic – one might almost say occult – imagination.

One instance of this concentration would be the four lines from *Purgatorio* XXVI that Eliot quotes in a note to line 428 of *The Waste Land:*

'Ara vos prec per aquella valor
'que vos guida al som de l'escalina,
'sovegna vos a temps de ma dolor.'
Poi s'ascose nel foco che gli affina.

('Now I pray you, by that Goodness which guideth you to the summit of the stairway, be mindful in due time of my pain.'
Then he hid him in the fire which refines them.)

In addition to providing a context for one of the lines in the poem's final pastiche, Eliot is introducing without comment a passage central to his spiritual life, one that he pondered for a lifetime and returned to again and again in his poetry. The last line is, of course, embedded in the close to *The Waste Land; Ara Vos Prec* was the title of the Ovid Press version of *Poems 1920; Som de L'Escalina* was the title of Part III of *Ash-Wednesday* when it was published separately; and "*sovegna vos*," part of the discarded poem "Exequy" in the *Waste Land* manuscript, ultimately found its home in Part IV of *Ash-Wednesday:*

143

Made cool the dry rock and made firm the sand
In blue of larkspur, blue of Mary's colour,
Sovegna vos

This exhaustive exploration of a single passage as if it were a
sacred text is the source of the intensity and concentration we
feel in the allusions drawn from it. But Eliot's final understanding of Dante's meeting with Arnaut Daniel took a form beyond
conscious allusion or even subliminal suggestion, and his poetic
life leads us inevitably toward that transformation.

After *The Waste Land* and "The Hollow Men," Eliot's use of
allusion turns in a manner that neatly reflects the other turnings
in his personal and artistic life. "Journey of the Magi," the first
ambiguous product of his new life, opens with five lines from a
Nativity sermon by Lancelot Andrewes.

'A cold coming we had of it,
Just the worst time of the year
For a journey, and such a long journey:
The ways deep and the weather sharp,
The very dead of winter.'

The lines are dropped into quotation marks, clearly acknowledging a source, but I suspect few readers feel a compelling urge to
locate it. On the other hand, I can vividly remember my first
reading of "Gerontion" and my fascination with the riddling lines

The word within a word, unable to speak a word,
Swaddled with darkness.

I knew that behind the mesmeric words there lay a background
that I needed to understand (the source, once again, is a Nativity
sermon by Andrewes). In "Journey of the Magi," by contrast, the
relaxed lines from Andrewes flow into the continuous narrative
of the poem, establishing a voice rather than appealing for inter-
textual engagement.

This absorption of sources is paralleled in Eliot's literary criticism, where touchstone passages that are interpreted allusively
give way to a more continuous argument. At the same time, the
personal element is embraced with less reserve, especially after
Eliot's 1932–3 visit to America led to the release of long-sup-
pressed feelings and anxieties. An unmediated line like "Twenty

years and the spring is over," in the landscape poem "New Hampshire," would have been assigned to a voice other than the poet's in the early verse.

Eliot's comments to John Hayward and others on the making of *Four Quartets* show how conscious he was of a new method, where the source or personal reference is folded under the surface of the poetry, reinforcing the emotion without appealing for conscious identification.[8] John Hayward had queried the line in a draft of *Little Gidding*, "He turned away, and in the autumn weather":

> 'Autumn weather': I do not get the significance of *autumn*? It struck me as having a greater significance than you may have intended it to have."

Eliot replied:

> 'Autumn weather' only because it *was* autumn weather – it is supposed to be an *early* air raid – and to throw back to Figlia che piange . . . but with less point than the children in the appletree meaning to tie up New Hampshire and Burnt Norton (with a touch, as I discovered in the train, of [Kipling's] 'They' which I don't think I had read for 30 years. . . .)[9]

This may be the most revealing passage in all of Eliot's correspondence about *Four Quartets;* it compounds his immediate sense of time and place (the autumn of 1940 and the London blitz) with the landscapes of time lost in "New Hampshire" and *Burnt Norton* and then links these emotional landscapes with that most poignant of the early poems, "La Figlia che Piange," where the poet-spectator stands at a Jamesian remove from experience. The point here is that the complex references, some intended, some only half-conscious on Eliot's part, do not insist upon conscious recognition in the way many of the earlier allusions do. It is hard to imagine Eliot saying of any of them, as he did of the tag from Dante "I had not thought death had undone so many," that he *meant* the reader to recognize it "and know that he would have missed the point if he did not recognize it." Existing as much for Eliot as for us, the connections give the phrase "autumn weather" the emotional force that Hayward felt but could not define.

When he came to write *Little Gidding* Eliot was faced with the formidable challenge of not only closing the sequence but of repeating a set pattern for a third time. He feared "signs of flagging"[10] and told Hayward that the "defect of the whole poem, I feel, is the lack of some acute personal reminiscence (never to be explicated, of course, but to give power from well below the surface) and I can *perhaps* supply this in Part II."[11] Eliot had in mind his creation (in the second half of Part II of *Little Gidding*) of a modern equivalent to a canto from the *Inferno* or *Purgatorio*, an enterprise that cost him, as he said in "What Dante Means to Me," "far more time and trouble and vexation than any passage of the same length that I have written." The method was different from that employed in *The Waste Land*: "I was debarred from quoting or adapting at length . . . because I was *imitating*."[12]

When we trace the revisions of *Little Gidding* II(b), the implications of "imitation," as against direct allusion, become apparent: The general movement is from an encounter with "the dead masters" of the poetic tradition, modeled after Dante's emotional meeting with Brunetto Latini in *Inferno* XV, to a more mysterious encounter with "a familiar compound ghost" who is both the masters of the past and Eliot's complex Anglo-American other self. It is as if the dramatic meetings of the *Inferno* and *Purgatorio* had been merged with the psychological drama of Henry James's "The Jolly Corner," which Eliot had already used in *The Family Reunion*. In the first draft the poet's strange meeting at dawn is specifically Dante's with Brunetto in *Inferno* XV, and Dante's appalled cry is directly repeated:

> And I, becoming other and many, cried
> And heard my voice: 'Are you here, Ser Brunetto?'

But Brunetto was soon replaced by a more ambiguous figure.

> So I assumed another part, and cried
> Hearing another's voice cry: 'What? are *you* here?'

When Hayward questioned the disappearance of Ser Brunetto, Eliot replied that he "wished the effect of the whole to be Purgatorial" rather than Infernal.[13] But he had another reason for enlarging the alter ego: the insistent presence of the ghost of William Butler Yeats. Eliot told Hayward that "the visionary figure has now become somewhat more definite and will no doubt be identified by some readers with Yeats though I do not mean anything so precise as that. . . . I do not wish to take the responsibility of putting Yeats or anybody else into Hell and I do not want to impugn to him the particular vice which took Brunetto there."[14]

Memories of Yeats are intimately bound up with the making of the last three quartets. Two early versions of *Little Gidding* IV were drafted on the versos of pages that contain notes for the memorial lecture Eliot delivered in Dublin in June 1940, and the attitude toward the "dead master" expressed in that lecture is reflected in the moving first part of *East Coker* V. Eliot had come late to an appreciation of Yeats's achievement,[15] but by the time *Four Quartets* was well underway he had recognized Yeats as "the greatest poet of our time," a master who spoke to all of Europe precisely because his poetry was grounded in the local and the personal. In the 1940 memorial lecture Eliot speaks of the process by which Yeats made himself "universal," returning once more to his old theme of "impersonality" in a way that clarifies many of the earlier comments:

> There are two forms of impersonality: that which is natural to the mere skilful craftsman, and that which is more and more achieved by the maturing artist. . . . The second impersonality is that of the poet who, out of intense and personal experience, is able to express a general truth: retaining all the particularity of his experience, to make of it a general symbol.[16]

It is exactly this process of turning "intense and personal experience" into a "general symbol" that Eliot followed in the recasting of *Little Gidding* II(b).

At the same time that Eliot was transforming the dead masters Brunetto and Yeats into a "familiar compound ghost," he was looking about for "some sharpening of personal poignancy" to animate the canto. Such personal urgency was already there in the last twenty-four lines of the first draft, which were later replaced by the more austere movement beginning, "But, as the passage now presents no hindrance / To the spirit unappeased and peregrine." The canceled lines open:

> 'Remember rather the essential moments
>   That were the times of birth and death and change
>   The agony and the solitary vigil.

Remember also fear, loathing and hate,
　　The wild strawberries eaten in the garden,
　　The walls of Poitiers, and the Anjou wine,
　The fresh new season's rope, the smell of varnish
　　On the clean oar, the drying of the sails,
　Such things as seem of least and most importance. . . .

Here there is "acute personal reminiscence" in abundance, memories of Cape Ann, of London in the autumn of 1940, and of the
visit to the south of France made with the Pounds in the summer
of 1919. Hayward objected to the Whitmanesque catalogue, and
Helen Gardner felt that the passage "is slackly written and the
'essential moments' lose their individual poignancy and are triv-
ialized by being set in a catalogue."[17] I do not agree. I find the
passage extremely moving, but it did not match the austere Dan-
tesque style Eliot was aiming at, and I suspect the "essential
moments" were too openly biographical for his taste – they would
be more at home in one of Pound's later cantos. In any case, Eliot
began to rework the passage by writing a prose draft in which the
details of Yeats's exemplary life replaced moments from his own,
yet he ended the draft with a reference to Canto XXVI of the
*Purgatorio,* always a touchstone to his deepest feelings:

> Those who have known purgatory
> here know it hereafter – so shall you
> learn when enveloped by the coils
> of the fiery wind, in which you
> must learn to swim.

A later prose version, which ends with a Yeatsian echo, "[T]here
is only the one remedy, pain for pain, in that purgative fire which
you must will, wherein you must learn to swim and better
nature," was then versified:

> From ill to worse the exasperated spirit
> 　Proceeds, unless restored by that refining fire
> 　Where you must learn to swim, and better nature.

Hayward queried "swim," Eliot's literal rendering of Guido's disappearance in Canto XXVI, "like a fish going through the water"
(*come per l'acqua pesce andando al fondo*). Eliot changed "swim"

to "move," then brilliantly recast the line to combine Yeats's favorite image of the dancer with the experience of joyful pain dramatized by Dante. Eliot surely did not know that one of the influences behind Yeats's Byzantium poems was Blake's illustration to *Purgatorio* XXVII, where the figures entering the fire are portrayed as dancers, but it seems entirely fitting that he should have inherited this Romantic image from Yeats and used it to recall the moment in the *Divine Comedy* that had haunted him throughout his poetic life: Arnaut Daniel's willing acceptance of the purifying flames:

> From wrong to wrong the exasperated spirit
>   Proceeds, unless restored by that refining fire
>   Where you must move in measure, like a dancer.

Part II(b) of *Little Gidding* contains, in Grover Smith's words, "an astonishing phalanx of allusions and imitations"[18] (by actual count it is denser than any comparable pages of *The Waste Land*), but most of these are light touches that act on us subliminally or provide Eliot with a turn of phrase. The power of the canto comes from what we might call its umbra, or surrounding shadows, inhabited by ghosts that may be scarcely visible in the text but are powerfully felt by Eliot and therefore by his readers. We have already noted James's "The Jolly Corner" and Dante's meeting with Arnaut Daniel; two other echoes inhabit the final tercet and then ring back through the entire canto:

> The day was breaking. In the disfigured street
>   He left me, with a kind of valediction,
>   And faded on the blowing of the horn.

Here the actual scene – the hooter sounding an "All Clear" after an infernal night over London – is framed by our recollection of the opening scene in *Hamlet,* where the ghost "started like a guilty thing / Upon a fearful summons" and "faded on the crowing of the cock." This is allusion of the conventional kind, but between Shakespeare and Eliot we sense the shadowy presence of Tennyson, who in Poem VII of *In Memoriam* anticipates a

Hamlet-like encounter with the ghost of Hallam in the light of a
London dawn, only to find nothing but blankness:

> Behold me, for I cannot sleep,
> And like a guilty thing I creep
> At earliest morning to the door.

> He is not here; but far away
>   The noise of life begins again,
>   And ghastly through the drizzling rain
> On the bald street breaks the blank day.

We know from Eliot's criticism that this poem had a special hold
on his imagination, and we know from the *Quartets* themselves
that the voice of Tennyson was one Eliot could comfortably adopt
in his later poetry. In order to identify the central presences in
Eliot's late poetry, as against the more tangential references, one
often must be familiar with the entire record of his life as a poet-
critic, since – as with Pound – all his writings are part of a single
enterprise. In *Four Quartets* the intense, concentrated allusions
of so much of the early poetry have yielded to a more pervasive
appropriation of other voices, other personalities:

> Not the intense moment
> Isolated, with no before and after,
> But a lifetime burning in every moment
> And not the lifetime of one man only. . . .

(East Coker, V)

## Notes

1  *To-Day* 4 (September 1918): 6–7.
2  Ronald Bush, *The Genesis of Ezra Pound's Cantos* (Princeton: Princeton University Press, 1976), 205–9.
3  Alex Preminger, ed., *Princeton Encyclopedia of Poetry and Poetics* (Princeton: Princeton University Press, 1965), entry on "allusion," 18.
4  James Longenbach, *Stone Cottage: Pound, Yeats, and Modernism* (New York: Oxford University Press, 1988).
5  *Translations of Ezra Pound* (New York: New Directions, 1953), 214.
6  Peter Ackroyd, *T. S. Eliot: A Life* (New York: Simon and Schuster, 1984), 120.

7  T. S. Eliot, *To Criticize the Critic* (New York: Farrar, Straus & Giroux, 1965), 128.

8  See Helen Gardner, *The Composition of Four Quartets* (New York: Oxford University Press, 1978), 24.

9  Ibid., 29.

10  Ibid., 22.

11  Ibid., 24.

12  Eliot, *To Criticize the Critic,* 128.

13  Gardner, *Composition,* 176.

14  Ibid.

15  See Eliot's 1936 lecture "Tradition and the Practice of Poetry," and my Afterword, *Southern Review* 21 (October 1985): 873–88.

16  T. S. Eliot, *On Poetry and Poets* (New York: Farrar, Straus & Giroux, 1961), 299.

17  Gardner, *Composition,* 185.

18  Grover Smith, *T. S. Eliot's Poetry and Plays* (Chicago: University of Chicago Press, 1956), 286.

# Forms of Simultaneity in The Waste Land *and* Burnt Norton

ALAN WILLIAMSON

In a celebrated essay Joseph Frank invented the term *spatial form* to describe various effects of simultaneity in modernist works, beginning with Pound's definition of the image as presenting "an intellectual and emotional complex in an instant of time." The instantaneousness, Frank argues, suppresses the inherently consecutive quality of a verbal art, thus creating "that sense of freedom from time limits and space limits" that Pound describes in almost mystical terms. In consequence, Frank suggests at the end of his essay, modernism tends toward a rejection of "the historical imagination" in favor of something like Mircea Eliade's concept of "the myth of eternal repetition," according to which, in primitive cultures, only trivial events belong to history; significant ones always occupy the same "mythic time" or "mythic space" of "the center" or "the origin."[1]

One purpose of this paper is to show that Eliot's earlier and later work have much more in common, in terms of the kinds of "freedom from time limits and space limits" they seek, than is often acknowledged. Another is to set this kind of transcendence, or "mythic time," in tension – as Frank himself, I think, fails to do – with the more usual concept of "mythic method." For the mythic method is by no means ahistorical. It uses the terms of one period to pass judgment on those of another, the present, which is generally assumed to be inferior – "the immense panorama of futility and anarchy which is contemporary history," as Eliot wrote in his essay on *Ulysses*.[2] In this unidirectional reading of history, Goldsmith's lines " When lovely woman stoops to folly" – in which the proper response to loss of chastity is "to die" – tell us how trivial a response it is to "[smoothe one's] hair with automatic hand, / And [put] a record on the gramophone." But the possibility that Goldsmith's lines are culture-bound, sentimental, or even false does not seem to enter the poem's field of play. Such passages endeared Eliot to readers who wished to be morally conservative while remaining aesthetically modern. But the leering, campy recitation of this particular one in the film of *Brideshead Revisited* shows better than I could how equivocal is its relation to puritanism as well as to titillation.

There is another possibility. In "mythic time," a healing meaning comes from beyond the present, but not from the terms or standards of any particular culture, rather from a Jungian or Frazerian depth within all cultures. Rather than a unidirectional comparison, there is a kind of palimpsest, in which events participating in this meaning on different levels seem to take place simultaneously, without excluding each other. (I think Jessie Weston's *From Ritual to Romance* was such a palimpsest for Eliot, because she was able to make Frazer's kind of connections back to the primitive and the erotic without ceasing to respect – indeed, urge the literal truth of – the "highest religious teaching" for which the Mysteries became the "vehicle."[3]) The depth we are talking about is an intrapsychic depth as well, the depth of the Jungian archetypes, which, Jung says, always involve both instinct and spirit. And I shall argue that, in the passages in which Eliot creates "mythic time," his own psychological history is always one of the elements in play, that a work of self-integration (to use the Jungian terms) is going on, which makes the

moral teachings less exclusionary than they are when the traditional "mythic method" is in control.

The first clear instance of "mythic time" seems to me to come
in the fifth – the inspired – part of *The Waste Land,* written in
the clinic at Lausanne. Here, stories from different epochs are
suddenly told in an interpenetrative way, as if they were a single
story. The section begins as an evocation of the Passion of Christ;
then, there is a subtle shift:

> After the agony in stony places
> The shouting and the crying
> Prison and palace and reverberation
> Of thunder of spring over distant mountains

Although "Prison and palace" come clearly enough from the Gos-
pels, "thunder of spring" does not, but it makes what the
Poundians would call a subject rhyme with the earthquake in
Matthew, the "darkness over all the land" in three of the Evan-
gelists. Where it does come from is Weston's account of the Indian cults surrounding the flooding of the Ganges, which form the
anthropological background for the story from the Upanishads
retold later, just as the sacrifice of vegetation deities, at the same
time of year, forms the anthropological background for the Christian story. In one line, the palimpsest has come into being, drawing together two great religions and their respective primitive
sources.

But what happens in the next three lines is, I think, even more
extraordinary:

> He who was living is now dead
> We who were living are now dying
> With a little patience

We suddenly hear again the voice of the very beginning of the
poem, the slightly querulous, weary, self-mocking voice of the
living dead, waiting for death "With a little patience." When even
this death is set in liturgical parallel with the death of Christ, an
immense dignity is conferred on it, as well as a burden of hope,
since what participates in the Crucifixion can, by an inexorable
logic, participate in the Resurrection as well. The psychological

dimension of the palimpsest has been established, and established with considerable implicit compassion.

As the second develops, Eliot continues to tell several stories as if they were a single story. The main strand now is the Grail knight's journey toward the Chapel Perilous, but the note on the journey to Emmaus keeps the Christian story active and moving forward while adding a modern instance of quest and psychic extremity, Shackleton's Antarctic expedition. As the travelers ascend, the perspective broadens, first spatially, to "the present decay of eastern Europe," the "hooded hordes swarming," then temporally, to the successive incarnations of the "mind of Europe," the "city" that

> Cracks and reforms and bursts in the violet air
> Falling towers
> Jerusalem Athens Alexandria
> Vienna London
> Unreal

Finally, the East as well as the West enters this inclusive picture. As the knight actually reaches the Chapel Perilous and the end of the drought approaches, we are led back, through Weston, to the first meanings of rain as a sacred term; the mountains become the Himalayas, and Brahma speaks in the thunder.

Put this way, it might all sound like a rather dry exercise in symbolism. But in the marvelous orchestrations of the actual poem, it all moves at the same speed toward crisis. In all three stories, healing spiritual powers are near at hand, but first there must be a test, an interrogation. "He who was living" is now alive again, but the disciples have not yet recognized Him. The knight has almost reached the Grail, but first he must keep his vigil in the Chapel Perilous, facing apparitions, corpses that come to life, in some versions the Devil himself, with the "dry bones" of failed predecessors all around him. The thunder has spoken, but its word must be interpreted. There is no assurance of a successful outcome; rather, in all three stories, we are brought simultaneously to that razor's edge where everything is promised and everything is in question. There is rain, but it has not arrived; there is "a damp gust / Bringing rain" – perhaps the most successful suspensive participle in all of literature.

As the action becomes thus archetypal, transcending the terms of any single culture or story, it becomes, like all archetypal actions, intrapsychic as well. Since Eliot ceased to be the poet of Impersonality, critics have gotten more and more interested in the Hieronymus Bosch–like passage beginning, "A woman drew her long black hair out tight," and in its psychoanalytic overtones: the seductive, crazed mother-muse, the verminous infantilized self. But from our point of view, what is most interesting is that this material is there at all, without the kind of frame that, say, the dirge from *The Tempest* gives to the implications of castration and the disintegration of the ego in "I think we are in rats' alley / Where the dead men lost their bones." Eliot's own involvement in the story of the Grail quester (whose trials include Bosch-like visions) is so intense as to permit a framelessness, a free-associative release of psychic chaos, utterly uncharacteristic of Eliot's poetic methods. So that we are in a sense prepared for the most drastic inward turning of all, when the commands of the Thunder are addressed not, as in the Upanishads, to all classes of conscious beings, but to "We who were living" or, even more narrowly, to that particular, shadowy modern figure whom Calvin Bedient calls the protagonist and whom I, in my post-Lowellian heresies, am tempted to call T. S. Eliot.

But what needs to be emphasized, most of all, is how much larger and more paradoxical the moral world of the poem becomes in the answers to these commands or questions. In "The Fire Sermon" – the section that most subjects its characters to "mythic method" put-downs of the Goldsmith kind – *The Waste Land* veers toward rejecting sexuality altogether:

O Lord Thou pluckest me out
O Lord Thou pluckest

burning

Now the protagonist is able to acknowledge that "The awful daring of a moment's surrender" to a forbidden sexual impulse was the moment in which he truly "existed," because he acknowledged and gave expression to his whole self. And he can also understand that that surrender, "blood shaking my heart," was a form of generosity, of "giving," because it put him at the mercy of the "friend" to whom he made the avowal; it broke down, for an instance, that impenetrable wall between separate consciousnesses that forms again in the answer to the second command, *Dayadhvam*. Similarly, in the response to the third command, Eliot has altered the meaning of the Sanskrit term, *Damyata*, from "self-control" to "control" over others, to suggest that sexual initiative can be a virtue, and failure to exercise it a betrayal of the other as well as the self. There is a work of integration, in the Jungian sense, going on in these lines, bringing together values that conventional wisdom keeps separate: aggression and sensitivity, the dirty secrets that will not be found by "the lean solicitor," and the highest virtues of generosity and truth to oneself.

Is it a successful work? This is, perhaps, another way of asking the much more common question: Is the end of *The Waste Land* optimistic or pessimistic? The protagonist's own testimony is ambiguous. He has, in a momentary, paradoxical sense, "given," but he has failed to "sympathize" or "control." The jumble of quotations at the end similarly points in both directions, "*Le Prince d'Aquitaine à la tour abolie*" suggesting despair, impotence, and death, whereas "*Poi s'ascose nel foco che gli affina*" suggests purgatorial suffering leading to salvation. My own opinion is that Eliot intentionally leaves the poem on the same razor's edge of unresolved crisis to which he has brought the three principal stories. In doing so, he hands the problem back to the reader as a problem in life: "Why then Ile fit you."

But in a certain sense, the accomplishment of "What the Thunder Said," for modern poetry and for Eliot's spiritual growth, lies beyond optimism and pessimism. It lies in the poem's greater human self-tolerance, its almost seamless unification of the inner psychic journey with the history of myth and religion, its pursuit of an image of human wholeness that is found in all cultures but confined to none.

The kind of interpenetrative time and space created in "What the Thunder Said" remains characteristic of Eliot's major poetry, despite all the apparent changes. In *Four Quartets* we are no longer concerned – or not, at any rate, consistently concerned – with different periods of history, rather with the intersection between specific but, as Eliot himself said, hidden moments in his personal history and the "timeless moment" of mystical vision. But we are also concerned with the different times and spaces of discourse – the linearity of argument, the fusion or confusion of Symbolist lyric, the looping back of lost time in narrative lyric. And the overriding, contentless metaphor of music suggests that the poem itself is a kind of abstract space in which these different spaces can overlap, like the voices of different instruments. Yet all of it somehow unfolds out of, folds back into, the dominance of literal place: Burnt Norton, East Coker . . .

We do not have space, here, for a complete reading of *Four Quartets* or even of *Burnt Norton.* I propose, instead, to show how, in the first part of *Burnt Norton,* real space is generated out of rhetorical space and how both in turn become the "mythic space" of Eliade's "center," of Eliot's "first world."

*Burnt Norton* opens, famously, in philosophical argument, without locality or appeal to the senses. The "rose garden" enters the poem first as a kind of allegorical equivalent for "what might have been," a place that, if we are tough-minded enough, we will acknowledge has only a negative, or a mental, existence. Yet the sentence negating the garden tells us just enough to make it unequivocally take shape, to make it belong to a particular house: One gets to it through a "passage" that has an echo and then through a door. The next line, which turns the poet's words into the echoing footfall ("My words echo / Thus, in your mind"), has a curious double effect. In one sense, it dissolves the whole scene back into a rhetorical device. In another, it makes the poem itself a kind of special space that poet and reader inhabit together – as in Whitman's "Crossing Brooklyn Ferry" – even if the reader's echoing associations are unimaginable to the poet, even after the poet is dead.

The next lines are a reversion against the wish to create such imaginative spaces:

> But to what purpose
> Disturbing the dust on a bowl of rose-leaves
> I do not know.

These lines begin to activate some of the traditional associations of roses: love and lost youth. (But where exactly is this bowl?

Surely, as one of the appurtenances of an aristocratic house like the one Eliot is describing, it makes that house ever more real to us.)

Thus the whole thrust of the poem is to create the garden, in spite of all resistances and disclaimers. Indeed, creation proves unnecessary: A line drops, and we are already there. The "echoes" are now not questionable substitutes for reality, but inhabitants, things in their rightful place. And as the poem goes on, the garden becomes unobtrusively ever more specific, the garden of an English country house, with its "box circle" and its "drained pool."

But where is this garden? To what context does it belong? There are, I think, two simultaneously valid answers. One is that it belongs to the imagination and to literature. It is called into being by a voice, "the deception of the thrush." This voice sings in response to "unheard music," which cannot help being, in part, the "unheard melodies" of a great precursor work, Keats's "Ode on a Grecian Urn," in which art itself is a special space, a stillness implying motion, and the repository of the perfection that "breathing human passion" cannot quite attain. (The association of a rose garden with not quite consummated love and with love as a spiritual education takes us straight back to the *Roman de la Rose* of Guillaume de Lorris and, of course, to Dante.)

But the garden also belongs to a series of synchronicities in Eliot's private history, elements, as he said, of "acute personal reminiscence (never to be explicated, of course, but to give power from well below the surface)."[4] In Eliot's own "first world," his childhood world in St. Louis, as Ronald Bush has pointed out, there was a "gate" (no longer a "door," which in itself tells us that there is a conflation of landscapes), which led from his family's backyard to the schoolyard of a girls' private school, the Mary Institute – an access to the world of women, of otherness, the world beyond the prohibitions of the family and the self.[5] In September 1935, having half-escaped the self-imposed prohibition of fidelity to a mutually tormenting marriage, Eliot visited Burnt Norton with Emily Hale, who had been, in Ronald Bush's words, "more than companion, less than fiancee" at Harvard two decades earlier. The seed-poem of *Burnt Norton*, "New

Hampshire," conveys the bittersweetness of their reunion, which would end in another parting:

> Black wing, brown wing, hover over;
> Twenty years and the spring is over. . . .

But the mood of September 1935 seems, by all accounts, to have been one of overpowering release and happiness.[6]

This reminiscence is, of course, "never . . . explicated" in the poem, but I think the reader does feel it giving "power from well below the surface." By the line "So we moved, and they, in a formal pattern," the "we" has invisibly but unequivocally narrowed from a large, philosophical "we," clearly including the reader, to a very specific cast of characters. This "we," in their very specific garden, are accompanied by an unidentified "they," who seem to be the end of a shift of referents going back to "echoes" and then to "What might have been" – now mysteriously turned into living creatures, as the garden itself has become real. At the end of the passage they metamorphose, as in "New Hampshire," into "children." Helen Gardner was the first to suggest a source in Kipling's story "They," where the invisible guests are dead children, appearing through the mediumship of a childless woman. Ronald Bush has mentioned Eliot's preoccupation at about this time with Henry James's "The Jolly Corner," in which the protagonist meets the ghost of the person he would have become if he had stayed at home in America.[7] I suspect that all of these associations lie behind the "they" whom Eliot never "explicates." "They" are the lovers Eliot and Emily Hale might have become if he had not emigrated; "they" are the children he might have had, the child-self he might have recovered, in a more peaceful, trusting marriage. I disagree with Bush only in his suggestion that "they" are also identical with the "they" of *The Family Reunion* and therefore represent a punitive sense of guilt, inadequacy, or illusion.[8] This seems to me to go against the tone of the passage, which is the tone of ritual peace surrounding the numinous, "dignified," "without pressure," accompanied by "unheard music" that makes the air "vibrant." It takes place at the paradoxical season ("autumn heat") that, throughout the *Quartets,* stands for release from chronological time. "They" are like Pound's "Rustle of airy sheaths, / dry forms in the *aether*," except that they are wholly "invisible." And their relation to the "we" is a benign one, though not without tension or pain. "Accepted" by the "we" as "our guests," they are, perhaps more importantly, "accepting" – not condemning or excluding the dwindled figures who have failed to give them a real existence.

And, of course, they do finally consent to become visible, in a moment of mystical ecstasy:

> Dry the pool, dry concrete, brown edged,
> And the pool was filled with water out of sunlight,
> And the lotos rose, quietly, quietly,
> The surface glittered out of heart of light,
> And they were behind us, reflected in the pool.

It is the quintessence of imaginative space, a pure absence that light fills with the surfaces first of water, then of a flower, then of the "heart of light" itself. We have reached the "center," and there – in the mind of God, as it were – "what might have been" is as real as "what has been," emotional plenitude as actual limitation.

It is extremely important, I think, that Eliot, though now writing as a convinced –even, in his prose, a bigoted – Anglican, allows the same slippage between major religions that occurs at the beginning of "What the Thunder Said." The lotos, the sacred flower of Buddhism, replaces the expected rose. The crucial moments, it would seem, still demand this universality. The two symbols have an overlapping meaning: the flowering connection of the created world to the Absolute, its invisible stem. In Christianity, the connotations lead toward love: the rose window of Our Lady's cathedrals, the *Paradiso*. In Buddhism, they lead to the position assumed in meditation, the integration of the self. Both associations are relevant. For, looking into the mirror of the flower, the lovers see what they cannot see in reality, their fulfilled and united selves.

These lines, I think, refute those critics who would have all of Eliot's poetry agree with the bitterer passages in his criticism that hold that romantic love is inherently disillusioning and intended only to lead the soul, by its own despair, to love of God. Romantic love is, indeed, "completed in the higher love" in *Burnt Norton*, but "completed" does not, here, mean "discarded." As in *The Waste Land*, the culminations of the poetry involve a work of self-integration of which Eliot the day-to-day thinker was not always capable. Its tolerance extends not only to Eros itself, but to the more tender-minded side of the poet, which would like to believe that the gentler, not quite lived-out possibilities of life are in their own way "real." And so, at the end of the passage the meaning of what was initially a tough-minded, dismissive statement, "What might have been and what has been / Point to one end [conclusion], which is always present [the real situation]," has changed, without the alteration of a single word, to "What might have been and what has been / Point to one end [purpose, *telos*], which is always present [immanent, accessible]."

But perhaps the most telling instance of this integration lies in the simultaneity with Eliot's own earlier poetry in the phrase "heart of light." The passage it comes from is in some ways one of the most puzzling in *The Waste Land*:

"You gave me hyacinths first a year ago;
"They called me the hyacinth girl."
– Yet when we came back, late, from the Hyacinth garden,
Your arms full, and your hair wet, I could not
Speak, and my eyes failed, I was neither
Living nor dead, and I knew nothing,
Looking into the heart of light, the silence.
*Oed' und leer das Meer.*

The vocabulary is that of religious ecstasy or the ecstasy of courtly love. Yet it turns the speaker away from the beloved, from all power to communicate with her, into a glittering expanse whose darker side is picked up by the German, the "desolate, empty sea" where Isolde's ship does not appear. And the tone of the beginning of the passage seems one of Prufrockian regret – a moment not seized, a relationship that has stagnated, un-clarified, for a year.

It is small wonder the critics have had trouble with this passage. For Robert Langbaum it is a moment of failure, failure to "break through to fertility, creativity," though "We know he failed only through the last line." For Calvin Bedient it is a "meta-physical success" because the speaker, in "discovering the noth-ingness of romantic love (its foundation in two narcissistic wants) . . . then discovers the Absolute."[9] Both readings avoid certain difficulties, Langbaum understating the rhetoric of religious vision, Bedient not seeing how it is altered by the German. I hope it is not just filial piety that makes me prefer the implications of George Williamson's brief reference to "a state neither living nor dead, describing the effect of the vision of the Grail upon the impure."[10]

"We had the experience but missed the meaning": My own sense is that it was because the passage was a tonal failure, reflecting an obscurity in self-understanding, that Eliot had to return to it. The older man who can, at least for a moment, look into the "heart of light" and at the same time see – and love – the human being at his side, has relived his earlier experience

> In the completion of its partial ecstasy,
> The resolution of its partial horror.

That is what standing outside time means in the *Quartets*.

At the end the garden is banished by a voice, as it has been called into being by one: "human kind / Cannot bear very much reality." If I have emphasized the garden's aspect of fiction, or of Reality, as well as its aspect of reality, it is to suggest that "freedom from time limits and space limits" is a characteristic not only of the works overtly drawing on myth, but of all of Eliot's innovations in the art of poetry. (Under other circumstances I would go on to try to relate the interplay of different times and spaces to the interplay of poetic voices in *Burnt Norton* as a whole.) I have also argued that Eliot's steps into mythic space are generally accompanied by an unusual effort to integrate instinct and spirit. I do so with some temerity, knowing that this conflicts with some of Eliot's consciously held opinions. But I think the text bears it out, as does the direction Eliot's life finally took. And for me, it makes him a larger poet.

## POSTSCRIPT

I am aware that many of the concepts taken for granted here – archetypes, self-integration, "freedom from time limits and space limits," a repository of value outside of history – are not popular ones in recent literary criticism. They are held to be, at best, an easy escape from life-giving elements of contradiction and contingency; at worst, a mystification covering an authoritarian and fascist agenda. The poems I have been discussing are vulnerable, to some degree, to both charges. As Carol Christ has observed, Eliot's anger, whatever we think of it morally, was a spur to good poetry, and anger is not part of the experience of the still point. When anger does flare out in "What the Thunder Said," it is an antidemocratic revulsion – the "red sullen faces" that "sneer and snarl," the "hooded hordes swarming." (One should, however, remember that "the present decay of eastern Europe," even in 1921, included protofascist as well as Communist upheavals. Eliot's horror of mass violence is impartial, not a right-wing polemic.)

One could simply retreat to a high historical line of defense. Then one would say that, whatever we think of archetypes or "mythic time," the modernists, writing in the wake of Frazer, Jung, and the Freud of *Totem and Taboo*, saw themselves as being on the cutting edge of exploratory new thought. The new ideas gave a structure, a way of integrating private and public, immediate experience and cultural lore, to the best long poems of a generation. Since the image of collectivity they informed could be profoundly democratic, as in Williams's *Paterson* or Crane's *The Bridge*, the connection with the authoritarian in contemporary criticism may prove more plausible than deeply true.

But I prefer to be more candid. I think these conventions have their basis in religious experiences that occur in almost all cultures whether or not they interest current critical fashion. Nor do all religious traditions see such experiences as negating the reality of historical time, defining the meaning of life once and for all. In Jung's concept of individuation, the role they play in the history of the individual is neither exclusionary nor static, rather a progressive, shifting dialogue and often a way of including what has previously been excluded. To confuse oneself with an archetype, for Jung, is the beginning of madness. To me, the Jungian concept provides the best model for thinking about the very complex way in which personal history and transcendent glimpses are related in the modernist long poem. And so I have tried to argue that Eliot in fact becomes larger, more flexible, more tolerant of contradiction in his view of himself, his past, and moral issues generally as he approaches what he sees as the mystic center. Eventually, I hope to make this argument part of a study that will include the more democratic and agnostic modernists, Williams and Crane, and show to what extent they were all involved in a common enterprise of the archetypal imagination. But for now, the argument must seem as strong or weak as my close readings.

## Notes

1 Joseph Frank, "Spatial Form in Modern Literature," in *The Widening Gyre* (New Brunswick, N.J.: Rutgers University Press, 1963), esp. 60. See also Mircea Eliade, *Cosmos and History: The Myth of the Eternal Return* (New York: Harper & Row, 1959), 3–62, esp. 35–6.

2 T. S. Eliot, "Ulysses, Order, and Myth," *Selected Prose of T. S. Eliot,* edited by Frank Kermode (London: Faber & Faber, 1975), 177.

3 Jessie Weston, *From Ritual to Romance* (Garden City, N.Y.: Doubleday Anchor, 1957), 158.

4 Eliot, letter to John Hayward, 5 August 1941, quoted in Ronald Bush, *T. S. Eliot, A Study in Character and Style* (New York: Oxford University Press, 1983), 227.

5 See Bush, *T. S. Eliot,* 132–3.

6 See especially Virginia Woolf's diary entry, quoted in ibid., p. 186. Bush has had the great generosity to show me a letter from Helen Gardner, disputing his own view that the disillusionment of *The Cocktail Party* was in any way part of Eliot's mood in 1935, and citing other contemporary testimony.

7 Helen Gardner, *The Art of T. S. Eliot* (New York: Dutton, 1950), 159–60; Bush, *T. S. Eliot,* 2–3, 192.

8 Bush, *T. S. Eliot,* 189–92.

9 Robert Langbaum, "New Modes of Characterization in *The Waste Land,*" in *Eliot in His Time* edited by A. Walton Litz (Princeton: Princeton University Press, 1973), 112; Calvin Bedient, *He Do the Police in Different Voices: The Waste Land and Its Protagonist* (Chicago: University of Chicago Press, 1986), 32.

10 George Williamson, *A Reader's Guide to T. S. Eliot* (New York: Farrar, Straus and Giroux, 1953, reprint 1966), 131–2.

## PART FOUR

# The History and Future of Modernism

# Eliot, Lukács, and the Politics of Modernism

MICHAEL NORTH

One of the minor roles in "The Ideology of Modernism," Georg Lukács's diatribe against the aesthetic avant-garde, is assigned to T. S. Eliot, who appears in the guise of an angst-ridden solipsist.[1] Lukács is perhaps repaying a slight quite unconsciously delivered by Eliot in the "falling towers" section of *The Waste Land.* Eliot glosses these lines by reference to Hermann Hesse's pamphlet *Blick ins Chaos:* "Already half Europe, at all events half Eastern Europe, is on the road to Chaos. . . ."[2] Eliot and Hesse apparently have in mind the wave of revolution coming out of Russia in 1917, in which Lukács played a minor part as deputy people's commissar for education and culture in the soviet republic established in Hungary for a few months in 1919. Hesse's pamphlet links these revolutions to the influence of Dostoyevski, and no one could epitomize this link better than Lukács, who published an article in Berlin in 1922 claiming that Dostoyevski is "the very person who convinces one most clearly of revolution's necessity."[3]

This rather distant antagonism would seem to reinforce certain assumptions about the relationship of aesthetic modernism and radical politics. The personal politics of modernists like Eliot, Yeats, Pound, Lewis, and Lawrence have led to a suspicion that seems to grow stronger every year, that aesthetic modernism is in some essential way reactionary.[4] On the other hand, Lukács's blind resistance to writers like Joyce and Kafka, what one critic has called his "heroic incomprehension" of modern literature in general, has made his revolution seem aesthetically reactionary.[5] But the relationship between Eliot and Lukács is neither so distant nor so antagonistic as it might seem. In fact, this reactionary modernist and this conservative revolutionary shared, for at least a few years, a single position that was both modernist and anti-modern, revolutionary and conservative.[6]

As young men, Eliot and Lukács shared a number of intriguingly odd literary enthusiasms. Somewhere around 1908 Eliot began reading John Ford, the Elizabethan dramatist, whose example, he says, was crucial to his earliest attempts to write poetry.[7] If Eliot had been able to read Hungarian in 1908, he could have read Lukács's essay "John Ford: A Modern Dramatist from the Age of Shakespeare."[8] Eliot read Charles-Louis Philippe's *Bubu of Montparnasse* in Paris in 1910 and, according to A. D. Moody, borrowed some of the atmosphere of this story of pimps and prostitutes for the third and fourth "Preludes."[9] In the same year, Lukács wrote his essay on Philippe, which first appeared in print in the German edition of *The Soul and the Forms* in 1911.[10] These rather minor coincidences suggest that Eliot and Lukács were both interested in a politically ambiguous way in society's outcasts and that they both found it quite natural to look for modernism in literature of the past.

The interests of the two writers converged again, more significantly, on the works of the politically ambidextrous Georges Sorel. Eliot placed Sorel first on the reading list he offered to define classicism in 1926, but he had mentioned Sorel in print as early as 1916 and had discussed him in the lecture series delivered in the same year.[11] Even in 1916, Eliot saw Sorel as a reactionary, reacting violently "against bourgeois socialism" and developing "toward royalism."[12] Within a few months of Eliot's lectures, Lukács began reading Sorel under the instruction of Ervin Szabó. Like Eliot, Lukács listed Sorel as one of the major sources of his own philosophy, "the greatest influence on my intellectual evolution," but Lukács read Sorel as a revolutionary, a stirring example in the year of the Russian revolution.[13] That Sorel could have been enlisted as royalist and as revolutionary in the same year tells us a good deal about him, but it also reveals an affinity between two positions and two men who seem very much at odds.

This affinity was expressed in more concrete relationships as well. In the early years of the century, Lukács studied under Georg Simmel, the celebrated sociologist, who had also attracted as a disciple a young student of art history, Wilhelm Worringer. Lukács and Worringer read one another's work and carried on a correspondence based on their common ideas and interests.[14] Through Worringer, some of these ideas became influential beyond Simmel's circle. For instance, they reached the ears of T. E. Hulme, who met Worringer in 1913.[15] Worringer had adapted to art history one of Simmel's central ideas, the split between subjective and objective culture. In his book *Abstraction and Empathy* Worringer argues that the very advances of modern civilization in scientific and technical proficiency have reduced humankind to the position it held in primitive times: insignificant, fearful, and alienated from nature and its own handiwork.[16] Hulme seized on these ideas as propaganda for an art alienated from its audience, an art that would be provocatively modern and at the same time express total rejection of social and political modernity. This potent combination obviously appealed to Eliot as it had earlier to Lukács.[17]

Another student of Georg Simmel was to play an even larger role in Eliot's life. As a young man, Karl Mannheim attended Simmel's lectures in part because Lukács had, and Lukács was Mannheim's model in everything intellectual. In 1910 Mannheim placed himself completely under Lukács's guidance, and he followed this lead even after breaking with Lukács personally. Mannheim's first German publication was a review of *Theory of the Novel,* and the first course he taught was a year-long seminar on Lukács's Marxist writings.[18] In the years during and immediately following the First World War Mannheim was a member of the Sunday Circle that met under Lukács's tutelage, but by the time of the Second World War he was himself the center of a very similar group called the Moot, a loose organization of Christian intellectuals. This group took so much of its impetus from Mannheim that on his death it ceased to meet. Eliot was, of course, a charter member of this group, and his social ideas during the war years were largely shaped by what he heard from Mannheim at its meetings. For example, *Notes Towards a Definition of Culture* was hammered out in response to Mannheim's theory of elites.[19] Thus the unfinished work of Lukács's Sunday Circle, which was to define the role of intellectuals in a renovation of culture, remained for Eliot to address two decades later.

These coincidences and relationships are not meant to be explanatory, but it is significant that Eliot's career touched Lukács's at the very beginning, in the case of Worringer, and at the end, in the case of Mannheim. It should not be surprising, then, that when Eliot first formulated his political and social beliefs he should have arrived at a slogan and a program remarkably similar to Lukács's of the same period. In his 1916 lectures, Eliot announces as his theme "a return to the ideals of classicism." These Eliot lists as "*form* and *restraint* in art, *discipline* and *authority* in religion, *centralization* in government."[20] Almost exactly two years after Eliot delivered these lectures, Lukács published, appropriately in a eulogy essay on Simmel, his belief that the European world was on the verge of "a new classicism" characterized by "firm and stringent, but all-encompassing forms."[21]

Though the two men clearly agree on art, they might be expected to diverge when the same standards are applied to politics. But Eliot was well aware that his ideas had affinities with socialism. The phrase "centralization in government" is followed by the parenthesis "either as socialism or monarchy." He notes in a later lecture that socialism and royalism have much in common since both "express revolt against the same state of affairs."[22] For his part, Lukács was conscious of the connections between socialism and the sort of religion described in Eliot's lecture. In 1913 he said, "The last culturally active force in Germany, naturalist-materialist socialism, owes its efficacy to hidden religious elements." Nor was this a connection Lukács rejected for himself.

He is reported by members of the circle around Max Weber as having voiced "rapturous praise for Catholicism."[23]

This seemingly contradictory combination of religious reaction and political revolution is embodied in a single literary figure, Thomas Mann's Herr Naphta, the Jewish Jesuit, preacher of authority and terror, rigid Catholicism and total revolt, who was modeled at least in part on Lukács.[24] In *The Magic Mountain* Naphta seems preternaturally distorted, so intellectually convoluted as to be physically deformed, and yet his ideas are not so far from those Eliot announced in the same year. In a 1924 issue of *The Criterion*, Eliot praised Hulme as "classical, reactionary, and revolutionary," as the very opposite of the "eclectic, tolerant, and democratic mind of the end of the last century."[25] Nine years later he warned that for those who take politics seriously "the difference between revolution and reaction may be by the breadth of a hair. . . ."[26] Lukács looked back on Herr Naphta with a thrill of disgust for precisely this reason, because Mann had exposed the connection between the socialism that had won Lukács's mind and the reaction with which it had once coexisted.[27]

Lukács later gave this coexistence the pejorative title "romantic anti-capitalism."[28] The ideological core of romantic anti-capitalism is its defense of culture as a principle of social unity against the economic and political fragmentation of modern civilization. This protest has a long history in England, going back at least to Carlyle, and in Germany, going back at least to Schiller.[29] But Mann's novel is in part about the intensification of this protest in the years immediately preceding World War I and its apocalyptic release in the conflict. The most extreme statement of this protest came from Lukács in 1919, after he had joined the Communist party: "[I]t is a pressing necessity, precisely in the interests of culture, in the interest of opening a new way to a new culture, to bring the long death process of capitalist society to its completion."[30] Eliot phrased the same protest in conservative terms, beginning as early as 1916 when he denounced utilitarianism and popular education. At least by 1921 he had begun to criticize "the world of mass-production" and to oppose it to an ever-weakening, ever receding culture.[31]

For Eliot, the chief culprit in the death of culture is liberal democracy, but in economics this role is played by industrial capitalism. F. O. Matthiessen may have surprised his readers in 1935 when he informed them that Eliot's desire for traditional culture grew out of "his revulsion against the lawless exploitation" of the end of the nineteenth century, but by that time Eliot had made his opposition to industrial capitalism perfectly clear. He may have felt, as he says in *The Criterion* in 1931, that "unrestrained industrialism" tends to harm the upper classes before it harms the workers, but he opposed it nonetheless.[32]

The most complete analysis of this protest against capitalism and liberal democracy was developed, appropriately enough, by Karl Mannheim. Mannheim tries to correct the assumption that the critique of capitalism was originally a proletarian socialist movement. Instead, he says, "this criticism was initiated by the 'right-wing opposition' and . . . was only subsequently transferred from here to the designs of the 'left-wing opposition.'" This original opposition represents the resistance of precapitalistic forces like the landed aristocracy to the growing power that was to displace them. The terms of this original protest are taken up by later, quite different, groups on the left.[33] But this is not to say that romantic anticapitalism is ideologically incoherent. Instead, the convergence of right and left should suggest a theoretical realignment in which left and right join against a common enemy: the liberalism behind modern democracy and laissez-faire economics. For both conservative and socialist proponents of romantic anticapitalism see humankind in collective terms rather than as individuals, both stress historical values over ahistorical principles, and both decry the effects of the capitalist economy.[34] Thus the coexistence in Lukács's prewar circle of conservative and revolutionary ideas, and the similarity between Lukács himself and Eliot, should not be seen as an anomaly but instead as an entirely logical result of the resistance to modern society.[35]

Of course, the ideal that conservatives locate in the past is located instead in the future by socialists, but the two groups have in common both their opposition to modern society and certain problems created by that opposition. According to Jürgen Habermas, the common idea uniting all aspects of modern society is that of "subjective freedom." This idea "was realized in society as the space secured by civil law for the rational pursuit of one's own interests; in the state, as the in principle equal rights to participation in the formation of political will; in the private sphere, as ethical autonomy and self-realization. . . ."[36] But what may seem, in comparison to feudal society, an increase in freedom may be accompanied by an equal but opposite decrease. According to Lukács, subjective freedom, based as it is on the abstract principle of individuality, leads not to difference but "towards ever greater uniformity."[37] As Eliot puts it, liberal democracy is merely "a sum of individuals," a chaos that replaces "the variety and uniqueness of persons" with a "purely material individuation."[38] In other words, when the individual is defined against society, then society can never be anything more than a mere sum of individuals, and the increasing gap between the individual and the social will abstract and devalue both.

Culture, the goal for both critics, means the reintegration of individual and society, particular and general. But how is this reintegration to be accomplished? How is an individual to oppose modern society without exploiting and thus exacerbating the very subjective freedom on which it is based? How is such a critic to create a society that doesn't exist, using tools that make such a society impossible? Can a new society be created or an old one revived by individuals who must, under the conditions of modernity, be antisocial and oppositional? As Roger Scruton admits, "the conservative who has risen above the fragments of his inheritance and reflected on the desolation that has been wrought in it, cannot return to an innocence which his own thinking has destroyed."[39] Or as Eliot says, the writer "born into an unsettled society" cannot transcend the conditions of his birth merely by wanting to do so.[40]

Antimodernism of the kind advanced by Eliot and Lukács can only work through modernism, through what Habermas calls "the subversive force of modern thought itself."[41] Attacking on the basis of a lost ideal does nothing more than juxtapose an empty abstraction to the facts of the present.[42] The ideal must somehow be extracted from the inescapable givens of the present, a new norm from what seems relative, social unity from individualism itself.[43] Two of the best-known literary manifestos of the early twentieth century do just this.

"*Ulysses*, Order, and Myth," which Eliot first published in 1923, and *Theory of the Novel*, written in 1914–15 but not published in book form until 1920, are both meant to shake loose a particular literary form from the constraints of the immediate past. To do so, however, they must confront the philosophical and social problems carried forward by modern society.[44] For both writers, the novel is the form of an age of formlessness, or as Eliot puts it, "the expression of an age which had not sufficiently lost all form to feel the need of something stricter."[45] Lukács's analysis is more extensive and more overwrought, and interestingly, it is more religious than Eliot's: "The novel is the epic of a world that has been abandoned by God."[46] This loss of meaning and form distinguishes the modern world from a past characterized by unity and clarity.

Both works are polemical in that they demand for the future a stricter form than the novel, but both deny that this form can be achieved simply by returning to the past. Eliot remarks quite snidely that a writer can seem to be classical by rejecting modern materials and "selecting only mummified stuff from a museum" (SP, 176–7), but this is clearly not his way. Though Lukács begins *Theory of the Novel* with a rapturous hymn to Greek completeness and roundedness, he opposes "any resurrection of the Greek world" (TN, 38).[47]

Instead, the future is to be achieved on the basis of the present, a new, stricter form on the basis of the novel's formlessness. Lukács insists that "the very disintegration and inadequacy of the world is the precondition for the existence of art and its becoming conscious," and that new forms must somehow "carry the fragmentary nature of the world's structure into the world of forms" (TN, 38–9). Eliot makes the same point rather more specifically. He praises Joyce and Lewis not for reconstituting the novel but for dismantling it, for writing novels "more formless than those of a dozen clever writers" (SP, 177). He proposes the same course of action for poetry in "The Metaphysical Poets" when he proclaims that modern poets "must be *difficult.* . . . The poet must become more and more comprehensive, more allusive, more indirect, in order to force, to dislocate, if necessary, language into his meaning" (SP, 65).[48]

Aesthetic modernism thus appears as a method of arriving at new forms by accelerating the destruction of present forms. The novel is for Lukács merely transitional to the renewed epic he envisions only dimly at the end of his book. The hero of his work, Dostoyevski, who symbolizes the new world, "did not write novels" (TN, 152).[49] Eliot says the same of Joyce and Lewis. The mythical method that Eliot defines in his essay is also transitional; it is a method and not a form. Eliot calls it "a step toward making the modern world possible for art, toward that order and form" that is so earnestly desired (SP, 178). As a transition, it is actually destructive, more formless than what it replaces, but only through this dismantling can the renewed form appear. The "order" of "*Ulysses*, Order, and Myth" does not appear *in* the text of *Ulysses* but is instead promised by its very lack of order.

The relationship between this dismantled novelistic form and the myth suggested by it is therefore an ironic one, since it is the very disintegration into ultimate formlessness of the novel that signifies the unified form of the renewed epic. The final step in Lukács's theory of the novel is therefore a theory of irony. For Lukács, wholeness is present by negative implication in the chaos of the novel. There is, he says, a "unified world in the mutual relativity of elements essentially alien to one another" (TN, 75).[50] Lukács calls irony "a negative mysticism to be found in times without a god" (TN, 90).[51] Since the wholeness of the lost world cannot be revived directly, it can only be glimpsed in inverted terms in the very disintegration that makes it impossible. Irony acquires, according to Paul de Man, "the positive power of an absence."[52] The ironic stance is therefore a peculiarly modern antimodernism, since it advances through the fragmentations of modernism toward a classical wholeness. This stance also combines the revolutionary, the relentless overturning of forms, with the reactionary, the renewed form promised in the end.

Lukács's theory of irony seems to be one of the few ways out of the impasse of modernism. Yet in its desperation to find some relationship, any relationship, between the particular and the general, it settles for a relationship that is purely negative. And as J. M. Bernstein says, the theory "appears to lack the power to turn the negating power of irony into something positive."[53] This inability dogs the works of both Eliot and Lukács for the rest of their lives, remaining as the sign of the unresolved problems of modernism.

*The Waste Land,* for example, dismantles the epic and the novel at once, rushing through all literary history as if in a race to the future.[54] Virtually since the beginning, critics have looked for a way to stop this rush at some point of coherence and harmony. In "The Fire Sermon," for example, Eliot seems to balance contemporary lives dismembered by the division of labor with a classical wholeness represented by Tiresias, but Tiresias can sum up those lives only *because* they have been reduced and standardized. The young man carbuncular is so transparent because he is "One of the low" (1. 233) and Tiresias has "walked among the lowest of the dead" (1. 246).[55] Tiresias represents not the truth of some timeless humanity but an image of modern totality, the negative plenitude arrived at by the addition of innumerable loveless couplings; only by negative implication does he suggest another sort of life. *The Waste Land* does not totalize itself in such figures but rather manifests a deep fear of totalization. What else is the Sibyl, betrayed by a handful of dust, but a drear figure of an eternity born out of repetition, an all-encompassing whole arrived at simply by extending its parts into infinity?

At the end of the poem a different sort of whole is promised, but this, "the Peace which passeth understanding," is by definition ineffable, apprehensible only in ironic contradistinction to the cacophony preceding it. Linguistically, "Shantih," the single word from the root language of the West, acquires its meaning through a paradox described by Walter Benjamin: "[T]he plurality of languages signifies an original unity of language."[56] But this significance exists, again, only in ironic counterpoint, in the very distance separating the babble beginning with "London bridge is falling down" and the final peace. Thus the mixture of styles, languages, and genres in *The Waste Land* may signify a lost linguistic unity, but only by dramatizing its loss.[57]

Eliot's religious conversion did not change, but instead merely sanctified, the irony of *The Waste Land.* Lukács says of the writer's irony that "through not-desiring-to-know and not-being-able-to-know he has truly encountered, glimpsed and grasped the ultimate, true substance, the present, non-existent God" (TN, 90). Nothing could better describe the negative mysticism of "Ash-Wednesday" and *Four Quartets,* in which human life comes to signify by its very limitation the limitless grace of God. The same irony marks Eliot's later criticism, in which dogmatism races neck-and-neck with diffidence. There is a negative rhetorical moment in even the most categorical essay, the moment at which Eliot refuses to define his terms. He refuses to define "use" in *The Use of Poetry and the Use of Criticism*, "idea" in *The Idea of a Christian Society*, "education" in "The Aims of Education," and, finally, declines to define "definition" itself.[58]

This habit simply reveals the pervasive ironic relationship in Eliot's work between the eternal and absolute order, which exists but is never to be revealed to humankind, and the relative order that obtains at any one time.[59] Eliot often sounds like an absolutist, but in the application always reveals himself as a relativist.[60] This is especially true of his social criticism, in which unity can best be approached, as Eliot himself says in *Notes Towards a Definition of Culture*, "through a consideration of the useful diversities." In this work, as in *The Waste Land*, unity exists as an implication of diversity, yet so tenuous is its existence "that it is something we cannot *imagine*. We can only conceive it as the logical term of relations between [specific] cultures."[61] Though Eliot is often dogmatic and narrow-minded, though he can be prejudiced, he is not philosophically totalitarian. On the contrary, the real danger of his social criticism is that it may make its ideal so ineffable that it disappears, that it may accommodate itself so well to the realities of the present as to forget its original opposition to the current order in complacent conservatism.[62]

For Lukács, of course, the dangers were quite different. *Theory of the Novel* was to have been completed by a theory of social utopia.[63] Though this was not written, it is reasonable to assume that such a theory would have looked something like what appears in *History and Class Consciousness*, where Lukács insists that "the intellectual restoration of man has consciously to take its path through the realm of disintegration and fragmentation."[64] Only by a dialectical realization of the unity implied in capitalist disunity could a new society come about. Adorno charges that Lukács writes as if this realization has already been accomplished so that the negative moment of disunity can simply be ignored.[65] Indeed, Lukács's later criticisms of modernist literature all see psychological isolation and stylistic fragmentation as obsessions that a mature dialectic would overcome. It remained for Adorno to use the negative dialectic of *Theory of the Novel* against the later Lukács, as he does when he defends modernist literature by asserting that "loneliness will turn into its opposite: the solitary consciousness potentially destroys and transcends itself by revealing itself in works of art as the hidden truth common to all men."[66]

The quarrel between Adorno and Lukács over modernist literature illuminates the two possibilities facing modern critique, either to insist as Adorno does, and as Eliot does implicitly in both poetry and prose, that the negativity of the modern is its only route back to unity or to decide, as Lukács apparently did, that a positive relationship between particular and general can be brought into being by sheer will. What Lukács himself defined as a leap of faith into the Communist party took him very far from the position once shared with Eliot. Yet the two remain locked together even in stark opposition. For Lukács criticizes the stylistic fragmentation and emotional negativity of modernist literature from the position of one who has penetrated beyond the negative to the positive value it promised. Eliot's conclusion, mirrored in the incessantly halting repetitions of his later style, is that to claim these values is to lose them. Modernist literature is prevented from solidifying precisely because it cannot solve the political and cultural problems of modernism. That it continues to try keeps it both modern and antimodern at the same time.

## Notes

1 Georg Lukács, *The Meaning of Contemporary Realism*, translated by John and Necke Mander (London: Merlin Press, 1963), 25–6. Eliot is mentioned four times in Lukács's massive *Die Eigenart des Aesthetischen*. In both works Lukács takes "The Hollow Men" as typical of Eliot's work.

2 Hermann Hesse, *In Sight of Chaos*, translated by Stephen Hudson (Zurich: Verlag Seldwyla, 1923), 46. Hesse's book was originally published in Zurich in 1922, and Eliot, who read it then and visited Hesse, urged Sidney Schiff (whose pen name was Stephen Hudson) to translate it. Hudson's translations of the first two essays in the book appeared in English in the same year. See *The Letters of T. S. Eliot*, vol. 1, edited by Valerie Eliot (New York: Harcourt Brace Jovanovich, 1988), 509–10.

3   Georg Lukács, *Reviews and Articles from Die rote Fahne*, translated by Peter Palmer (London: Merlin, 1983), 48. The article in question is entitled "Stavrogin's Confession." The Dostoyevski cult was widespread in the Hungarian and German circles Lukács frequented before the war. For details, see Mary Gluck, *Georg Lukács and His Generation 1900–1918* (Cambridge, Mass.: Harvard University Press, 1985), 26–7. See also Zoltan Tar's Introduction to *Georg Lukács: Selected Correspondence 1902–1920* (New York: Columbia University Press, 1986), 21–2. *Theory of the Novel*, which appeared in Germany in book form in 1920, ends with a dramatic equation of Dostoyevski and a "new world . . . to come." See *Theory of the Novel*, translated by Anna Bostock (Cambridge, Mass.: MIT Press, 1971), 152–3. According to Hesse, Dostoyevski and his acolytes preach "an entirely amoral concept" (p. 16), a moral freedom that goes "beyond prohibitions, beyond natural instincts, beyond morality" (p. 20). This amorality is identified with "Revolution, accompanied by slaughter and violence . . ." (p. 26).

4   This charge is made with such frequency and in such a variety of ways as to elude summary. For a recent discussion, see Ronald Bush, "But Is It Modern?: Eliot in 1988," *Yale Review* 77 (Winter 1988): 193–206.

5   The critic in question here is Francisco Fernandez-Santos, quoted in Neil McInnes, "Georg Lukács," *Survey* 72 (Summer 1969): 138. Peter U. Hohendahl says that it was "The Ideology of Modernism" itself that "helped to discredit Lukács as a philosopher and critic among young West German intellectuals of the 1950s and 1960s." "Art Work and Modernity: The Legacy of Georg Lukács," *New German Critique* 42 (Fall 1987): 33. In *Modern Poetry and the Tradition* (Chapel Hill: University of North Carolina Press, 1939), Cleanth Brooks calls Eliot the maker of a critical revolution and complains that the poetics of Marxist critics are not revolutionary at all (pp. 51, 53).

6   Stephen Spender speaks of the "intense hatred and contempt for modern life" that is inseparable from the modernist's "will to be absolutely modern." See *The Struggle of the Modern* (Berkeley: University of California Press, 1963), 208. Marshall Berman makes the same point, "that to be fully modern is to be anti-modern," in *All That Is Solid Melts into Air* (New York: Simon and Schuster, 1982), 14. A study that specifically locates this antimodernism in the United States in the late nineteenth century is T. J. Jackson Lears, *No Place of Grace: Antimodernism and the Transformation of American Culture 1880–1920* (New York: Pantheon, 1981). Lears con-

cludes his book by calling Eliot an "antimodern modernist" (p. 312). In "The Routinization of Charismatic Modernism and the Problem of Post-Modernity," *Cultural Critique* 5 (Winter 1986–7): 49–68, Russell A. Berman also uses the term "modernist anti-modernism" (p. 54), relying in part on Lears for support.

7   T. S. Eliot, *To Criticize the Critic* (New York: Farrar, Straus & Giroux, 1965), 18. A. D. Moody dates this study at around 1908–9. See *Thomas Stearns Eliot Poet* (Cambridge: Cambridge University Press, 1979), 5.

8   Gluck, *Lukács and His Generation,* 107. Lukács's essay was published in *Pester Loyd* on 5 January 1908. It has not been translated into English. It should be mentioned here that when Eliot came to write his essay on Ford in 1932, he quarreled with Havelock Ellis's attempts "to present Ford as a modern man." *Selected Essays 1917–1932* (New York: Harcourt, Brace, 1932), 178.

9   Moody, *Thomas Stearns Eliot Poet,* 23. Lyndall Gordon sees the influence of Philippe's novel on Eliot's "Interlude: In a Bar," dated February 1911. *Eliot's Early Years* (Oxford: Oxford University Press, 1977), 39. See also Eliot's Introduction to Charles-Louis Philippe, *Bubu of Montparnasse* (New York: Avalon, 1945), 10.

10  See Georg Lukács, *Soul and Form,* translated by Anna Bostock (Cambridge, Mass.: MIT Press, 1971), 91–106. Lukács's treatment of the book is surprisingly romantic and apolitical. See especially p. 99: "Poverty is a way of seeing the world. . . ."

11  See "A Commentary," *Criterion* 4 (January 1926): 5, and the discussion in William M. Chace, *The Political Identities of Ezra Pound and T. S. Eliot* (Stanford: Stanford University Press, 1973), 126–7. Eliot mentions Sorel in a book review published in *The International Journal of Ethics* 27 (October 1916): 15–17. According to the chronology in Valerie Eliot's edition of the letters, the review of Sorel's *Reflections on Violence* in *The Monist* 27 (July 1917): 478–9, is by Eliot. See p. xxiii. This review parallels quite closely the argument given in the lecture outlines. The lecture series is discussed and Eliot's annotated syllabi reprinted in Ronald Schuchard, "T. S. Eliot as an Extension Lecturer," *Review of English Studies* 25 (1974): 163–73, and in Moody, *Thomas Stearns Eliot Poet,* 41–9.

12  Schuchard, "Eliot as an Extension Lecturer," 167.

13  Lee Congdon, *The Young Lukács* (Chapel Hill: University of North Carolina Press, 1983), 134. See Congdon's whole discussion, pp. 132–6, and also Michael Löwy, *Georg Lukács – From Romanticism to Bolshevism,* translated by Patrick Camiller (London: NLB, 1979), 123. Lukács's denunciation of Sorel in *The Destruction of Reason,*

translated by Peter Palmer (1962, reprinted, London: Merlin, 1980), 30–3, represents part of the complex, almost destructive self-criticism he carried on during the Stalin years (this part of the book is dated 1952).

14 See Gluck, *Lukács and His Generation*, 182–3. Worringer's thesis, *Abstraction and Empathy*, originally published in 1908, was republished in 1948 with a rapturous acknowledgement of Simmel's influence. See also Lukács's slap at Worringer in *The Meaning of Contemporary Realism*, 87.

15 The most complete discussion of the history of Hulme's interest in Worringer is in Michael Levenson, *A Genealogy of Modernism* (Cambridge: Cambridge University Press, 1984), 94–101. See also one of the earliest such discussions, Frank Kermode, *Romantic Image* (1957, reprinted, New York: Random House/Vintage, 1964), 119–37.

16 See Wilhelm Worringer, *Abstraction and Empathy*, translated by Michael Bullock (New York: International Universities Press, 1953), especially p. 18. Perhaps the most important difference between Worringer and Hulme is that Hulme ignores Worringer's warning that modern man cannot simply recreate the society of the pre-Renaissance through copies of its art: "[M]an had become an individual and broken away from the mass" (p. 18).

17 The relationship between Eliot and Hulme is a very complex one often touched on in the criticism. Levenson is concerned to show that Eliot misunderstood what Hulme brought back from Germany (*Genealogy of Modernism*, 208–9). That Eliot was influenced at all by Hulme before the *Criterion* days was first established by Schuchard, "Eliot and Hulme in 1916: Toward a Revaluation of Eliot's Critical and Spiritual Development," *PMLA* 88 (October 1973): 1083–94. This is a particularly important achievement in that it demonstrates that Eliot's political and social interests were of long standing when he finally began to write polemically in the twenties. See also John D. Margolis, *T. S. Eliot's Intellectual Development 1922–1939* (Chicago: University of Chicago Press, 1972), 45–52. Hulme was the translator of the edition of Sorel's *Reflections on Violence* that Eliot reviewed in 1917.

18 For Mannheim's dedication of himself to Lukács's work, see *Correspondence*, 122. For an overview of the portion of Mannheim's career most influenced by Lukács, see David Kettler, Volker Meja, and Nico Stehr, *Karl Mannheim* (London: Tavistock and Ellis Horwood, 1984), 35–40. For Mannheim's early academic career, see the Introduction by Kettler et al. to Mannheim's *Conservatism*, translated by

David Kettler and Volker Meja (London and New York: Routledge & Kegan Paul, 1986), 6–8.

19 The most complete history of the Moot is to be found in Roger Kojecky, *T. S. Eliot's Social Criticism* (London: Faber and Faber, 1971), pp. 169–97. For the origins of *Notes* and Eliot's tributes to Mannheim, see Kojecky, pp. 196–7, and Chace, *Political Identities*, 194–201. Chace concentrates so heroically on the differences between Eliot's elite and Mannheim's that he undervalues the plain fact that both men agree on the necessity of having an elite. For a good discussion of the affinities between Mannheim and Eliot, see Pamela McCallum, *Literature and Method: Towards o Critique of I. A. Richards, T. S. Eliot and F. R. Leavis* (Atlantic Highlands, N.J.: Humanities Press, 1983), 140–2.

20 Schuchard, "Eliot as an Extension Lecturer," 165.

21 Andrew Arato and Paul Breines, *The Young Lukács and the Origins of Western Marxism* (New York: Seabury Press, 1979), 77. The slogan "new classicism" had a certain currency in Lukács's circle. See Gluck, *Lukács and His Generation*, 143. For a discussion of Lukács's "classicism" covering the whole of his career, see Ferenc Feher, "Lukács in Weimar," in *Lukács Reappraised*, edited by Agnes Heller (New York: Columbia University Press, 1983), 75–106.

22 Schuchard, "Eliot as an Extension Lecturer," 165, 166.

23 Löwy, *Georg Lukács*, 96, 38.

24 Mann met Lukács in 1922 but had admired his writings for some time. Naphta is discussed in many works on Lukács, but the most extensive discussion is Judith Marcus, *Georg Lukács and Thomas Mann* (Amherst: University of Massachusetts Press, 1987). See also Michael Löwy, "Naphta or Settembrini? Lukács and Romantic Anti-capitalism," *New German Critique* 42 (Fall 1987): 17–32.

25 "A Commentary," *Criterion* 2 (1924): 231.

26 T. S. Eliot, *The Use of Poetry and the Use of Criticism* (1933; reprinted, London: Faber and Faber, 1964), 73. See also the 1936 talk reprinted as "Tradition and the Practice of Poetry," *Southern Review* 21 (1985): 873–84: "[T]he truly traditional poet will be submissive, reactionary or revolutionary according to his perception of the need of his time and place" (p. 875).

27 In *The Destruction of Reason*, Lukács refers to Naphta's "mystificatory proto-fascism" (p. 91).

28 The most well-known use of the term "romantic anti-capitalism" is in Lukács's 1962 Preface to *Theory of the Novel*. See p. 19 in the edition cited in n. 3. The best analyses of romantic anticapitalism are Löwy's book and article cited in nn. 13 and 24 and Michael

Löwy and Robert Sayre, "Figures of Romantic Anti-Capitalism," *New German Critique* 32 (Spring–Summer 1984): 42–92. The chief objection to this term is the possibility of confusion with the "classicism" announced by both Lukács and Eliot, but this is a purely terminological difficulty. For discussions of the coexistence of these terms in Eliot's criticism, see Margolis, *Eliot's Intellectual Development*, 45 and Levenson, *Genealogy of Modernism*, 209–10. "Revolutionary culturism" is the term given to Lukács's position around 1918–19 in David Kettler, "Culture and Revolution: Lukács in the Hungarian Revolution of 1918/19," *Telos* 10 (Winter 1971): 35–92. Martin Jay distinguishes romantic anticapitalism and revolutionary culturism as different phases of Lukács's career. See *Marxism and Totality* (Berkeley: University of California Press, 1984), 99–101. But Löwy and Sayre produce a typology capable of embracing a romantic anticapitalism committed to revolution and one that is merely regressive.

29  For discussions of this protest tradition with particular relevance to Eliot, see Chris Baldick, *The Social Mission of English Criticism 1848–1932* (Oxford: Clarendon Press, 1983); Raymond Williams, *Culture and Society: 1780–1950* (1958; reprinted, New York: Columbia University Press, 1983); Robert Weimann, *Structure and Society in Literary History*, expanded ed. (Baltimore: Johns Hopkins University Press, 1984).

30  Georg Lukács, "The Old Culture and the New Culture" (1920), in *Marxism and Human Liberation*, edited by E. San Juan, Jr. (New York: Dell, 1973), 4. For a general discussion of Lukács's ideas about culture, see György Markus, "Life and the Soul: the Young Lukács and the Problem of Culture," in *Lukács Reappraised*, 1–26.

31  T. S. Eliot, "Mr. Leacock Serious," *New Statesman*, July 29, 1916, 405; "London Letter," *The Dial* 70 (April 1921): 451.

32  F. O. Matthiessen, *The Achievement of T. S. Eliot* (1935; 2d ed., New York: Oxford University Press, 1947), 144. T. S. Eliot, "A Commentary," *Criterion* 10 (April 1931): 485. Any number of other comments might be cited here. See, for example, "The Idea of a Christian Society," in *Christianity and Culture* (New York: Harcourt Brace Jovanovich, 1968), 17, 48–9.

33  Karl Mannheim, *Conservatism*, 66–7. Mannheim is, of course, not the only one to offer this analysis. See as well Williams, *Culture and Society*, 140; Fredric Jameson, *Fables of Aggression: Wyndham Lewis, The Modernist as Fascist* (Berkeley: University of California Press, 1979), 15, 18. Lukács himself saw romantic anticapitalism as an originally liberating movement that had turned conservative

with time. See *History and Class Consciousness*, translated by Rodney Livingstone (Cambridge, Mass.: MIT Press, 1971), 214; *The Historical Novel*, translated by Hannah and Stanley Mitchell (Lincoln: University of Nebraska Press, 1983), 26, 177–8.

34  The historical instance best illustrating this coalition against liberalism is the alliance in nineteenth-century England of conservative landowners and industrial workers against the laissez-faire doctrines of the liberals. See Guido de Ruggiero, *The History of European Liberalism*, translated by R. G. Collingwood (1927; reprinted, Boston: Beacon Press, 1959), 48. A number of recent works have studied the convergence of conservative and communist against liberalism. See, for example, Kirk F. Koerner, *Liberalism and Its Critics* (London and Sydney: Croom Helm, 1985); Ronald Dworkin, "Liberalism," in *Liberalism and Its Critics*, edited by Michael J. Sandel (Oxford: Basil Blackwell, 1984), 64–5. There are, of course, other brands of conservatism, notably that now linking classical liberalism to repressive social ambitions, and other versions of socialism, including that in power in Lukács's time, which combines an Enlightenment faith in science with materialism and social centralism.

35  For descriptions of the ideological ambiguity of Lukács's circle, see Gluck, *Lukács and His Generation*. 94–5; Arato and Breines, *Young Lukács*, 76; Löwy, "Naphta or Settembrini," 9, 18. It should be mentioned that not all Marxists will be comfortable with an alignment that opposes socialism to liberalism and industrial capitalism. Gareth Steadman Jones insists that nowhere in Marx "is there even the sign of a serious 'temptation' by either romantic anti-industrialism or utilitarian positivism." For Jones, Marx is the steadfast opponent of "feudal socialism" who stressed the progressive role of the material revolution made by the bourgeoisie. Appropriately, Jones scalds Lukács and insists that "the metaphors of *Capital* are never those of the *Wasteland*." "The Marxism of the Early Lukács: an Evaluation," *New Left Review* 70 (November–December 1971): 45.

36  Jürgen Habermas, *The Philosophical Discourse of Modernity*, translated by Frederick Lawrence (Cambridge, Mass.: MIT Press, 1987), 83.

37  Markus, "Life and the Soul," 18, paraphrasing Lukács's "History of the Development of Modern Drama" (1911). See the similar discussion of the same work in Arato and Breines, *Young Lukács*, 24. Lukács did not fundamentally alter this analysis even after joining the Communist party. In "The Old Culture and the New Culture"

he speaks of the necessity of overcoming "anarchic individualism" (p. 17).

38  T. S. Eliot, "Literature and the Modern World," *American Prefaces* 1 (1935): 20. Quoted in Lewis Freed, *T. S. Eliot: The Critic as Philosopher* (West Lafayette, Ind.: Purdue University Press, 1979), 108.

39  Roger Scruton, *The Meaning of Conservatism* (London: Macmillan, 1980), 191. See also Michael Oakeshott, *Rationalism in Politics* (London: Methuen, 1962), 21–2. It is significant that those who have reflected most seriously on the problems of immanent critique are either conservatives like Scruton and Oakeshott or Marxist-influenced critics like Adorno. See "Cultural Criticism and Society," in *Prisms*, translated by Samuel and Shierry Weber (Cambridge, Mass.: MIT Press, 1981), 17–34.

40  T. S. Eliot, *After Strange Gods* (New York: Harcourt, Brace, 1934), 27.

41  Habermas, *Philosophical Discourse*, 310. According to Andreas Huyssen, it has been a central belief of critical modernism that modernism must be passed through "before the lost unity of life and art [can] be reconstructed on a higher level." Postmodernism represents the debunking of this attitude. See "The Search for Tradition: Avant-Garde and Postmodernism in the 1970s," *New German Critique* 22 (Winter 1981): 36.

42  Seyla Benhabib, *Critique, Norm, and Utopia* (New York: Columbia University Press, 1986), 29.

43  Habermas, *Philosophical Discourse*, 7. For discussions of this problem, the problem of immanent critique, in relation to Lukács, see Maurice Merleau-Ponty, *Adventures of the Dialectic*, translated by Joseph Bien (Evanston, Ill.: Northwestern University Press, 1973), 30–1, 56; Jay, *Marxism and Totality*, 110.

44  See Franco Moretti, *Signs Taken for Wonders*, translated by Susan Fischer, David Forgacs, and David Miller. (London: Verso, 1983), 213. Two other very brief comparisons between Eliot and Lukács should be mentioned here. Congdon uses a passage from "Tradition and the Individual Talent" to gloss Lukács's theories of history (p. 178), and Peter Demetz makes a very oblique comparison in *Marx, Engels, and the Poets*, translated by Jeffrey L. Sammons (Chicago: University of Chicago Press, 1967), 223.

45  T. S. Eliot, *Selected Prose*, edited by Frank Kermode (New York: Harcourt Brace Jovanovich/Farrar, Straus and Giroux, 1975), 177. All further citations will be identified in the text by the abbreviation SP.

46 Lukács, *Theory of the Novel*, 88. All further citations will be identified in the text by the abbreviation TN.

47 See Löwy's discussion in "Naphta or Settembrini," 19–20.

48 Note Eliot's very interesting defense of Cubism, which he says "is not license, but an attempt to establish order." "London Letter," *The Dial* 71 (August 1921): 215. Obviously, Cubism does not establish order directly, but rather by demolishing the old forms that stand in its way.

49 See the analyses of Hohendahl, "Art Work and Modernity," 40; Jameson, *Fables of Aggression*, 173.

50 See the explanation of this point in J. M. Bernstein, *The Philosophy of the Novel: Lukács, Marxism and the Dialectics of Form* (Sussex: Harvester Press, 1984), 192.

51 See ibid., 196. See also the excellent discussions by Andrew Feenberg, "Reification and the Antinomies of Socialist Thought," *Telos* 10 (Winter 1971): 101–2; David Carroll, "Representation or the End(s) of History: Dialectics and Fiction," *Yale French Studies* 59 (1980): 213.

52 Paul de Man, "Georg Lukács,' *Theory of the Novel*," in *Blindness and Insight*, 2d ed. (Minneapolis: University of Minnesota Press, 1983), 56.

53 Bernstein, *Philosophy of the Novel*, 205. See also p. 215, where Bernstein comments on the madness of perpetual irony.

54 For a discussion of *The Waste Land* as a kind of unwritten *Aeneid*, see Hugh Kenner, "The Urban Apocalypse," in *Eliot in His Time*, edited by A. Walton Litz (Princeton: Princeton University Press, 1973), 38–40.

55 T. S. Eliot, *The Complete Poems and Plays 1909–1950* (New York: Harcourt, Brace & World, 1971), 44.

56 This is Bernstein's paraphrase; see *Philosophy of the Novel*, 72; Walter Benjamin, *Illuminations*, translated by Harry Zohn (New York: Schocken, 1969), 82.

57 Thus the difference between Lukács's irony and Cleanth Brooks's is that the latter is resolved within the text, which then becomes affirmative in character. Note, however, the similarities, as when Brooks ends his reading of *The Waste Land* by saying, "[T]he statement of beliefs emerges *through* confusion and cynicism – not in spite of them" (*Modern Poetry and the Tradition*, p. 172). On the other hand, the thoroughly negative reading of the poem, exemplified by Eloise Knapp Hay's *T. S. Eliot's Negative Way* (Cambridge, Mass.: Harvard University Press, 1982), removes all the critical power of negative comment.

58 *Use of Poetry,* 15; *Christianity and Culture,* 6; *To Criticize the Critic,* 74, 122. This list of examples could be extended almost indefinitely.

59 This distinction is first made explicitly in "Donne in Our Time," in *A Garland for John Donne,* edited by Theodore Spencer (Cambridge, Mass.: Harvard University Press, 1931), 5. See also *Use of Poetry,* 35–6, 98, 109.

60 A number of recent essays have begun to make this clear. See, in particular, Jeffrey M. Perl and Andrew P. Tuck, "Foreign Metaphysics: The Significance of T. S. Eliot's Philosophical Notebooks," *Southern Review* 21 (Winter 1985): 84; Victor P. H. Li, "Theory and Therapy: The Case of T. S. Eliot," *Criticism* 25 (Fall 1983): 349–50; Walter Benn Michaels, "Philosophy in Kinkanga: Eliot's Pragmatism," *Glyph* 8 (1981): 170–202. See also William Righter, "The Philosophical Critic," in *The Literary Criticism of T. S. Eliot,* edited by David Newton–De Molina (London: Athlone, 1977), 135. In a letter to Norbert Wiener, Eliot himself testifies to his relativism. See *Letters,* 79–81.

61 *Christianity and Culture,* 125, 136.

62 This is, in fact, the final criticism of one of Eliot's best critics, Raymond Williams. See *Culture and Society,* 241.

63 Arato and Breines, *Young Lukács,* 70.

64 *History and Class Consciousness,* 141.

65 Theodor Adorno, "Reconciliation Under Duress," in *Aesthetics and Politics,* by Ernst Bloch et al. (London: NLB, 1977), 176. In the same essay, Adorno defends Eliot, along with Joyce, against Lukács's criticisms (p. 162).

66 Ibid., 166.

# T. S. Eliot and Modernism
# at the Present Time:
# A Provocation

RONALD BUSH

Begin in the Paris of November 1922 and with the American poet John Peale Bishop. Bishop, five years out of Princeton and traveling on an extended honeymoon, decided to visit Ezra Pound in Montparnasse after his good friend, Edmund (Bunny) Wilson, editor at *Vanity Fair* and *The New Republic,* raved to him about a forthcoming masterpiece by T. S. Eliot. *The Dial* magazine had arranged to publish *The Waste Land* in November and had supplied Wilson with proofsheets for the purposes of a follow-up essay trumpeting Eliot's praise. There will be occasion to glance at Wilson's December essay in a moment. His first response, though, was more interesting. On 5 September, supplied with notes he had not yet had time to read, Wilson had written Bishop that "the poem, as it appears to me from two or three cursory readings, is nothing more or less than a most distressingly moving account of Eliot's own agonized state of mind during the years which preceded his nervous breakdown. Never have the sufferings of the sensitive man in the modern city chained to some work he hates and crucified on the vulgarity of his surroundings been so vividly set forth. It is certainly a cry *de profundis* if ever there was one – almost the cry of a man on the verge of insanity."[1]

Bishop, primed by this letter, read the now published *Waste Land* with enthusiasm and contrived after visiting Pound to invite him to dinner. The dinner was a success, and sometime before 29 November he wrote: "Dear Bunny.. . . . I wished many times that you might have been here to see the great 'Amurcan' poet work out. There was a lot of his past that came out after he had begun to get into his cups which was fairly soon, as well as a few points about 'Tears' Eliot (as some Paris wit has recently christened him)."[2] Concerning Eliot, Bishop in fact had a good deal to say. For example:

Eliot is tubercular and disposed toward epilepsy. On one occasion he decided to kill himself in Pound's house but funked at the final moment. The psychological hour in *Lustra* [Pound's 1916 collection of poems] gives E.P.'s reaction to T.S.E.'s wedding which was substituted on the spur of the moment for a tea engagement at Pound's. It seems that Thomas and Vivienne arrived in the hallway and then turned back, went to the registrar's and were wed, to everybody's subsequent pain and misery. She . . . is an invalid. . . . Eliot's version of her is contained in [the lines beginning] "The Chair she sat in like a burnished throne". . . . [The pub scene, on the other hand,] reflects the atmosphere immediately outside their first flat in London. Eliot, it seems, is hopelessly caught in his own prudent temperament. . . . Mr. Eugenides actually turned up at Lloyds with his pocket full of currants and asked Eliot to spend a weekend with him for no nice reasons. His place in the poem is, I believe, as a projection of Eliot, however. That is, all the men are in some way deprived of their life-giving, generative forces.

Needless to say, all of this made an impact on Bishop's reading of *The Waste Land,* so much so that he told Wilson to "disregard" his recent inquiries. "I think," he wrote, "I have cleared up the meaning of the poem as far as it is possible. . . . It's my present opinion that the poem is not so logically constructed as I had at first supposed and that it is a mistake to seek for more than . . . personal emotion in a number of passages. The Nightingale passage is, I believe, important: Eliot being Tereus and Mrs. E., Philomela. That is to say, that through unbalanced passion, everybody is in a hell of a fix; Tereus being changed to a hoopoe [i.e., a hawk] and T.S.E. a bank clerk. Thomas' sexual troubles are undoubtedly extreme."

Bishop's letter, until now almost unknown, will have to be accounted for. But I leave that accounting, as well as the task of sorting out the truth of what Pound told Bishop, for another place. More important here are the dynamics of transmission beginning with this moment very close on the composition of *The Waste Land* and opening out into its first public reception. For Wilson answered Bishop's letter immediately, and his response, penned a little short of three months after he advised Bishop that *The Waste Land* was "nothing more or less than a most distressingly moving account of Eliot's own agonized state of mind," was to leave a large mark. Between September and November, Wilson studied Eliot's notes, supplied to him with the Liveright proofs but unavailable to Bishop, who read the poem in the October *Criterion* or the November *Dial,* both without notes. And on the heels of his study Wilson changed his tune. Writing on 29 November 1922, he was as ever patronizing to Bishop, who, older than Wilson, had passed through Princeton a year behind him. He began the letter expressing interest in Pound's "gossip," but assuring his friend that, as he would discover if he read Wilson's "long thing" in *The Dial,* he had "the wrong dope about the nightingale." The bird, he assured Bishop, was a reflection of the "'sylvan scene' in *Paradise Lost,*" just as Tereus, the barbarous king, was "not Eliot, but the things which are crucifying Eliot," which Bishop would realize once he read *Titus Andronicus,* act IV, scene i. And while he was at it, Bishop would have to refresh his memory of *The Spanish Tragedy, Antony and Cleopatra, The Golden Bough,* and so forth.[3]

The rest, as the saying goes, is history. And as we are in the process of rediscovering, history tends to ride on ideological rails. Wilson's essay, which appeared in the December 1922 *Dial,* contained an extremely sensitive assessment of the personal and cultural resonances of *The Waste Land,* but it was dominated by an urge to explain to the public at large, as Wilson had already explained to Bishop, the significance of Eliot's "complicated correspondences" and "recondite references and quotations."[4] Wilson's patronizing, moreover, though an expression of his personality and of his editorial persona, was also part of his institutional charge. The editors of *The Dial*, Scofield Thayer and J. S. Watson, Jr., had in 1922 both awarded Eliot a large prize and commissioned Wilson's essay to advance the magazine's mission. They had bought *The Dial* to make the American spirit "count in the great world of art and affairs."[5] And co-opted into this project, *The Waste Land* in Wilson's description came to signify something different from what Eliot later called – not without guile – "the relief of a personal and wholly insignificant grouse against life . . . a piece of rhythmical grumbling."[6] Whatever the disjunctions of its formal and thematic cross purposes, in Wilson's account it was made to announce the achievement of American mastery and therefore to signify classical standards of high seriousness.

Nor did the appropriation stop there. One of the many themes Wilson attributed to the poem came to serve the interests of many who followed him. In "our whole world of strained nerves and shattered institutions," he speculated, *The Waste Land*'s symbolic landscape of "spiritual drouth" was especially telling. "The reflections which reach us from the past," he added, "cannot illumine so dingy a scene."

Wilson's keynote here is our "shattered institutions," our contemporary crisis of tradition and belief. And his characterization came to resonate with the changing emphases of Eliot's own concerns. To rehearse an old story, although in 1920 Eliot was quite willing to concede that poetry deals with "philosophic ideas, not as matter for argument, but as matter for inspection,"[7] by 1929 he had withdrawn his concession. In his essay on Dante of that year he insisted that in some sense we must assume that the poet "means what he says" and that "one probably has more pleasure in the poetry when one shares the beliefs of the poet."[8] And by then he had already indicated (in a preface added to the 1928 reprinting of *The Sacred Wood*) that his own interests had evolved. He was now less interested, he said, in poetry considered by itself than in "the relation of poetry to the spiritual and social life of its time and of other times."[9] Which is to say that he then considered it his task to ponder the relation of poetry to a particular order of belief – an order of belief that (to quote the same preface) elevated the poetry of Dante over that of Shakespeare because "it seems to me to illustrate a saner attitude towards the mystery of life."[10]

But if by the early thirties Eliot himself was ready to reenvision his earlier work along the lines Wilson had laid down, his disciples were even more so. Eliot, at least, had his moments of candor. When his friend Paul Elmer More, for example, suggested in an essay of 1932 that there was a cleavage between Eliot "the lyric prophet of chaos" and Eliot the critical exponent of classicism, he was taken aback.[11] In public, with much qualification, he implied that the contradiction was only apparent.[12] In private, in an unpublished letter dated 26 October 1932 and now at the Princeton University Library, he was more forthcoming. There he simply wrote that More had raised a problem to which he had no answer and that the contradiction would only be resolved when no one was interested any longer in his prose or his verse.

F. O. Matthiessen, however, had none of Eliot's qualms. In the first prominent full-length study of Eliot, published in 1935, Matthiessen found himself "unable to understand" More's naïveté and patiently explained that Eliot's classicism "steadily illuminates the aims of his verse" and that both were rooted in the themes of religious belief.[13] Then two years later Cleanth Brooks, an admirer of Matthiessen's, published one of the landmark essays by which New Criticism domesticated modernism. Despite the force of its corrosive ironies, Brooks explained, *The Waste Land* was in fact a calculated unity. Its "theme" was "the rehabilitation of a system of beliefs" which had been reduced to clichés, and its method of indirection, though lamentably "violent and radical," was necessary if the poet were to bring Christian truth back to life.[14] Thus was the shape and ideological import of *The Waste Land* fixed for a generation. What Edmund Wilson, albeit tentatively and against his own initial instincts, had been impelled by the politics of his sponsor to begin, the New Critics consolidated into dogma. And as *The Waste Land* became part of the academic curriculum, the testimony of Wilson's friend Bishop was forgotten.

As the nineties begin, there is some cheer in the fact that the New Critical appropriation of *The Waste Land* has at last lost its grip on literary history and that energies in the poem that were obvious to its first readers are once more being acknowledged. During the past ten years a number of careful and thoughtful studies have examined Eliot's early poetics and discovered not conformity with his later political and philosophical positions, but philosophical, formal, and psychological disjunctions of considerable force. In 1984, for instance, Michael Levenson's *A Genealogy of Modernism* examined the developing premises of Eliot, Ford, Conrad, Hulme, and Pound and concluded that they had changed radically over the course of modernism's first decade. The writings of these figures, according to Levenson, built on themselves in "conflicting and sometimes contradictory" ways, and these contradictions, rather than any ideological uniformity, conditioned their creative work. The case of *The Waste Land* was particularly interesting. It was, Levenson says, an attempt to restore the equilibrium of religious authority conditioned by a form derived from the philosophical pluralism of Eliot's doctoral dissertation. Wittingly or not, Eliot guaranteed that any unity achieved by his poem would be "provisional." And thus inexorably "the principle of order in *The Waste Land* depends on . . . an ever-increasing series of points of view, which struggle towards an emergent unity and then continue to struggle past that unity."[15]

There is also the resurgence of biographical and psychological interpretation, which started with the publication of *The Waste Land* drafts and lately has grown more subtle and better informed. Although this kind of criticism obviously eschews the broad theoretical and cultural questions raised by Eliot's poem and its reception, it does serve also to limit certain kinds of excesses. Once we have recognized the divided impulses driving Eliot's composition, for example, and the fact that the "different voices" of his working title ("He Do the Police in Different Voices") had strong unconscious sources, it becomes more difficult to credit an account like Brooks's, which gives us a poem sprung full-bodied from its author's conscious mastery. The New Critical line, it is worth remembering, was anticipated and pilloried by Eliot's close friend Conrad Aiken, who, in a *New Re-*

*public* review that appeared four months after *The Waste Land,* took pains to insist that "the poem is not, in any formal sense, coherent," that it is anything but "a perfect piece of construction." In Aiken's words, Eliot's "powerful, melancholy tone-poem" succeeds "by virtue of its ambiguities, not of its explanations."[16] And one would hope that as letters like John Peale Bishop's continue to appear, it will become easier for us to remember Aiken's admonishment and harder to accept any new totalitarian account.

I say one would hope, however, with some melancholy. For it is already becoming apparent that a new set of shibboleths have come into play that reinforces the New Critic's Eliot, this time not to praise the poet but to bury him. Simplifying, we may identify the source of these pressures with that wing of post-structuralist theory that has come to ascribe to postmodernism more and more of the oppositional values that were once seen as the essence of modernism and consequently has depicted the modernists themselves as homogeneous and reactionary. This kind of thing gets tricky with Joyce, Woolf, and even Pound, of course, and these three are intermittently designated postmodernists *avant la lettre.* But Eliot is a sitting duck because he himself prepared the ground in the latter phase of his career. Thus we find Fredric Jameson in his book *Fables of Aggression: Wyndham Lewis, the Modernist as Fascist,* blithely identifying Eliot's "aesthetic and political neoclassicism" with Lewis's celebration of Hitler and cautioning us that our admiration of the modernists indicates we live in a time "when new and as yet undeveloped forms of protofascism are in the making around us."[17]

At present, the chief exponent of this new school (and perhaps the chief obstruction to acknowledging modernism's contingent and contradictory history) is probably Terry Eagleton. Eagleton, in his 1976 *Criticism and Ideology,* shaped the Marxist commonplaces of today when he argued that *The Waste Land,* though it mimes the experience of cultural disintegration, in fact silently alludes by its "totalising mythological forms" to a "transcendence of such collapse." By means of its "elaborate display of esoteric allusion" and its "closed, coherent, authoritative discourse," the poem, Eagleton asserted, produces "an ideology of cultural knowledge" consonant with the "authoritarian cultural ideology" espoused by Eliot's prose.[18]

197

Yet Eagleton's position is simply Brooks's stood on its head. No less than Matthiessen or Brooks, Eagleton derides the idea of what Paul More called a "cleft Eliot." For Eagleton, too, Eliot and modernism are in practice and theory monolithic, only he would argue that they are also malign. This, in the face of the stark ideological contradictions that pervade the production and reception of modernist writing, beginning with the case of that arch-modernist Nietzsche, whose example since 1900 has underwritten thinkers as diverse as Derrida and Mussolini.

In the late 1980s, Eagleton's terms seemed pervasive. Consider the case of Richard Poirier, who once celebrated the subtlety of modernist writing but in *The Renewal of Literature* apes Eagleton and characterizes especially Eliot's modernism as a "snob's game." The modernists, Poirier now claims, having inculcated in us a respect for 'difficulty-as-a-virtue,' conned us into swallowing on updated terms the old elitist notion that literature is "a privileged and exclusive form of discourse" and cut us off from the springs of our imaginative power as readers.[19] Poirier's argument is particularly ironic because it relies on the sponsorship of Ralph Waldo Emerson and the American tradition, from which Eliot is pointedly excluded. And yet it is this last pinch of extremity that may provide leverage to use Poirier against himself and suggest a way of approaching Eliot that will resist the reductive force of his most recent metamorphosis.

Although Edmund Wilson attributed to *The Waste Land* the theme of failed belief, there were other strains in his 1922 *Dial* review. A second, less remarked, was his identification of Eliot's "constricted emotional experience." And when, nearly ten years later, Wilson set about revising his essay for inclusion in *Axel's Castle*, the latter theme seemed to him weighty enough to begin his discussion. For in the meanwhile Wilson had concluded that not only was Eliot a major representative of modern tendencies in literature, he was first and foremost "characteristically American. . . . a typical product of our New England civilisation."[20] "One of the principal subjects of Eliot's poetry," Wilson noted, "is really that regret at situations unexplored, that dark rankling of passions inhibited, which has figured so conspicuously in the work of the American writers of New England and New York from Hawthorne to Edith Wharton." "In this respect," Wilson continued, Eliot "has much in common with Henry James. Mr. Prufrock and the poet of the 'Portrait of a Lady,' with their helpless consciousness of having dared too little, correspond exactly to the middle-aged heroes of 'The Ambassadors' and 'The Beast in the Jungle,' realising sadly too late in life that they have been living too cautiously and too poorly."

Wilson's remarks quite rightly have become cornerstones of Eliot criticism. But one of his other phrases has not, and its provocation might serve the present moment well. One of the characteristics by which Eliot most clearly disclosed his New England heritage, Wilson suggested, involved a "combination of practical prudence with moral idealism." It is the latter that needs to be stressed now. Eliot's idealistic striving, as I have argued elsewhere, colored everything he did and wrote.[21] Not only did it form the self-conscious subject of most of his poetry (in the form of a drama in which men live in an idealistic dreamworld only to awaken to their own betrayal of real lovers), but it motivated his philosophy and poetics as well, launching his resistance to Emersonian excess from a platform of intellectual absoluteness and aloofness no less American than Emerson's own. No matter how hard the later Eliot tried to accept received dogma and received ritual, his striving betrayed an Emersonian quest to renew and purify the spirit. It was the negative side of this quest that his sister Ada recognized when she confided in Eliot's friend Frank Morley shortly after her brother's conversion. "She was both interested and concerned about Tom's 'Way of contemplation,'" Morley recounts, which she imagined "might divorce him from 'human' relationships and drive him into a shadow-world of 'dramatism,' into increasing tendencies of outward 'acting' and inward 'mysticism.'"[22]

But Eliot's Emersonianism had positive qualities as well – the very qualities that Poirier now endorses but, taking preaching for practice, refuses to credit in Eliot's creative work. I am thinking now of the impulse toward imaginative renewal, which most of us took for granted in modernism until it became fashionable to think otherwise. If Eliot's poetry returns us to the work of his great predecessors, it also, as Wilson concluded in 1922, lends "to the words of his great predecessors a new music and a new meaning." And if his most famous essay calls on us to write and read with a feeling for "the whole of the literature of Europe from Homer" onward, it adds that this knowledge must exist as a "simultaneous order" which is "modified by the introduction of the new (the really new) work of art" – modified, that is, by the "great labour" by which we remake the tradition for ourselves.[23]

W. H. Auden wrote in the introduction to the *Faber Book of American Verse* that no true European could have written those phrases. And if "Tradition and the Individual Talent" (1919) weren't enough to confirm Auden's judgment, Eliot, in a little-known lecture he gave to the Arts League of London at about the same time, articulates more clearly a similar Emersonian yearning to make it new. This lecture, which Eliot called "Modern Tendencies in Poetry" when he published it in an obscure Indian journal, was meant, he said, to complement "Tradition and the Individual Talent."[24] As in its more familiar counterpart, he employs the metaphor of the poet as catalyst. But far more than anything else in the reprinted piece, he takes pains to explain what it means to have a perception of the presence of the past. His point of departure is the often heard complaint that poetry is less future-looking than science. In Eliot's words, "while past work in science appears of value only because of its being the basis of present conclusions and future discoveries, past poetry retains a permanent value equal and alongside of contemporary and future work." Literature, in other words, often is reduced in our minds to dusty books on dusty shelves, all of which are of equal value because none affects our lives. To which Eliot replies that "the life of our 'heritage' of literature is dependent upon the continuance of literature." Imagine yourselves, he says, "suddenly deprived of your personal present, of all possibility of action, reduced in consciousness to the memories of everything up to the present." These memories, then, this existence (amounting to "merely the totality of memories") would be "meaningless and flat." That is, if "suddenly all power of producing more poetry were withdrawn from the race, if we knew that for poetry we should have to turn always to what already existed . . . past poetry would become meaningless." For, Eliot argues, the capacity "of appreciating poetry is inseparable from the power of producing it. . . . Life is always turned toward creation; the present only, keeps the past alive."[25]

"Life is always turned toward creation." The phrase is one Emerson would be proud of. And the statements that precede it inescapably recall, if one is in an Emersonian mood, lines from "The Divinity School Address" and "Self-Reliance":

> . . . [truth] is an intuition. It cannot be received at second hand. Truly speaking, it is not instruction, but provocation, that I can receive from another soul. What he announces, I must find true in me, or reject; and on his word, or as his second, be he who he may, I can accept nothing. . . . Let this faith depart, and the very words it spake and the things it made become false and hurtful. Then falls the church, the state, art, letters, life.
> . . . [I]mitation is suicide. . . . [T]hough the wide universe is full of good, no kernal of nourishing corn can come to [a man] but through his toil bestowed on that plot of ground which is given to him to till.[26]

Lest I be misunderstood, I need add that even in the essays Eliot wrote before *The Waste Land* the passage I have isolated represents one mood among many. Also, that in his writing the mood is usually counterpointed by a sense, not un-Emersonian, that the truth we create has been created in other forms before and by a definitely non-Emersonian suspicion of the creative imagination. Yet even when Eliot was most resistant, his Emersonian strain recurred, remaining part of his fundamental stance as late as *Four Quartets:*

> And so each venture
> Is a new beginning, a raid on the inarticulate
> With shabby equipment always deteriorating [etc.]

It therefore in the present critical climate seems more salutary to risk overemphasizing this mood and to represent Eliot as an American, a maker, a "toiler" who fashioned a tradition with "great labour" and knew that the next man would have to repeat the labor for himself. Better that than to continue revering the stolid master of the Anglophile New Critics, whose achievement was to wrench literature back from the barbarians and revitalize the great tradition. In the former account we at least keep the internal contradictions of man and poet in focus and make it harder to fall prey to the reductions of either right or left. And more importantly we keep in view the real power *The Waste Land* shares with *Ulysses*, the *Cantos*, *Women in Love*, *To the Light-house*, and the Yeats of *The Tower*. For that power derives not just from the renewed authority these works aspire to, but from their simultaneous awareness that in art such authority can never be permanently and legitimately embodied. And if it is true that this precarious tension could disintegrate into something politically unpleasant, it is also true that without it the works I have named would lose much of their energy, an energy that with few excep-tions has not been surpassed. In the words of a recent study of modernism by Alan Wilde, it is necessary to "assert, in response to those who see the shape of modernist literature as organic, its failure to fuse its contradictory elements." What moves us in this literature, Wilde says, is the spectacle of "desire straining against the constraining form it has itself devised as the only possible response to its own impossible hope for fulfilment." And if any-thing, this spectacle is more impressive in the age of postmoder-nism. In the supermarket of postmodernist tolerance, whose characteristic gesture is a "willingness to live with uncertainty, to tolerate, and in some cases, to welcome a world seen as random and multiple," the moral idealism that Edmund Wilson recog-nized in *The Waste Land* continues to have its attractions.[27]

## Notes

1 Edmund Wilson, *Letter on Literature and Politics* (New York: Far-rar, Straus and Giroux, 1977), 94.
2 This and other parts of Bishop's letter are taken from Elizabeth Carroll Spindler, *John Peale Bishop: A Biography* (Morgantown: West Virginia University Library Press, 1980), 79–82.
3 Wilson, *Letters*, 98–9.
4 This and subsequent citations are taken from Wilson's "The Poetry of Drouth," *The Dial* 73 (December 1922): 611–16.
5 See William Wasserstrom, "T. S. Eliot and *The Dial*," *The Sewanee Review* 70 (Winter (1962): 81–92, esp. 86. These issues have been taken up more recently by Richard Sieburth in "Pound's *Dial* Letters: Between Modernism and the Avant-Garde," *American Po-etry* 6 (Winter 1989): 3–10. But Sieburth seems reluctant to point out how the *Dial*'s appropriation of Eliot runs against the poet's grain.
6 Valerie Eliot, ed., *The Waste Land: A Facsimile and Transcript of the*

*Original Drafts Including the Annotations of Ezra Pound* (New York: Harcourt Brace Jovanovich, 1971), 1.

7  *The Sacred Wood: Essays on Poetry and Criticism* (1920; reprint, New York: Barnes & Noble, 1966), 162.

8  *Selected Essays* (1932; reprinted and expanded, New York: Harcourt, Brace & World, 1960), 230–1. The standard study of the subject is Kristian Smidt, *Poetry and Belief in the Work of T. S. Eliot* (Oslo: Jacob Dybwad, 1949; reprinted and expanded, 1961).

9  *Sacred Wood*, viii.

10  *Sacred Wood*, x.

11  See Paul Elmer More, "The Cleft Eliot," *The Saturday Review of Literature*, 12 November 1932; reprinted in Leonard Unger, ed., *T. S. Eliot: A Selected Critique* (New York: Rinehart, 1948), 24–9, esp. 27.

12  See *After Strange Gods: A Primer of Modern Heresy* (New York: Harcourt, Brace, 1934), 30–1.

13  See F. O. Matthiessen, *The Achievement of T. S. Eliot: An Essay on the Nature of Poetry* (1935; reprint, New York: Oxford University Press, 1972), 98–9.

14  Cleanth Brooks, "*The Waste Land*: An Analysis," originally published in *The Southern Review* 3 (Summer 1937): 106–36; reprinted in Brooks's 1939 *Modern Poetry and the Tradition*. I quote from the 1965 Oxford University Press edition, p. 171.

15  Michael Levenson, *A Genealogy of Modernism: A Study of English Literary Doctrine 1908–1922* (Cambridge: Cambridge University Press, 1984), x, 192–3.

16  Aiken's review, "An Anatomy of Melancholy," appeared in the *New Republic*, 7 February 1923, and is reproduced in C. B. Cox and Arnold Hinchliffe, eds., *The Waste Land: A Casebook* (London: Macmillan, 1969), 93–9, see esp. 94–5, 98.

17  Fredric Jameson, *Fables of Aggression: Wyndham Lewis, the Modernist as Fascist* (Berkeley: University of California Press, 1979), 116–23.

18  See Terry Eagleton, *Criticism and Ideology* (1976; reprint, London: Verso, 1985), 145–51.

19  Richard Poirier, *The Renewal of Literature: Emersonian Reflections* (New York: Random House, 1987), 98–9.

20  This and the following citations are taken from Edmund Wilson, *Axel's Castle: A Study in the Imaginative Literature of 1870–1930* (1931; reprint, London: Collins, 1967), 87.

21  See "T. S. Eliot: Singing the Emerson Blues," in *Emerson: Prospect and Retrospect,* edited by Joel Porte (Cambridge, Mass.: Harvard

University Press, 1982), 179–97; "Nathaniel Hawthorne and T. S. Eliot's American Connection," *The Southern Review* 21 (October 1985): 924–33.

22  See Frank Morley, "A Few Recollections of Eliot," in *T. S. Eliot: The Man and His Work*, edited by Allen Tate (New York: Delta, 1966), 110.

23  *Sacred Wood*, 49–50.

24  The essay was published in *Shama'a* (India) I (April 1920): 9–18. As Donald Gallup notes in his *T. S. Eliot: A Bibliography* (New York: Harcourt, Brace and World, 1970), 206, a five-line excerpt was "printed under the heading 'T. S. Eliot on Poetry' in the *Bulletin of the Arts League of Service* . . . with a note that the lecture 'will form the theme of an essay on Poetry ["Tradition and the Individual Talent"] which will be published shortly by 'The Egoist.'"

25  "Modern Tendencies," 12. I am indebted for this text to James Longenbach, who quotes it in part in his *Modernist Poetics of History: Pound, Eliot, and the Sense of the Past* (Princeton: Princeton University Press, 1987), 209.

26  See Stephen E. Whicher, ed., *Selections from Ralph Waldo Emerson* (Boston: Houghton Mifflin, 1957), 104, 147–8.

27  Alan Wilde, *Horizons of Assent: Modernism, Postmodernism, and the Ironic Imagination* (Baltimore: Johns Hopkins University Press, 1981), 37, 44. About the relative value of modernist and postmodernist art, even Terry Eagleton has had second thoughts. See his 1985 essay "Capitalism, Modernism and Postmodernism," in which he grudgingly acknowledges the impressiveness of modernism's "struggle for meaning" in the light of the postmodern artwork's disturbingly casual acceptance of its own commodity status. Terry Eagleton, *Against the Grain: Essays 1975–1985* (London: Verso, 1986), 131–47, esp. 140, 143.

# Index

# CAMBRIDGE STUDIES IN AMERICAN LITERATURE AND CULTURE

*Editor*
Albert Gelpi, Stanford University

Brook Thomas, *Cross-Examinations of Law and Literature: Cooper, Hawthorne, Stowe, and Melville**

Albert von Frank, *The Sacred Game: Provincialism and Frontier Consciousness in American Literature, 1630–1860*

David Wyatt, *The Fall into Eden: Landscape and Imagination in California**

Lois Zamora, *Writing the Apocalypse: Ends and Endings in Contemporary U.S. and Latin American Fiction*

*Now available in hardcover and paperback